I LOVE YOU,
NICE TO MEET YOU

I LOVE YOU,
NICE TO MEET YOU

A Guy and a Girl Give the
Lowdown on Coupling Up

Lori Gottlieb and **Kevin Bleyer**

St. Martin's Press   New York

www.stmartins.com

Design by Jamie Kerner-Scott

Library of Congress Cataloging-in-Publication Data

Gottlieb, Lori.
    I love you, nice to meet you : a guy and a girl give the lowdown on coupling up / Lori Gottlieb and Kevin Bleyer.—1st ed.
        p. cm.
    ISBN-13: 978-0-312-34008-7
    ISBN-10: 0-312-34008-7
    1. Dating (Social customs)   2. Dating (Social customs)—Humor.
3. Man-woman relationships.   4. Man-woman relationships—Humor.
5. Single people—Social life and customs.   I. Bleyer, Kevin.
II. Title.

HQ801.G598   2006
306.73—dc22   2006041066

First Edition: June 2006

10 9 8 7 6 5 4 3 2 1

For Z. J.—a guy who
was definitely worth the wait
—Lori Gottlieb

For the gal who stomped on my heart.
No, not that one.
The other one.
—Kevin Bleyer

CONTENTS

PART ONE: THE BALL IS IN YOUR COURTING

PART TWO: THE EXCLUSIVE ON BEING EXCLUSIVE

PART THREE: SERIOUS BUSINESS

PART FOUR: IT'S ALL OVER BUT THE POUTING

ACKNOWLEDGMENTS

We'd like to thank Jennifer Enderlin at St. Martin's Press, Liv Blumer at the Blumer Literary Agency, and Anna Barber at Slamdance Media Group, who, despite all being happily married, shared an unwavering enthusiasm for our essays on being unhappily single.

Jen's keen editorial savvy, respect for our words, and constant cheerleading helped us stay the course, in both writing and dating. (If she weren't already spoken for, we'd marry her.) Liv always laughed with us and not at us, no matter how mortifying the stories we shared. Anna believed in this project before it *was* a project and somehow always had the patience to take our calls, even when we acted like an old married couple.

We'd also like to thank, in advance, our future significant others and/or spouses for not freaking out about the fact that we've publicly shared our sordid dating histories. We're decent people, we swear.

AUTHORS' NOTE

The names and identifying characteristics of most of our exes have
been changed.

PROLOGUE

We Said . . .

You could call it fate. Serendipity. Kismet.

When we first met on a clear spring day in 2001, the connection between us was obvious. We had so much in common: our career ambitions, our addiction to orange juice, and most of all, our hopeless romanticism. It seemed inevitable to us that we would ultimately enjoy a life of happily ever after. Just . . . with other people.

So you *could* call it fate, serendipity, or kismet, but you'd be wrong. We never became a love match. Not now, not then.

At the time, in fact, we were both entrenched in our own serious relationships, but nobody believed that we were "just friends." Not even Kevin's girlfriend (who soon became Kevin's ex-girlfriend). Not even Lori's boyfriend (who didn't give a shit either way).

Even our colleagues at a television show we worked on together were sure that we'd collaborated on more than each other's dangling modifiers. But behind closed doors, all we shared was our respective relationship troubles, eager for some friendly understanding and commiseration.

Instead, we noticed we'd often side with the other person's partner, because, after all, men understand men and women understand women. Or at least, that's how we justified having our friend side with our enemy. But then Kevin got dumped, Lori did the dumping, and our exes replaced us.

Newly single and licking our wounds, we entered the dating scene once again. But this time, we paid close attention to advice from the other camp.

It wasn't long before those post-date debriefings became more entertaining than the dates themselves. Come the end of the night, we'd find that the best part wasn't the date part, it was the pick-the-date-apart part. In fact, a date was a waste of a night if we didn't come away with a good anecdote or two.

Finally we admitted to each other that we weren't going on dates at all. We were going on something far more interesting and, we think, valuable: *anecdates.* Bad news for us, but good news for you. Because while our dates sometimes, well, sucked, these anecdates generally instruct: *Why did he just order for me? Why is he crying on our second date? If I broke up with her right now, would it ruin this restaurant for me?*

Despite its obvious appeal, dating can be a dangerous ritual with a very particular set of pitfalls. Fortunately, we've fallen into most of them, so you don't have to. Unfortunately, we don't have all the answers. We don't even understand some of the questions. Heck, half the time, we're not even listening. (Frankly, our dates talk too much.)

But we can offer you this: the male and female interpretation of what happens when two people who love each other try not to hate each other. Twice the perspective. Half the insight. All the details. None of the pain. And a few good reasons to keep the faith.

After all, even we eventually found new relationships. (Again, just not with each other.)

Kevin's Note: Names have been changed to protect the miserably cruel.

Lori's Note: Names have been changed to protect the narcissistic and commitment-phobic.

PART

ONE

THE BALL IS IN YOUR COURTING

1

That Whole "One True Love" Thing

IS YOUR SOUL MATE YOUR SOLE MATE?

He Said . . .

My soul mate broke my f-ing heart.

I met her, my supposed "one true love," a few years ago. She was beautiful, and funny, and I just knew it: We were meant to be. Her name was Katrina. Actually, her name *wasn't* Katrina, but I'll call her that, because by the time our relationship was over, she had devastated me with such hurricane-force brutality my heart involuntarily evacuated my body. I was romantically MIA for years. Two years, to be exact.

Frankly, sometimes I'm still nowhere to be found.

But I'm getting ahead of myself. At the beginning, when the first winds of romance were just starting to blow, I was in love with her, and my soul was in love with her soul, and her soul and my soul and she and I double-dated while sailing off the coast of San Diego.

We were, I thought, perfect for each other, and quickly we went from being too nervous to hold each other's hand to being willing to pop the most disgusting pimple on each other's forehead. Our love went from clammy to grotesque, as true love so often does.

One beautiful Saturday morning, after setting our course offshore, we hung a hammock from the mast, and as we lay nestled within it, gently buffeted by the rolling Pacific, I had never felt closer to a woman in my life. Our bodies just . . . fit. The way the bodies of soul mates should. Sure, it may have had more to do with the fact that her long legs made up the difference in our heights (once I even wore her leather pants for a Halloween party), but at the time I preferred to chalk it up to something greater than anatomy. Katrina and I simply . . . clicked. Within months, we had already discussed marriage and children and who to invite to the wedding and where to live in retirement.

Then, feeling flirty one morning, I snuck into her shower naked and began soaping her back. But instead of luxuriating in my touch, she screamed and punched my head into the shower caddy.

Uh-oh, I thought. *My soul mate wouldn't do that.* My soul mate wouldn't respond to my caress with a roundhouse to my temple. Would she?

Oh, she apologized for hurting me. And I apologized for surprising her. So after the stitches came out, I didn't lose the faith. I still clung to the belief that Katrina was my soul mate. After all, there was the hammock, the leather pants, the apology.

Then my soul mate embarrassed me in front of my boss. I had brought my soul mate to an office Christmas party and my soul mate told the guy who signs my paychecks that she didn't think he, as the host of a television show, treated his female guests fairly. *Uh-oh, I* thought again. *Soul mates don't get you fired, do they?* I hadn't had a soul mate before, so I wasn't entirely sure, but I suspected that my soul mate wouldn't endanger my livelihood.

Plus, my soul mate started making demands of me. "Call me at least once a day." "Stop by the cleaners on your way over." "Wipe your feet." *Soul mates aren't pushy, are they?*

Then my soul mate broke up with me. *Soul mates don't break up with you, do they?*

Three weeks later, after we got back together (we were soul mates, after all), my soul mate asked me if it would be all right if she stayed registered with the dating service she had joined during our time apart. She had spent a lot of money on it, she pointed out, and it would be "a waste" to just stop showing up. "Plus," my soul mate added, "it's kind of interesting, you know, sociologically speaking." *My soul mate wouldn't go out with other people, would she?*

I said no. Screw sociology.

As the days wore on, sometimes my soul mate seemed like my soul mate, other times she seemed to not even like me that much. I feared that the part of my soul mate who was my soul mate was just one of her many personalities, a few of which flew over the cuckoo's nest. Oh, I wanted it to work, but before I could convene a meeting of her personalities and find a way we could all get along, they apparently assembled without me, took a vote, and the majority ruled that the best plan of action was to break up with me. Again.

"This just isn't working out for us," they said in unison.

A year later, after my soul mate had become engaged and gotten married to someone else, moved to Dublin, gotten pregnant, and delivered twins, I started to lose hope. *That's not what soul mates do,* I thought. *They don't run off, meet a new guy, and start a family within a year of breaking your heart, do they?*

"You really dodged a bullet with that one," my friends told me a couple weeks later. I considered whether they had a point. *Soul mates aren't bullets to be dodged, are they?* At the very least, if Katrina was my one true soul mate, then my soul was a masochist.

It's tempting to conclude that I was mistaken, and that Katrina wasn't my soul mate after all. That when it comes to soul mates, either love is blind, or my soul needed Lasik. Yet, there's no denying that I was deeply in love with her, so looking back, I've come to the (albeit convenient) conclusion that Katrina *was,* in fact, my soul mate, but that there would be others as well.[1] Perhaps Katrina was simply my ideal soul mate when my soul needed to fall in love and have its heart broken—so that when the next soul mate comes along, my soul will know to prize her that much more. It may be delusional thinking, but it's necessary for our sanity and therefore, just a little genius. After all, we hamstring ourselves when we believe we'll only be happy with our perfect match and conclude there's no point in bothering with anyone who doesn't measure up.[2] At the beginning of any soul mate search, it's important to realize that those perfect-match soul mates are like truffles: rare, hard to come by, and perhaps overrated. That the more we keep our mind open, be open to new soul mates, and bounce around the Whitman's Sampler of love, the more likely we'll find something that satisfies. Try as we might to guarantee we won't be disappointed by what we find, there's no way of knowing if it's what we were hoping for until we take a bite.

After all, I doubt when Alfred Stieglitz fell in love with Georgia O'Keefe, he thought, "Gee, I'm really into southwestern artists with Irish names who paint vaginal flowers."

---

1. There had better be. If you assume there's only one soul mate out there, the odds a soul mate will be in the same city, let alone the same bar, at the same time you are . . . well, it boggles the mind. Consider: A few years ago, in the middle of the ocean between Hawaii and Japan, an American submarine named the *Ehime Maru* surfaced under a Japanese fishing trawler. Nine Japanese fishermen died. The American captain was forced to apologize, since he apparently should have known it was a distinct possibility he'd come up underneath the Japanese vessel. I spent a full afternoon calculating the odds that a submarine the size of a submarine would happen to be in the same place at the same time as a fishing boat the size of a fishing boat in an ocean the size of an ocean. (I mean, have you *seen* the ocean? It's like . . . an ocean.) I came up with a number: 1 in 800,000,000. Point is: It wasn't the captain's fault. It was fate. It was a miserable, horrible once-in-a-lifetime tragedy. Like soul mates.
2. We're writing a particularly delectable recipe for self-defeat if we only date women who are our "type." Some men, for example, only date blondes. Others date Latinas. Or blond Latinas. Or married women. Or married blond Latinas. Or long-legged Polynesians. Or short-haired Poles. Or big-breasted redheads. But regrettably, the more specific we get, the harder it is to convince ourselves we're not at a dog show. ("And up next, a lovely bitch Norwegian. Look at her fine grooming!")

I doubt Mary Matalin thought, "I'm really into snake-headed Cajuns who disagree with me."

I doubt Soon-Yi thought, "I'm really into nebbishy curmudgeons twice my age who married my mom."

And yet, they've found their soul mate, their "one true love." Or at least something that gets them one step closer to their one true love.

Something like Katrina.

She Said . . .

I know women who believe in a soul mate but not in God.

Never mind that saying "I want to find my soul mate" is a bit like saying, "I want to find my fairy godmother." If you're older than ten, you know there's no fairy godmother, no Santa Claus, and no such thing as age-defying cosmetics. But from our very first princess-finds-her-prince story, women—Catholics, Protestants, Jews, and Buddhists alike—are brainwashed to believe that soul mates exist. God, we're not so sure about. After all, if there were a God, wouldn't He have sent us our soul mate by now?

"There's no evidence that God exists," these women say.

Well, where's the evidence that soul mates exist? We see people get married, divorced, and married again (and again), each time to the "love of their life." We see people who stay married to their so-called soul mates, but tell you with no prompting how much they despise every fiber of his or her being. We've spent most of our adult lives sleeping next to men we say are our soul mates but who can't even begin to fathom our souls.

And still, we're looking in bars, on the Internet, at parties—we're even scoping guys out at the office's sexual harassment seminar—in hopes of finding our "one true love." Meanwhile, we come up with all sorts of theories to explain why He (our soul mate, not God) hasn't appeared yet.

An interior designer friend was sure that she hadn't met her soul mate because everyone in her field was female or gay.

"My soul mate won't know Herman Miller from Herman Munster," she said, explaining that she "just knew" her soul mate—whom she had yet to meet—was a "guy's guy." At a particularly low point, she even considered changing careers ("I could do sports marketing") right before meeting her current boyfriend, an architect, at a conference of, well, designers. *Hallelujah, sister! I believe!*

Another friend was convinced that geography separated her and her soul mate. "Maybe I haven't found him because I'm in the wrong city," she said. She even turned down Yale Medical School for a less prestigious one because, she told me, "I don't think my soul mate is in a tiny town in Connecticut." Well, it turns out he's not in New York either. And now she's got her M.D. from a third-rate medical school instead of Yale. (Oddly, she started going back to temple.)

The other day, I was flipping through my college alumni magazine and every person who announced their marriage wrote, "I finally found my soul mate!" After I finished gagging, I read their stories. Someone who met her husband online gushed, "It's magical that we finally found each other!" Well, if it were so "magical," why did they need to spend $24.99 a month on Match.com in order to hook up?

Sadly, *my* soul mate wasn't on Match.com. Oh, several guys claimed to be my soul mate. But apparently my soul mates aren't very photogenic and can't spell. In the real world, when I'm attracted to someone, there's an intensity between us that can mean only one of two things: either we'll become soul mates (except there's no such thing—see above), or we'll rip each other's souls out (there is such a thing—see chapters 27–32).

Other than that, it's confusing. Once I thought a guy was my soul mate because we both ate the same brand of chocolate chip cookies—for breakfast. Instead, it just meant that we had terrible nutritional habits. Sometimes what you think is a spark really is a spark, but sometimes it's just static electricity from your seamless bra rubbing up against your rayon tank top. Most times, it's your unconscious zeroing in on the part of his unconscious that resembles the unconscious of the person who hurt you the most in your formative years. But instead of calling him "devil," your unconscious calls him "soul mate."

I used to have fantasies of meeting a male alter ego, but who could also fix the dishwasher. I thought my soul mate would be like me, until I remembered that half the time I hate myself. In fact, the whole point is to find someone better than me, someone who doesn't succumb to jealousy, selfishness, or five-hour bouts of TiVo watching. So then I'd fall for guys not like me—the opposite of me—only to realize we had nothing in common. No wonder so many of us are single; we're single-minded. In our minds, we've created such a specific portrait of The One that we don't allow for the guy who falls outside of our mental map. But our "dream guy" isn't out there precisely because *we've dreamed him up.* (Besides, I can't help thinking that if soul mates really do exist in the cosmic sense, there's sure to be divine retribution.)

Which is why instead of waiting for The One, I'm just waiting for One. One guy I deeply connect with. In a twisted way, it would be a lot easier to believe that there's a single soul mate out there and I can't find him, than to believe that there are dozens of potential soul mates and I can't even find *one* of them. I mean, what kind of loser am I, when the odds are that high? And yet . . . I've let go of the sole soul mate idea.

Dozens, on the other hand?

Now that's something I can believe in. *Amen.*

Dating Out of Your League

DOES IT GUARANTEE A STRIKEOUT, EVEN
BEFORE YOU STEP UP TO THE PLATE?

He Said . . .

I once had short fling with somebody who ended it by telling me
that she was getting back together with Prince Albert of
Monaco. Not some guy she nicknamed "Prince Albert of
Monaco." The *actual* Prince Albert of Monaco. To this day, I'm not sure
what that dumping says about me. Should I assume I'm in Prince Albert's league? Unlikely. But should I be flattered that I got dumped for
Prince Albert instead of, say, the FedEx guy? Don't know. Maybe.

After all, I didn't just get dumped. I got royally dumped.

Figuring out your dating league—the league where you win some,
you lose some, but at least you're playing with your romantic peers—is
imperative. Without an attuned self-awareness of who plays at your
level, you run the real risk of truly embarrassing yourself next time you
show up for batting practice. And although your league is constantly
evolving, there are certain boundaries that will likely never change. Inviolable walls separating you from the rest of the field that can never be
breached. (And even if they could, they shouldn't.)

For example, I've never dated a celebrity. My college roommate once "boinked" (his word) a famous actress in my bed while I was in Houston visiting my parents, but me, no, I've never dated a celebrity. Celebrities, I'm not ashamed to say, are out of my dating league.

I've come close, however. And by that I don't mean to suggest that I once asked out Nicole Kidman and she said, "Um, I don't know. Can I think about it?" Rather, I've dated a number of women who themselves dated celebrities. In the dating game, I've batted clean-up to *Saturday Night Live*'s Charles Rocket, *American Pie* director Paul Weitz, and Black Flag frontman Henry Rollins. I've even been within two degrees of Kevin's bacon. So I've dated a celebrity if you use the transitive theory from algebra: If A boinked B and B boinked C, then A boinked C. (After all, isn't that how they used to warn us about STDs back in high school: If you sleep with ten people, you've slept with the ten people they've slept with?)

Now, in any other town—or so I like to tell myself—I'd be comfortable in my own league. After all, I'm reasonably pleasant-looking, coiffed, and hygienic. I've got my wits about me, and I've been known to make a beautiful woman laugh. But in LA, simply being able to play in your own league won't get you to the all-star game—because in LA, people don't just have a league; they have a Q-score.

For those lucky but uninitiated daters in the rest of the country (what people in the 213 and 310 area codes—as well as those eastern residents of 212 and 917—cynically call "flyover land"), a Q-score is an actual number that movie studios have assigned movie stars to quantify how "in demand" they are. The lower the better. Take the Toms, for example. Hypothetically, Tom Hanks is a 3, Tom Cruise is a 9, Tom Selleck is a 93, and Tom Arnold is a 390. You get the picture.

So really, why should dating in LA be any different? To this day, I'm still surprised when I ask a woman for her number (which, in any other part of the country, would naturally imply *phone number*) and she doesn't say, "Well, this month I moved up a few notches to 72—thanks to the Botox, the new yoga place that opened up on my block, and the fact that I dated Jimmy Fallon's agent last month."

For my part, I lived in "Beverly Hills, 90211" for six years—as zip codes go, a desirable number if there ever was one. I told dates familiar with 90210 that my address was "one better." But *I* was always joking. If they didn't take it as a joke, and instead seemed impressed by my zip, I knew I was sitting across from a Q-score social climber.

And that's the problem: In a league, you get to play ball with people similar in talent. But in LA, most women will play ball with us (to say nothing of playing with our balls) only if they deem our Q-score to be better than theirs. And usually by the seventh inning stretch (which falls after the main course, but before the tiramisu), they've already determined if they'd rather go home with the batboy because he's got ripped abs while our Q-score wouldn't even fit on the JumboTron screen.

Am I plain wrong in thinking that dating in LA is more superficial than in, say, Missoula? Probably. All towns are company towns, after all, and if you want company in your town you have to play by the rules. Even Missoula has its roster of beautiful, brilliant, and billionaire men and women, which leaves us men all of two options: either go on the road and rope countless homers slumming it on a farm team in someplace even more podunk—Poughkeepsie or Puyallup, for example—or stay in the (moderately) big leagues and resign yourself to the fact that, with an undesirable Q-score like yours, she'll always have home field advantage.

She Said . . .

I want a man who can expand both my mind and my vagina. You know, someone who can talk and chew gum at the same time, intellectually and sexually speaking. I don't think that's too much to ask for. I'm not saying he has to be a Rhodes Scholar with genitals in the *Guinness Book of World Records*. But I deserve to be with someone relatively smart and sexy since I'm considered, on a very good day, to be relatively smart and sexy.

It's fair, it's Darwinian, and heck, it's downright American.

But of all the unsolved mysteries in the universe—global warming, UFOs, whether to go Atkins or South Beach—the one we single women have the hardest time grappling with is why our equals won't date us.

So we have a choice: We can stay home with our vibrators in one hand and TV remotes in the other, or we can lower our expectations and date below our league.

Our mothers euphemistically call this kind of trading down "not being so picky." I call it "unfair." Because while women are simply trying to find a comparable mate, men often seem interested in dating women completely out of their league. Just look at any family sitcom, where the sensible, hot wife (the lovely Leah Remini) is married to the fat, clueless husband (the waiting-to-die-of-a-heart-attack Kevin James).

Things were much easier growing up, when the prom queens dated the prom kings, the drama groupies dated their costars, the honor students dated their study partners, the cheerleaders dated the jocks, and potheads dated their dealers. Like attracted like. You rarely saw couples who didn't belong at their partner's lunch table. You knew where you stood.

As adults, though, you can't simply find someone who shares the same extracurricular activities. Now, you have to weigh several factors—wealth, success, beauty, age, intelligence, kindness, sense of humor, sense of style, level of emotional dysfunction, amount of hair—run them through the computer, and calculate your league relative to your potential date's.

As a general rule, men can date out of their league physically, while women can date out of their league financially. This explains why a very attractive woman might be in the same league as a short, bald, paunchy man in an Armani suit; but not why a famous fifty-year-old playwright might be in the same league as her hot twenty-five-year-old assistant-slash-boyfriend. When we see mismatched couples, the first thing we do in our minds—if not aloud—is try to figure out why they're together. I don't know whether it's worse to be the person who traded down ("Something must be wrong with him") or the one who traded up ("She must be really good in bed").

Personally, I wouldn't want to be either, which is why I try to stay in my own league. If only I could figure out what league I'm in. The other day, I learned that an ex-boyfriend (charming, successful, and attractive—did I mention the trust fund?) is dating a woman ten years older and five times duller than him. What makes her in his league? And if she's in his league, had I been dating below my league but didn't know it? Or am I just in a lower league than I'd thought?

Sometimes I'm tempted to date below my league because, oddly, dating a loser makes a woman seem like less of a loser than staying at home alone with her nonloser self. If you don't date anyone (since men in your league won't date you), people act as if you're the one who drools or laughs too loudly in restaurants. But if you date a guy who wears Speedo bathing suits with his pubic hair sticking out on public beaches, you seem "normal" simply because you're dating *someone*. People ask with concern and pity why seemingly eligible single women aren't in a relationship (any relationship, even with a guy who wears velour sweatpants), whereas seemingly eligible single men are considered a national treasure (fit only for dating another national treasure—supermodels). But what's wrong with a little solitude? It worked for Thoreau. (Although, if Thoreau had been a woman, *Walden* would be considered a tragic, cautionary tale.)

For now, though, I'm holding out for someone in my own league. I'm not ready, as my married friends put it, to "settle down." (There's a reason they don't call it "settling *up*.") Because I'll compromise, but I won't settle. Because something isn't always better than nothing. And also because a part of me believes that there *is* a man out there who can expand both my mind and my vagina.

3

Freakers

IS THERE ANY WAY TO AVOID THEM?

He Said . . .

So you're about to start trolling for a date, and you want to avoid your past mistakes.

The good news is . . . you will.

There's no way, if you put your mind to it, that you'll make the same mistakes you made in your previous attempts at dating. Rest assured—you'll make *entirely new ones,* and they'll be named Jenny, Joanie, Carla, Pamela, and Beth. They'll seem normal—they'll have driver's licenses, carry cell phones, and blink regularly—but odds are they won't be. Odds are they've got a defect of some kind. Let's face it: At this point, they're like a house that has curbside appeal but somebody got murdered in there. There's probably a reason they're still on the market.

Just like you.

Just like me.

Personally, I think there's something lovable in everyone I meet, with murderers possibly being the lone exception. Everyone in moderation, as they say.

But my laudable open-mindedness aside, occasionally there are those dates who make me wonder why I unlocked my car door, let alone why I called ahead for a reservation.

Take Lara. Bless her—she was pretty. Jennifer Connelly with freckles. And what's more, she came highly recommended: we had been set up on a blind date by a mutual friend I trusted. Already two reasons to be optimistic: she was pretty, and I was pretty certain her references would check out.

But from the get-go, her oddity was on display. We both arrived at the movie a little late, and immediately after we sat down, she got up, apologized, and excused herself to go to the bathroom. She was back barely two minutes before she excused herself to go to the bathroom again. *Huh.* When she got back to her seat, just as the lights began dimming, I was alarmed.

"Everything all right?" I whispered.

"Oh sure," she said, "I just have to pee a lot these days. . . . What with the pregnancy and all."

Oh. Wow. Pregnancy. *Huh.* My friend (who, it bears repeating, I trusted) hadn't mentioned that Lara was pregnant (not to be picky, but wouldn't that fall under the category of "anything I should know?"). And yet—I'm so proud of myself—when Lara let that little nugget of information slip, I didn't blink for a slightest moment. Sadly, it had already gotten too dark in the theater for her to notice my perfect composure, but let the record show I reacted as if the news of her pregnancy was 100 percent anticipated, as if there was *nothing to see here, move along.* As if, instead of saying "what with the pregnancy at all," she had said something as innocuous as, "what with the four bottles of water and all."

After the credits rolled, we went to a bar known for its apple martinis. "Mmm, apple. That sounds delicious," she said. So, of course, she immediately ordered an apple *juice.* "No alcohol for the baby," she laughed. (Again, I remained perfectly composed. At this point, even *you'd* be proud of me.)

Near the end of the date, after she skipped to the loo for a third time, I thought the gentlemanly thing to do was to ask when she was due—to "take an interest," as my mother used to advise me. It was the baby elephant in the room, after all.

"Due to what?" she asked.

"Due to deliver," I said.

"Deliver what?" she asked.

"The baby," I said.

"What baby?" she asked.

I told her I thought she was pregnant.

"Why would you think that?" she asked, as if I had just said, "I think pretzels are evil." (*Pretzels? Evil? Why would you think that?*)

When I explained that I'd taken her pregnancy remarks seriously, she started laughing. She even told the waiter how ridiculous I was. *WHAT?!*

I mean, it's not like we knew each other well. It's not like I could read her tone with such a featherweight delicacy or tell she was joking by the way she held her chin at that rakish angle she always does when she's being delightfully sarcastic.

No, I'd done what I had to do. I did a gentleman's work: hear the news that your date is pregnant and *be perfectly all right with it.* And here, now, my date was making fun of me for being so gullible. Never mind that if I had said, "You're pregnant? EWWW!" and stormed out of the theater, she wouldn't have applauded me for my sensitivity.

I'm told there's a word for people like her: *freak.*

Then there was Liza. I met Liza buying coffee New Year's morning, and we spent the entire day together—three meals, sixteen hours, and nine holes of golf. By evening we already had several inside jokes and kissed a few times (I doubt that's true, but in my memory I like to believe I'm a fast operator). Naturally, I asked her when I'd see her again. She looked at me the way a nurse looks at a patient who's dying but doesn't know it quite yet. But the look was less surprising than what she was about to say: she told me she was flying out of the country in a week because, well, perhaps she should have explained this earlier but, well, you see, "I'm in a relationship with Prince Albert of Monaco."

"Really?" I asked.

She was offended by my incredulity. "Yes. I'm pretty sure he's going to ask me to marry him this time."

Yeah. Me too. Yet when she got back from Monaco (or at least *said* she "just got back from Monaco"—I never saw a wedding ring), I saw her a few times. I told myself I wanted to figure her out—separate the truth from the fantasy—but the likelier explanation is that I wanted companionship. She may have been a little crazy, but I was a little lonely. Plus, if the story were true, I wasn't about to let Prince Albert win without a fight. If the story *weren't* true, if Prince Albert was indeed a figment of her imagination, how sad would it be to come in second to an *imaginary* boyfriend who lives on the other side of the earth?[1]

I thought Liza could be the woman of my dreams. Liza thought she was living in dreamland. Where freaks live.

That's what I was talking about: *Entirely new mistakes.* So as a public service, I've provided some rules of thumb that lessen the chances your next date will be one you regret. Consider these behaviors as relationship firing offenses: conduct unbecoming a girlfriend, as it were. If at all possible, don't date anyone who:

Pretends to be pregnant.

Fancies herself a princess.

Unfortunately, that's about as specific as I can get, frankly, because men can't afford to be so picky. But more important, we'd best be

---

1. Where the hell *is* Monaco, anyway?

patient and forgiving of women's freakiness, because there will come a time when they'll be the ones who brand *us* with the "freak" label. (Talk about freaks.)

So keep this list handy. Embrace it. Laminate it. Carry it in your wallet. Refer to it often. But don't be a freak about it. Remember, your date will have a list as well.

She Said . . .

I was on a first date with a cute guy when I asked if he had any siblings. Yes, he said. An older brother. Married, two kids, happy.

"Are you close?" I asked. Yes, the guy said. Then his eyes welled up with tears. I wondered if he was allergic to the walnuts in the waffles, but no, he was actually *crying*. As he wiped his eyes with his napkin, he said, "Wow, sorry, I don't know why I'm having this reaction. I guess I just really love my brother."

Freaker, I thought. But instead of asking for the check, I dated him for two years.

After we broke up (yes, he cried then, too), I was five minutes into a candlelit dinner at another guy's house when he told me how badly he wanted to get married and have children. The problem, he continued, was that women are unstable.

"Excuse me?" I asked.

"That's not misogynistic," he replied. "I mean, women are unstable, but men are assholes."

"Or maybe unstable women date assholes," I huffed, thinking, *What a freaker.* Still, I agreed to go out with him again. (Which, I guess, makes me unstable.)

The problem with freakers, as opposed to genuine freaks, is that freakers present as normal—even delightfully charming—in every other way. So when they say or do the freaky thing, it doesn't compute.

It's a strange blip that you simply delete from your mind, like it never happened.

Until, of course, you get your friends on the phone for a reality check:

◆ *"He won't go out to eat on a first date because he says the way people's faces look when they're chewing is distracting—that's weird, right?"*

◆ *"He has a condom full of cum in his freezer that he's saved for sentimental reasons because it was the last time he had sex with his girlfriend from five years ago—that's mental, huh?"*

◆ *"He calls his therapist his 'mentor' and goes to Alcoholics Anonymous meetings for what he calls 'a prior dependence on Prozac'—freaky, right?"*

These questions are, of course, rhetorical. I'm not talking about the dime-a-dozen, garden-variety freaks: men who do origami, call their cars by human names, or judge you for watching foreign films dubbed instead of subtitled. Freakers are more confusing. They make you wonder, "Is he a genius or is he insane?" and it's hard to tell. They seem quirky—and after dating enough straight-laced accountants, a dash of insanity seems oddly refreshing.

Meantime, we avoid telling the freaker how freaky he is, because if we call him on his freakiness, he'll not only deny it, but he'll project it onto us. When I told a guy I'd seen three times that it wasn't okay to call me at 1:00 A.M. on a weeknight just to say hi, he sighed, "Wow, you're really uptight." When I told another guy that compulsive exercise combined with fasting wasn't healthy, he accused me of being jealous of his willpower. Freakers justify their freakiness by saying that we're too uptight or jealous—it's not that they're totally out of line.

Rationally, we know we're not the problem here. In fact, we stay in these relationships precisely because we're on a mission to prove that we're not crazy—which, of course, only makes us seem *more* crazy.

Case in point: I went out with a guy who said constantly that I was "the whole package" and that he'd never felt this strongly about anyone before. So when I asked why suddenly he wanted to be "just friends," he called me "needy" for asking. Then, in a valiant attempt to prove I wasn't needy, I slept with him then promptly dumped him.

These are not the actions of a sane person. But freakers turn even the most sensible of women into, well, freakers. (If you ever ask a freaker why he broke up with any of his girlfriends, his answer inevitably will be, "She was a total psycho." And she probably was—because of him!)

Friends will hear the litany of stories and say, "So why are you dating this guy?" I've asked my women friends this same question. Part of the answer is: It's hard not to be intrigued by somebody so unembarrassed by their weirdness. You've got to admire the lack of self-consciousness of a guy who admits that he calls to check on his perfectly healthy parents when he hears an ambulance go by because he's afraid it might be headed to their house; or that he performs a compulsive ritual in which he says good-bye to the sun as it sets each evening. You think, *Gosh, I wish I could be that shameless. I wish I could care that little about what other people think of me.*

But here's the thing: maybe he *should* care more. A lot more! Maybe the fact that he blurts out every freaky thought that rages through his brain doesn't make him seem happy-go-lucky or ultra-confident. It means he has major boundary issues: He either doesn't know what's appropriate, or doesn't care.

Like any good sociopath, though, freakers are tenacious at sucking you in. They flatter you. They tell you you're special, that they're only being this open about their creepy inner lives with you (a dubious honor, if you stop to think about it). They make you think that sharing their freakiness with you is a sign of intimacy, when really it's a sign to get a restraining order.

So when you're with a freaker, you hand over your passport and willingly enter his alternate reality. You tell yourself the guy's an eccentric. He's not vanilla. But we forget that a guy can be chocolate almond fudge without being wacko nutso freaky. Having an "edge" doesn't mean, like one guy I dated, that he carries knives to the local upscale sushi place in case we get attacked.

If women weren't so analytical, we probably wouldn't give freakers the time of day. (When *women* exhibit the first signs of freakiness, on the other hand, men forget to return our phone calls.) But women become obsessed by baffling behavior: If he's fabulous 90 percent of the time, then what accounts for the deviant 10 percent? We can't just walk away. We have to *figure him out.*

Which is why you can try to avoid freakers altogether, but often you have to let them run their course. When the guy finally reaches a Critical Mass of Freakdom (he says he can't fall asleep in the same bed with another person, so he ties a black T-shirt around his head like a hostage and sleeps in the closet so he won't hear any noise), that's when you'll get over it. Dating a freaker is exhausting.

"Go be your freaky self on someone else's clock," you'll say. Because there will always be another woman who can't wait to figure this guy out, too.

4

Blind Dates

He Said . . .

It began with an e-mail.

To: <Kevin Bleyer>
From: <Sharon Li>
Subj: You're annoying my boss

Peter tells me he's getting frustrated because every time he calls you to talk about the script you end up complaining about your ex-girlfriend. (What's her name—Katrina? Betina? Dina?) And when he gets frustrated, he takes it out on me, so now I'm taking it out on you, otherwise I'll take it out on my husband, and there's no sense in breaking up my relationship just because you ruined yours, right?

BTW—Why are you still obsessed with Katrina/Betina/Dina? Didn't you two break up, like, TWO WEEKS AGO?

I think you need to move on.

Call me—I've got just the girl for you . . . ;)

Shar

P.S. Trust me on this. When it comes to my matchmaking skills, I'm batting a hundred.

I wanted to trust her on this. I really did. Frankly, I needed to trust her on this. I was lonely. I was desperate. (The fling with the Princess of Monaco didn't work out, hard to believe.) Between you and me, it had been so long since a woman laid her hands on me I was tempted to fly internationally just for the pat-down at airport security.

I had a hard time trusting Sharon, however. First off, I've always been suspicious of the common ;) emoticon because, while it's intended to suggest a "just between you and me" or "what do you think of this inside joke" sentiment, I can't help but think it's a "don't really listen to me because I'm lying through my keyboard" sentiment. And here was Sharon—not my best friend, but as friendly as a work associate could be—telling me she had found "just the girl for me." True, I should have known that when she said she's "batting a hundred," it may have evidenced something more than a profound misunderstanding of baseball statistics. But I hadn't had a successful inning in a while, so I was game.

After all, she was right. It *had* been two weeks. And if you can't get over the loss of the love of your life in a fortnight . . . ;)

So I said yes, and a few days later I went to a dinner party at Sharon's place to meet "just the girl for me": Trisha. Lovely, pretty, great sense of humor, charming, clever, witty. The thought even entered my mind: *Where have you been all my life?*

Frankly, I was thrilled.

Which made one of us.

Oh, she *seemed* to be having a great time. For most of the night, all signs pointed to yes. When we were introduced at the doorway, there was a definite spark between us—not, I was certain, merely from static electricity from the shag carpeting. When we sat for dinner, she made a point of placing herself next to me—not, I insisted to myself, so she didn't have to look me in the eye. When, after dinner, we played Scrabble, she demanded we be on the same team—not, I hoped, simply to keep from owing me anything if we competed and I hadn't let her win.

Which I would have.

Shucks if she didn't seem to be flirting with me. And by the end of the night, even I couldn't cling to any lingering suspicion that, despite her every flirtatious action, she secretly found me repulsive—when, to my delight, she kissed me after I walked her to her car.

Another thought entered my mind: *Blind dates rock!*

The next morning Sharon called me. *No doubt to congratulate me on a job well done,* I suspected.

Instead Sharon began to read aloud. Apparently Trisha had sent her an e-mail:

Dear Sharon,

    Thanks for the setup. What a guy. Clever, cute, charming, great sense of humor. Quite a catch, and in this town that's hard to come by. You know, Sharon, it's so hard out there, it's great to know that there are good guys still available. Speaking as a woman, however, I can't date anyone who's shorter than I am. But thanks for thinking of me! Hey, are we going hiking tomorrow? Call me ;)

    Trisha

That's what she had said: "Speaking as a woman," she thought I was too short for her. Speaking as a woman, apparently she couldn't stand to stand by me. Speaking as a woman, she thought I was just too damn close to the ground. Wow. If Trisha was, in fact, "just the girl for me"—my perfect match, so to speak—then I was apparently one of the most superficial people on the planet. Is that what Sharon thought of me?

I suppose it's poetic that it began with an e-mail, and it ended with an e-mail. God forbid that it began with an e-mail, and ended with lasting happiness.

Now, *speaking as a man* . . . never mind the era we seem to have entered, in which a woman who "knows what she wants" in life is expected—nay, encouraged—to judge a man on his looks/chest hair/stature, while if *I* had e-mailed Sharon and written, *Gosh Sharon, she's everything I'd ever want in a woman, but speaking as a man, I can't date anyone whose breasts are smaller than mine. Hey, are we going spelunking on Friday?* I wouldn't be described as simply "knowing what I want," I'd be described as "a pig." I'd be told, quite frankly, to go spelunk myself.

Speaking as a man, it seems clear that the unintentional consequence of blind dates is the further empowerment of women. It used to be that a man would see a woman—"scope her out," was the phrase of my teen days—to determine if she was someone he'd like to ask out before wholly embarrassing himself by stammering through an invite for Friday night. Though we failed often, men were the prime movers. Blind dates, however, take that judgment away from the man and put it squarely in the lap of the woman. Truly, blind dates are feminist. Messy, uncomfortable, and feminist.[1]

Speaking as a man, the whole blind date enterprise is inherently suspicious. If my single friends are setting me up with single women, why aren't they dating them themselves? To be sure, if *I* thought a woman was worth dating, I'd want to keep her for myself. And if I thought they were nothing to sneeze at, and you were my good friend, I wouldn't want to burden you. I'd consider our friendship a fraternity: friends don't let friends blind date—that sort of thing.

But really, what's most troubling about blind dates is not what we learn about ourselves, or our dates, but rather what we learn about what our friends think of us. What kind of a woman you set me up with

---

1. A quick side note, if you will. Consider it a dating service announcement: As a species, we've overcome so many dating obstacles. In many parts of the world, humans of the same gender can date, be granted civil unions and benefits, even marry. Overwhelmingly, we've embraced interracial dating. Now we need to embrace *interspatial dating*—the odd coupling of two lovers whose heads happen to exist in different planes in the atmosphere simply due to genetics, nutrition, and high heels. I'm just saying, perhaps we need an adjustment in our attitudes toward altitudes. Can I get a diminutive "amen"?

speaks volumes about JUST WHAT KIND OF MAN DO YOU TAKE ME FOR?!

After I had just broken up with a very tall woman I dated for over two years (she stoops, he conquers!), every time I was out with my friends and we walked past a woman vaguely six feet tall, they would nudge me and wink, as if to say, "Hey, what do you think of her? She's your type, right?" And no surprise, these same close friends set me up on a couple blind dates with women who were equally giraffelike, apparently thinking that my first criterion was dating a woman I could, well, look up to. *Likes: sunset walks on the beach, the novels of Charles Dickens, craning my neck . . . Dislikes: mean people, reality television, keeping my head level at all times . . .*

But at least I knew what that came from. They had seen me in a relationship with a tall woman, so naturally they thought that's who interests me. But where did Sharon get the idea that petty shallowness turns me on? Where were the Trishas in my dating past?

I don't think I am merely *speaking as a man* when I say that when it comes to our friends' attempts to nudge us along the path to romantic bliss, our good friends don't make good pimps. Sure, they love us, and look out for us, and want us to be happy, but no matter how insightful they think they are when it comes to our love lives, it's still a matter of the blind leading the blind dates.

She Said . . .

Unless you've actually dated your friends, you have no idea what they're like in a relationship. Which is to say, the person you know as a friend (even a very close friend) is a *completely different person* when romance is involved.

Over the years, I've set up friends—male or female, doesn't matter—who, I thought, were so "together." They were, for all I knew, "catches." But inevitably, in the course of the relationship I helped to create, they'd act completely nuts. My college roommate harangued my closest guy friend for "gawking at hookers" after he casually mentioned that he felt bad for the prostitutes he saw while driving on Sunset Boulevard. Another guy friend ordered a latte and a mocha espresso for himself and his date and when the Starbucks guy said, "That'll be $5.40," my guy friend replied, "Actually, these are separate." ("What?" he replied defensively when I asked him about it. "I didn't want her to think I was being presumptuous by paying for her drink.")

I'd heard the play-by-play of these friends' respective bad dates for years, but suddenly I was hearing both sides of their stories. And often, what I heard didn't compute. *He said what? She did what?* I'd never seen these sides of my friends before.

So now when a friend says, "I've got a great guy for you," my response is, "Have *you* ever dated him?" Andrea, a friend I didn't know well, set me up with a friend she'd known since college. On our first date, he said, apropos of nothing and without a trace of irony, "Whenever I make a woman come, she falls in love with me."

"He'd *never* say that!" Andrea insisted. But I was crossed off her set-up list because somehow *I* appeared to be the weird one—either delusional, or a liar. (Lesson learned: Even if you don't like the guy, try to make him fall in love with you simply so the friend who set you up will think you're desirable and set you up again.)

I've found out the hard way that a friend saying, "I want you to meet this guy. You're perfect for each other," is a declaration that can only lead to false expectations. (Like, in one case, I didn't expect him to have a girlfriend.) She may say that he "has good taste," which later you realize means that he brings the chef to your table at restaurants to discuss the food: "The salmon was nice but the swordfish was disappointing." Or that he's a writer, when what he writes are pharmaceutical brochures. Or that he's "a diamond in the rough" when he's cubic zirconium set in cheap plastic metal. Or that he's "versatile" ("He's an accountant-slash-poet!" "He's a lawyer-slash-musician!") when, in fact, he's a half-assed accountant and no-talent poet, or a sleazy lawyer and wannabe musician. (Always question a setup with a guy described as something-slash-something.)

Other friends take the used-car salesman approach. They'll tell you how handsome, smart, funny, and interesting a guy is, and just when you close the deal—"Great, I'll meet him"—they drop the bomb.

"Excellent," they'll say, "there's just one thing. You know how I said he's a producer? Well, he's kind of in between things right now, so he's working as a dog walker. But it's just temporary." Or, "You know how I said he's eccentric? Well, he lives on somebody's boat. Isn't that cool?"

No. It's not cool. It's degrading. After all, what does that say about your friend's impression of you? Does she think this guy is *in your league* (see chapter 2)?

The set-ups I dread most are the ones where your friend says, "I want you to meet Joe." So against all better judgment, you say okay. Then she gets back to you the next day. "Okay, I talked to Joe, and he wants to know if we can all go out together, do a group thing. You know, less pressure."

Less pressure? I'm sorry, but going on a date with a stranger and having your best friend give you looks all night (*D'oh! Don't talk about that!* or *Oooh. I think he likes you!*) is not my idea of a relaxing evening. And if the conversation lags, your friend is sitting there going, "Joe, did you know that Lori is also a runner?"

"No, I didn't," Joe says, before reluctantly turning toward me. "Where do you run?"

"The Canyon," I say. "You?"

"The Canyon," Joe says. Then we both look away and sip our drinks.

"Lori, Joe just got back from a trip to Paris," our mutual friend says in her peppy voice usually reserved for dogs or babies. "Joe, Lori loves Paris. Lori, tell Joe about the time you got stuck in Paris!"

There's a reason "group date" is an oxymoron. A date is a meeting between two—and no more than two—people. Unless it's an orgy, as my date once suggested on a "group date." I didn't laugh and he didn't call.

When single female friends set you up with their guy friends, they'll say they're not dating these guys because "there's no chemistry." This is a lie. There's always chemistry—at least for him. Unfortunately, *she* didn't feel any chemistry, they became "friends" (read: He pined away for her while she pretended not to notice but secretly felt flattered and sexy around him), he complained about not meeting quality women (read: Women like her), and she agreed to set him up.

Problem is, if you and her guy friend actually do connect, she'll start to resent it. Not because she's interested in him, but because he's no longer pining away for her and she misses the ego-boost. So she'll make passive-aggressive comments like, "Really? You find him sexy? Because he's definitely funny, but he *is* kind of scrawny. Which is fine. I just didn't know you'd go for that, but if you do, great!"

Ultimately, the biggest problem with the friend setup is the conflict of interest. It's like a real estate agent who's representing both the buyer and the seller. You each need your own agent who's looking out for your interests alone. But since your friend is also representing your date, you can't complain about him. If I date a stranger and he's not interested, my friend—my "agent"—will say he's a jerk. That he's not good enough for me. That he's blind if not gay. But if her friend—her "client"—rejects me, she won't take my side and vilify the guy, which is the duty of any good female friend.

Add to that the frustration you'll feel if she has the information you want, but won't spill. She's poker-faced when you tell her the date was amazing . . . and the next day he doesn't call. She knows why he thought the date was a disaster—in fact, why he thinks *you're* a disaster—but she's tight-lipped. She'll have heard that you talked too much or too fast or had bad breath—but she'll say she has "no idea what his deal is."

Representing both sides in a dating transaction isn't just unethical, it's doomed to fail. Because even if a relationship takes off in the beginning, chances are it'll crash and burn eventually. And in that case, both members of the couple compete to stay friends with the friend who set them up. They'll try to plead their case—*See, I took the high road. He's the one behaving badly. You have no idea what she's like behind closed doors*—but instead make the person who set them up so uncomfortable that she'll stop taking both of their calls. Especially because during those first two weeks after a breakup, both parties feel the need to share every horrible-creepy-obnoxious thing the other person did. Once the anger settles down, they'll be more polite. But during that critical period, you'll learn more about your two friends than you ever wanted to know.

So if you let your friends hook you up, prepare by asking for the equivalent of a pre-setup prenup. Decide in advance who gets to stay friends with whom. Same with the person doing the setting up. Otherwise, you'll never be able to have comfortable dinner parties again. Maybe it's based on seniority—who's been your friend longer? Maybe it's based on gender—the same-sex friend wins.

Or maybe you'll wise up and stop trying to get your friends laid. Because in the end, everybody gets screwed.

5

Venue Ask Her Out

IS "LOCATION, LOCATION, LOCATION" THE KEY TO
GETTING A SECOND DATE?

He Said . . .

T he who, what, and when are easy. But after deciding to ask
the who (a woman) out on the what (a date), and after picking the when (next Friday), we'll have to start talking the
where. If we want to show her a good time, we have to show her a good
place. It's a troubling detail, and I've often wondered if dating would be
easier if it were mandatory to hold all first dates at a prescribed site.
Someplace romantic but unthreatening. Like a candle shop. Or a mat-
tress warehouse.

Nonetheless, we have options, and it's the prudent dater who carefully considers them all before deciding which venue is the most likely
to facilitate success in the romance department.

Let's take a quick tour:

Starbucks. It's often the first place that comes to mind, as in, "Let's
grab a cup of coffee." The pros: If the date sours, you can end it without a waiter asking you if you'd like to see a dessert menu. Further,
picking Starbucks in particular proves that you're solvent enough—and

employed enough—to drop a healthy ten-note on two flavored waters without batting an eye. It says, "I'm not a barista; on the contrary, baristas do my bidding. Baristas are my bitch." The cons: If the date goes well, you either have to drink nineteen cups of caffeine or propose that you continue the date somewhere else (like, say, the Starbucks next door).

An art gallery. Bad move. The only man who can look at a piece of art for more than thirteen seconds and not appear to be bullshitting interest is the guy who painted the thing. You don't want your date to think you're a total fraud. That comes later.

The zoo. Sure, it's childish, but childish sometimes works. And meandering among primates provides a nice contrast to your own charms. It says, "Compared to these monkeys, I don't throw feces."

Dinner and a movie. Depends on the dinner. And the movie. And the woman. Spago, *Being John Malkovich,* and the girl you've been obsessed with for weeks? Maybe. KFC, *Caligula,* and the girl who's been stalking you? Still maybe.

Movie and a dinner. You've no doubt committed the first date faux pas of "Let's just catch a movie before dinner." The premise is sound: Attend a cultural event and spend the next couple hours discussing and dissecting it over a fine late-night meal. But inevitably what happens is you show up, say hello, and then spend the next two hours sitting silently next to this perfect stranger jockeying for elbow position while impossibly better-looking people rattle off impossibly better conversation fifty feet high before you. Worse, in a mere two hours these matinee idols meet, fall in love, face a daunting romantic obstacle, and fall again back into each other's arms as they motor off to Martinique. You, however, wrestle over the armrest and then motor off to the Olive Garden. Puts a little pressure on your next two hours when, in the last two hours, your date just got power-horny for Orlando Bloom.

A gay bar. Yes, everyone there will be dressed better than you, but there are two advantages to going to the local homosexual haunt.

One, it shows you're *that* confident in your sexuality. Two, no one will hit on your date (because, after all, you're not *that* confident in your sexuality).

Your place. If you propose your place for your first date and she accepts, she obviously trusts you more than she should at that point. She's trouble. Hang up. Run.

Her place. Hard to say. I've never mustered the courage to ask a woman out to her place, though I've been tempted. Often, when I pick up a woman at her doorstep, I'm amused by the thought that if all goes well—heck, if all goes stupendously—my ultimate goal is merely to return to this very spot. Her doorstep. (Often, before I knock on her door, I'll take a good look around—it's still daylight, and in the best case scenario I'll be returning to this spot well after the sun has gone down and moonlight will be the only illumination, so now's my only chance to scope the place out. Case the joint, if you will.)

After all, the intervening hours between the pickup and the drop-off (or hookup) is but an exhausting, puddle-jumping sojourn from romantic restaurant to chichi bar to classic movie theater to late-night coffeehouse—a minimum three-hour tour whose only utility is to prove to my date that I have the capacity to squire her around the town and return her to her home sweet home without letting her be pillaged by pirates, kidnapped by renegade truckers, or audited by the IRS. In my hands, she'll be unscathed by the cruel, cruel world. And as I turn the corner to her apartment building at the end of the night, see the staircase to her front door in the distance, and slow my car to a crawl on the approach, I'm desperate to interpret her subtle sighs and ministrations as a sign that I should stop the car instead of just letting it idle. That I should park, rather than double-park. Because at the end of the day, and the end of the date, if we men have done our jobs, if we've performed valiantly, we get to try our luck at a possible goodnight kiss at the place where it all began: Her doorstep, the best venue of all.

She Said . . .

When choosing where to live, women want to be near a gourmet grocery store, a friendly dry cleaner, the office, the gym, and the Korean guy who cuts our hair. But when choosing a place for the very first date, all we want is to be near our car. Our car is our get-away vehicle should disaster (or mind-numbing boredom) strike.

Let me make this easy for you guys: Women have enough to deal with before a date, like preparing ourselves for post-date disappointment and plucking our lip hairs. So we want the logistics to be easy. We don't want to schlep across town—but nor do we want to be picked up. We're not cleaning our apartments, lighting scented candles, and stocking drinks and crudités in the fridge for someone who hasn't even taken us to dinner yet. Basically, we're looking for the location equivalent of Switzerland: neutral territory. So please, pick a place where we can meet you halfway.

If you get there before us and are talking on your cell phone, don't hold up a just-a-sec finger signal when we arrive, then keep talking for the next three solid minutes. It's awkward—we can't look at you, since that would invade your privacy, and we can't whip out our own phones and start making calls, since you indicated that you'd be off in a second. What are we supposed to do with our eyes? On the other hand, try not to arrive after us. Because then we're forced to whip out *our* cell phones (so we don't look like losers sitting alone in a café, possibly about to be stood up) even if we don't need to make a call. (Usually I just check my home messages, and let them run in a loop until the guy shows up.)

The place you pick shouldn't be a "cool dive bar." Nor should it be a stuffy hotel bar, or any place considered "romantic" (especially if there are singing waiters involved). We're looking for hip but not velvet rope. Classy but not piano bar. Casual but not free pitchers. We don't like it when you steal glances at the TV in a sports bar and say, "Oh, sorry—but it's the *playoffs*."

Don't choose a place that's so loud we have to ask "What?" after each sentence you utter. It doesn't make you look "popular" if you pick a place where you just happen to see ten of your closest friends. Running into your parents doesn't make you seem "family-oriented." Being on a first-name basis with the hostess doesn't impress us. Flirting with the hostess pisses us off. Giving the bartender the thumbs-up sign essentially ends the date.

Some guys add "activities" into the equation. Instead of asking for a simple meal, they'll tack on a movie, museum, or amusement park. Save these for later dates. We don't want to be trapped in a movie theater with an aspiring film director who spends the entire two-hour dinner bragging about his accomplishments, only to hear him whisper during the movie previews, "I could have done that so much better." We don't want to stare at naked female bodies at a photo exhibit before we've seen you naked. And despite the name, there's nothing amusing about going to an "amusement park" and puking our guts out on the double loop.

Other men suggest athletics—hiking, tennis, Rollerblading. I don't know who put the "multiple location" idea in men's heads, because there's not a sane woman anywhere who welcomes this itinerary the first time out. It's like packing for a trip: What are the weather conditions? What's comfortable for the activity but also attractive for the meal afterward? Will there be showers nearby? Even worse, we never know how a guy might respond to our athletic performance. Some men may be turned off if we're uncoordinated, others may resent us if we're better than they are. Which is a problem, because we'll no longer be near our cars to make a quick get-away.

Remember, there's a purpose to a first date. We're trying to get as much information as possible about each other in as short a period of time, in order to see if we want more information over a longer period of time. But men and women acquire this information differently. Men like to go to events so they can observe us *(Did she cheer for the wrong team at the baseball game? Can she dance to alt-rock?)* while women prefer sharing a meal so we can pepper our date with questions *(So, when was your last relationship?).* Which method is better: passive observation or active conversation? As my friend Michael put it, "I pick a place where I think she'll be happy. Because if I'm happy and she's miserable, in the long run, I'll be miserable, too."

Good advice. But when you ask us out, don't reveal all the angst that went into your decision. If you've got weird fetishes about location, keep them to yourself. Don't share tidbits like, "I can't go anywhere with checkered tablecloths. It has to do with what happened at my fifth birthday party." And please don't give us a choice of where to go. We don't ask you to choose whether we should wear the cropped black trousers or a Guess halter dress. Like a concierge in a hip hotel, casually toss the name of the restaurant off the tip of your tongue, as if there are dozens of equally perfect places you might have spontaneously suggested instead.

Because if you manage to pull this off, you might get lucky enough to pick a place for our next date, too.

6

Order in the Courtyard Restaurant

IS CHIVALRY DEAD?

He Said . . .

Y ou're sitting there at your table, and you're wondering if you should order for your date. On the one hand, it's bold, assertive, possibly sexy. She might like that. On the other, she might be offended by your presumptuousness and refuse to kiss you at the end of the night. You might not like that. Okay, maybe just the wine. She won't be offended if you pick just the wine, right?

Whoa there, buddy. Slow down. Let's put this date in some historical context.

I once wrote an eighteen-page report on chivalry. It was an assignment for Mr. Percini's seventh grade accelerated humanities class, and I remember it vividly because it was the longest paper I had ever written to that point in my schooling, and I was even prouder of its scholarship than its length. Plus, it had footnotes.[1] I got an A,[2] so evidently I know a thing or two about chivalry.

---

1. Like this one. (Cool. This brings me back . . .)
2. See transcript, Bleyer, Kevin. Chinook Junior High, 1984–5.

Now, if you remember, the knights of the Middle Ages were heralded for more than simply their ability to joust.[3] They were experts in chivalry. Above and beyond their call of duty, knights understood medieval chicks.[4] In between fighting battles and warding off plagues, Lancelot committed himself to figuring out just what made Guinevere tick, and more often than not he got it right—at least, right enough to convince Guinevere to cheat on her husband—who, it should be remembered, was a king.

By and large, the way to woo a woman in the world of King Arthur was simple: Keep her from having to think, act, or fend for herself. Instead, a man should think, act, and fend for her. He should, above all, be valiant not only in battle but also in romance: At all costs, make her decisions, tell her how she feels, and fight her battles on her behalf. Done right, what woman wouldn't swoon?

It was called "courtly love," and it involved a very particular kind of courting: namely, everything was in the man's court. It was a medieval man's responsibility to defend the weak and innocent that, in the day, included women. As a matter of fact, it was a knight's code of honor "to do to ladies, damsels, and gentle women succour upon pain of death."[5]

There was a time not so long ago—let's call it "the fifties"[6]—when that kind of behavior was still expected in a man. At a restaurant, a man would order for a woman. When a husband wanted his wife's opinion,

---

3. Bleyer, Kevin. *The Age of Chivalry.* Mr. Percini's Humanities Class (Accelerated). 1985. p. 2 (of 18!).
4. ibid.
5. Found on Internet. Must be true. (By the way, "succour" is the British variant spelling of "succor," which means "assistance in time of distress," and is not nearly as dirty as it sounds.)
6. The period between 1950 and 1959 (inclusive) when gender roles were particularly discrete and symbiotic: men brought home the bacon, women fried it up in a pan. To be followed by an era known as "the sixties," when men brought home the bacon, women burned their bras; "the seventies," when men brought home the bacon, women filed for a divorce; "the eighties," when men brought home the bacon, women drank Tab; "the nineties," when men brought home the bacon, women didn't eat bacon; and leading of course to the beginning of the current era, "the twenty-first century," when men and women were on Atkins.

he'd give it to her. If a woman was offended or challenged by someone or something, a man would defend her honor at all costs. Not upon pain of death, perhaps, but upon pain of emasculation.

But that was then. This is now. Things have changed. A week ago I held a door open for a woman (a stranger, not a date), thinking I was being polite. Instead of passing through, she stopped, looked at the door, and said sarcastically, "Oh, so *that's* how it works?" Although we were in the same era, we clearly weren't in the same decade. My gesture was vintage fifties; her acid sarcasm reeked of today. I was Montgomery Clift;[7] she was Janeane Garofalo.[8]

So I wonder: What's become of courtly love? Because I didn't experience the era firsthand, it's odd to miss the good ol' days when men were men and women were damsels in distress. Yet I do. I think I would have flourished during the age of chivalry. I enjoy offering pleasantries. I like to spoil. I even consider myself, on occasion, gallant. Yet today, I fear that if I were to take off my overcoat and throw it in a puddle so that my date wouldn't have to suffer the indignities of a damp heel, *I* would be the heel. My date would think I had taken leave of my faculties.

Or, maybe, she'd think I was the man of her dreams. Depends. These days, it's hard to tell.

I'm not alone in my confusion. Frankly, it's unclear what's required of a man today. If we hold the door open for a woman, is it a courtesy?[9]

---

7. Actually, I think I may have confused him with someone else.

8. A comedienne who has transformed into an acerbic social commentator on politics and gender issues.

9. Modern technology, it should be noted, is also no friend of chivalry. True, the advent of the car gave men a chance to showcase our chivalry—nothing said "you're one hip flapper" than opening the car door of our brand new Model-T and taking care not to close it on her fringe. But then came "keyless entry"—a so-called modern *convenience* that does nothing but shine a glaring spotlight on our choice to *inconvenience* ourselves by walking all the way to her side of the car and bothering to open her car door when a simple press of a button on our remote would have sufficed. It's awkward and obvious, and defeats the purpose. Half the battle of being convincingly chivalrous is to be casual about it.

Or are we suggesting that this pathetic creature is so fragile the door might break her arm?[10] If we order for a woman in a restaurant, are we indicating that, as men, we know exactly what we want? Or are we suggesting that she is so dim she couldn't possibly know what *she* wants?[11] Does our intention matter,[12] or merely her interpretation?[13]

The problem lies exactly where my overcoat never will: squarely at the feet of contemporary women, women who operate under a debilitating damsel dilemma. Namely, today's women can't decide if they want a man who will fight their battles for them or a man who will merely cheer them on as they fight battles for themselves. (On *Politically Incorrect,* we called it "convenient feminism": the modern woman's currently *en vogue* practice of subscribing to the tenets of feminism only when it suits her purposes. The rest of the time, such as when a spider needs to be killed, Gloria Steinem be damned. As I once put it to Bill Maher, women want to have their cock and beat it too.)

In such an environment, we men are lost. With no certainty that our gestures will be appreciated or even welcomed, the temptation for us is to do nothing. In fact, this new post-Lancelot, post-Lance Bass[14] era begs the question: Is chivalry dead? Is all that Algonquin romance gone?

As an expert in the subject,[15] I'm prepared to declare: No, chivalry is not dead, but it's most definitely dying, and those who attempt to resuscitate it are no more likely to be deemed a valiant hero for their efforts than to be sued for malpractice for crushing chivalry's sternum

---

10. No, we are not.
11. No, we are not.
12. No, it does not.
13. Pretty much, yeah.
14. Lance Bass was a late-twentieth-century troubador who performed with four other troubadors under the monicker 'N Sync. They were prized for their voices, their jaunty dances, and their evocative lyrics such as "Yeah . . . oh yes . . . Ohhh . . . yeah . . . baby yeah."
15. See Bleyer, Kevin. *The Age of Chivalry.* Mr. Percini's Humanities Class. 1985.

and forcing air down chivalry's windpipe. Sadly, today's chivalrous knights are not covered under any Good Samaritan laws.

It comes down to this: What is considerate in the twenty-first century? Does being considerate mean I should consult my date at every turn (which restaurant?) and on every decision (which wine?)? Or does it mean I should make unilateral decisions that I have honestly calculated are in her best interest—to be so in tune that I can read her mind?

It's exhausting, and designed to see us fail at least 50 percent of the time.

So fair maidens, don't think for a minute that we gallant knights don't calculate every chivalrous move we make. We're trying very hard to be princely and charming. We merely ask that you please forgive us when we overshoot the mark.

And gallant knights, don't think for a minute that any amount of calculation will ensure you won't overshoot the mark. Today's damsels in distress aren't even certain they want to be rescued.

Trust me. I'm an expert in the subject.

She Said . . .

Despite the bold headlines on magazine covers, chivalry is not dead in the new millennium. No, chivalry is alive and well. Nowadays, though, it's hard to tell the chauvinists from the chivalrous.

Get a group of single women together and within fifteen minutes the subject of men will come up. In particular, the fact that men can be assholes. Not all men, mind you—just the ones we happen to go on dates with. The great men, the gallant men, the chivalrous men, the ones for whom we've been scouring the planet (or at least, the city)— we know they're out there somewhere. Even if they're all John Cusack, standing outside our window with a boombox blaring "In Your Eyes."

Meantime, we meet assholes. Assholes who have sex with us but won't reply to our e-mails. Assholes who cancel an hour before the date, when we've already paid for a manicure and blow-out. Assholes who don't even have the courtesy to call in the first place. And we go around the table, each woman offering up her very own sad tale of less-than-chivalrous male behavior. Like an asshole buffet.

A few weeks ago, I offered up my own. I met a cute guy named Jason at a party. He called the next day and asked me on a date. He asked if there was anything I didn't eat, and anything I particularly liked to eat. At the restaurant, he held the door open for me. Princely behavior, I thought.

Until we walked inside.

"Would you prefer a table on the patio or inside?" the maître d' asked. "Patio," Jason replied, without asking whether I'd be cold. (John Cusack would have asked if I'd be cold.) When the waiter asked which wine we'd like with dinner, Jason ordered a bottle of pinot noir—again, no input from me. When the waiter asked if we'd like pepper on our shared salad, Jason said yes—seemingly uninterested in whether pepper might make me go into anaphylactic shock. It seemed like Jason had forgotten I was there. So did the waiter. He started speaking directly to Jason, like he assumed I was either mute or had a bad case of laryngitis.

Back in the car, I noticed that we were heading in the opposite direction from my house. I asked Jason if he was lost.

"Nope," he smirked. "We're going on an adventure." I wanted to know what kind of adventure.

"It's a surprise," he said. I hate surprises with strangers.

A few minutes later, Jason pulled into a lovely spot in the canyon, took his fancy guitar out of the trunk, and played some tunes. He complimented me on everything from my accomplishments to my appearance. But once the flattery wore off (and I'll admit, it took an embarrassingly long time to wear off), I felt like Jason had scripted his own date, and I was just a character in his movie.

"What an asshole!" one of my brunch friends said at this point in the story. Of course, we all knew that Jason was unbelievably considerate. But because he'd taken me on a more traditional guy-makes-the-decisions kind of date, we held it against him.

It's not that we don't appreciate chivalry. It's that ideally, we'd like to pick and choose from an à la carte menu of chivalrous acts. I'll pass on having him pull out my chair at dinner, but I'll take the meal payment plan. Yes to help carrying heavy packages but no to carrying my coat. I'd like him to bring me flowers in private, but not in public. I'd like the guy to choose the restaurant, but not what I'll eat at that restaurant.

I know this sounds wishy-washy, but when we deviate *entirely* from convention, everyone's left even more confused. The week before my date with Jason, I met a guy at a dinner party and we spent a good hour flirting in the kitchen. At the end of the night, he left without asking for my number. The next day, I got a form e-mail saying that he had invited me to become his Friendster on Friendster.com. No personal e-mail message saying that he enjoyed talking with me, much less asking me out. Since the networking site is called "Friendster" and not "Datester," I figured he wanted to be friends. (Although recently somebody told me the site is nicknamed "Fuckster.") A week later, though, I heard that he thought I wasn't interested because I never replied to his form Friendster invitation. Huh? I would have replied to a traditional "Want to go to dinner?" invitation.

Certainly women could take things into our own hands by doing the asking, but that causes other problems. If a woman asks a guy out, a man might see that not as equal opportunity chivalry, but desperation. And on the off-chance a man might appreciate the gesture, I still wouldn't know how to do it. If I asked a guy out, how would he know it was a date and not just a "friend thing"? Would he interpret, "Want to come to this party on Friday night?" as "with me" or "to meet other women"? (If a man asks a woman to a weekend party, on the other hand, we know it's a date.)

Even worse, what if he says yes and I realize midway through the date that I want to be just friends (or never see him again)? What's the sign to convey my newfound lack of interest (other than not returning his calls, which he'll interpret as me playing "hard to get" since I, after all, asked him out in the first place)? Inevitably, we revert to the perspective of traditional gender roles, even when they're no longer applicable to the situation. So much for modernity.

So we're back where we started—looking for a chivalrous guy, so long as he subscribes to our own peculiar brand of feminist-style chivalry. I want a guy who will threaten to beat up a bully who's mean to me, but who won't go through with it because he's afraid of getting hurt. I want a guy who will invite me over for a candlelit dinner, but nearly cause a fire with the candles. Which brings me back to John Cusack.

John Cusack's attempts at chivalry seem endearing partly because their clumsiness makes them feel authentic. Jason's slickness made his gallant behaviors seem canned. In the end, maybe it all comes down to this: There's a difference between a fancy guitar and a beat-up boombox. Even if only women can see it.

7

Topics du Jour

AT YOUR CANDLELIT DINNER FOR TWO, ARE SOME SUBJECTS OFF THE TABLE?

He Said . . .

S o, will we be having sex tonight?"
That's what most men would *like* to ask. That's the question most men would love to have answered right away, before the waiter even takes their order, if they were being perfectly honest. *Really, truly, sincerely, I'm interested in where you grew up and what school you went to and how many siblings you have, but first, if you don't mind: Will we be having sex tonight?*

But because "Will we be having sex tonight?" is one of those questions that tends to alarm their dinner companion, men rarely ask it. Not because they don't want to know the answer (oh how they do), but because they don't want to *affect* the answer. They don't want to spoil their chances. They don't want to startle this beautiful woman they just met and would, yes, ultimately, like to have sex with—perhaps even tonight. But "Will we be having sex tonight?" is one of those conversational catch-22s: You're damned if you do, and you're damned if you ask whether you will.

So we're left talking about other things: the weather, the traffic, the menu, where she went to school, what she majored in, and mmm, that looks good . . . what is that? Chilean sea bass? Isn't that endangered?

Scintillating.

Picking the right topic on a date can be a tricky enterprise. Say the wrong thing on the first date and you won't have to worry about saying the wrong thing on the second. It's no wonder we tread lightly. Unfortunately, we'll have to bite the bullet and pick a topic eventually, because I have yet to hear of a good first date that entailed two hours of chewing. At a bare minimum women seek "a good conversationalist."

Banter—the wittier the better—is the coin of the realm at this point. So pick carefully, and keep in mind: There are certain conversational land mines on which we should never step our first time on the battlefield, such as our recent surgery, our recent ethics review at work, or our recent therapy session. Remember, we want this woman to be interested in what we have to offer, not in what we contracted, defrauded, or cried about. We're trying to help her find us attractive. If, for example, we just had our palm read—or had a near-death experience—save that for dessert.

But we're not the only ones who go wrong. One unfortunate habit I've noticed in the women I've dated is their inclination to start talking dirty, even on the first date. I don't mean *pillow-talk* dirty, where she makes suggestive comments about body parts—with any luck, that comes later. I mean *pasta-talk* dirty. I mean dirty compared to what most other people in the restaurant are talking about. In a pasta-talk dirty conversation, there are no genuinely R-rated comments, just a few select PG-13 revelations about past dirty deeds—preemptive semigraphic disclosures designed to pique our prurient interest. Within ten minutes on our first date, for example, Gloria let it slip that she once had sex on a cliff in Ireland. By date two, Leigh told me she once had sex in a tree. My third date with Jennifer took place in the restaurant where—she was all too eager to divulge—she had had sex with her last boyfriend. On *their* first date.

Why did they do this? Because after a lengthy career of dating, most dating veterans have realized that a very quick way to force intimacy is to talk about intimate things. It's a sexual shortcut—go directly to sex without passing go. To a degree, it works; certainly, I get to know in a few minutes what it should take me a few months (or at least a few more martinis) to learn. But when we force intimacy, we have exactly that: forced intimacy. When a date confides her sexual peccadilloes to me, it's a manipulative tactic to imply that others have—and therefore I should—consider her a sexual being. But really, it's very desperate. When I heard about sex on a cliff, in a tree, under a table, and on a trampoline, I didn't conclude I was dating sexy women; I was dating the cast of Cirque du So-laid.

These disclosures often backfire: When Gloria also told me that recently she's been dating so much that she's been "doubling" and "tripling up" on a given night, she was trying to make me think she was popular, in demand, and objectively sexually attractive; I just thought she was a whore. Or at least, whorish.

We talk about our past (of which past sexcapades are simply a most interesting part) for a reason that is likely self-evident: because we want to determine if we're compatible.[1] When we do this, we're inclined to reveal details of our lives that make us seem interesting. But if we haven't had sex in a tree (what, you haven't had sex in a tree?), other details must suffice. I'm embarrassed to admit that, in my effort to impress a date, I've blurted out the fact that "I was a child actor!" (As if I wanted to be attracted to someone who was attracted to a child actor. It made no sense.)

---

1. I once read an article explaining why a dog, when it first greets another dog, sniffs its butt. It's the quickest way to determine where it's been recently and if it's eaten anything worthwhile—and therefore, whether the dog doing all the sniffing should hang out with the dog doing all the eating. An odd mating ritual, perhaps, but humans are no different. Upon first meeting someone on a date, we'll cram twenty-plus years of where we've been and what we've been up to and how long we've lived in town into the twenty-plus minutes we've allotted to that topic—before, of course, we should be moving on to the present and determining if we have a future. *Sniff, sniff.*

And sadly, a lot of the things that do make me an interesting person—if indeed I am an interesting person—don't exactly make me a romantic catch: the time I got my foot stuck in an escalator in East Berlin (wanna see my scars?); the time I overcame my obsessive-compulsiveness (wanna see my hotel shampoo bottle collection?); the time my soul mate got engaged to someone else (wanna see my scars?).

The conversational land mines are everywhere, so really, there's only one topic that will truly fly: her. Talk about her. Ask questions about her. If she asks a question about you, turn the question back around to her. "Her" is a topic she'll be fully briefed in, have insightful things to say about, and find endlessly fascinating. It may seem like a conversational black hole to you, but it won't to her, and at least the conversation will keep flowing, as long as you keep asking. Not to mention if you don't show an interest in who she is and what she has to offer (and where she grew up and where she went to college and how many siblings she has) . . . no, you will not be having sex tonight.

She Said . . .

Shortly after I got out of a long-term relationship (2.5 years and a dog) I went on a date with a guy who had just gotten out of a short-term marriage (2.5 years and a kid). Peter was handsome, successful, and, judging from our pre-date phone call, utterly charming.

But it was the first post-breakup date for both of us, and clearly we were out of practice. At the restaurant, we made awkward small talk about the bread ("Right out of the oven!"), the real estate market ("It's a bubble!"), and the weather ("I know! It's usually not this hot so early in the season!"). After a discussion about whether the seats in the booth were made of leather or pleather (we drew out this line of inquiry over the entire salad course), desperation set in as the entrées arrived. That's when we made the rookie dater's most fatal conversational gaffe: I asked him about his marriage; he asked me about my relationship. Needless to say, we became "just friends."

After that, it didn't take long for me to remember the Rules of Engagement (or the rules that might get a second date, which might eventually lead to an engagement). When looking at the menu, I established a common culinary bond (*You hate artichokes? Oh my God . . . so do I!*). When a date talked about his nephew, I mentioned my volunteer work with teen girls (date-speak for "I like children, but I'm still using birth control"). I made witty comments about the topics du jour (eBay, iPods, spray-on tanners).

Forget romance. A first date is like a job interview—except you alternate between interviewer and interviewee. When you tell a story about your friend who's dating a younger guy of a different race, your date knows you're testing his views on social politics. When you say that you can't believe how badly the man at the next table treated the waiter, he knows you're assessing his level of empathy. When you say, "I went to this wonderful exhibit of modernist art. I skipped over the old masters . . . what a bore," he knows you're judging his sense of aesthetics.

Similarly, your date will be evaluating you, so if he gushes about Aqualung, gush back for the sake of simpatico. ("Aqualung? Yeah, I love Aqualung!"—even if you've never heard of Aqualung). If he says his favorite movies are *A Clockwork Orange* and *Raging Bull*, there's no need to mention that yours are *Amelie* and *Lost in Translation*. If he says he doesn't eat junk food, stop yourself from talking about your love of double-stuffed Oreos. (The implication being: We both like healthy food, therefore we like each other.) It's natural to take on alternate personalities as we try to guess what type of person might appeal to the object of our affection (even as we somehow forget to consider: What type of person might appeal to *me*?).

As in a job interview, the goal is to impart general information without imparting Too Much Information. If the interviewer is interested, he or she will do a background check (i.e., Google) but there's no need to warn him or her up front about what he or she might find.

If, for instance, you're still deciding whether to write movies, open your own restaurant, or apply to business school for the third time, the vague and general "exploring my options" may go over best. Use appropriate judgment when offering up either your relationship history ("One day we were rehearsing a play at her place and, well, we both got rug burns—*if you know what I mean.*") or medical history ("I'm glad your mom recovered from breast cancer. My doctor once thought I had testicular cancer because one ball is smaller than the other—but it turns out everything was normal.").

Of course, it's natural to want to break the ice and let down your guard if you hope to end up naked together. You'll want to "be yourself." As if that were possible. To paraphrase Chris Rock: In the early stages of a relationship, you're not you, you're the *ambassador* of you. Which is why I cite the three most important words of first-date discourse: Better Left Unsaid.

Clichés are always safe. If asked why your last relationship ended, make it sound as if you both sat down and talked in a healthy and loving way about "wanting different things" (even if what you wanted was to have his children and what he wanted was to date his coworker). No need to say anything about marital ultimatums or being screwed out of half your furniture and your entire DVD collection. Bonus points for using the phrase "I wish him the best" with a straight face.

Try to remember that you don't have to fill every single silence. Sometimes it's nice to take a breather. Or chew. I once went out with a guy who would quiz me during the pauses: *Would you rather be blind or deaf? Smart or pretty? Die in a fire or plane crash? If you could have love or money, which would it be?* When I reported this to the friend who had set us up, she replied, "I think he was just trying to get to know you."

Fair enough. But sometimes, actions work better than words in moving things forward. Like at the end of that first date? Instead of mumbling some lame version of "I'll call you," just go home and pick up the phone. Because beneath the surface, that's what the entire first-date conversation was about anyway: Would there, or would there not, be a second date?

All the rest was just filler.

8

I Just Want a Guy with a Sense of Humor

ARE YOU SERIOUS?

He Said . . .

Three dates in, I couldn't decide if I wanted to ask Angela out for a fourth.

"Is she pretty?" Dennis Miller asked me. I told him she was.

"Is she smart?" he asked. *Yes, very,* I told him.

"Is she funny?" he asked.

Funny? Huh. I hadn't considered that before. And I didn't know quite how to answer. Or at least, I couldn't be concise about it.

"Well," I said, after some consideration, "she doesn't make *me* laugh hard. But on the other hand, she's funny in the sense that she seems to know what funny is, and she usually laughs at the right jokes. So I guess she has a sense of humor, but she's not funny herself. Is that what you mean?"

I looked up to see that Dennis had already left the room. Now *that* was funny.

But Angela? Funny? Maybe not so much.

Don't worry—I'm not going to make the argument that women

aren't funny, or aren't as funny as men. But I will say this: In the dating game, insofar as I've played it, funny is the man's responsibility.

Now, before I get strung up by my punch lines as a misogynist because I've announced there's a double standard in the humor department, keep in mind that women are the ones making these rules. Read the latest *Cosmo* poll, and you'll notice that the number-one quality a woman looks for in a man is a sense of humor. "I just want someone I can laugh with," is the usual refrain. I remember seeing my first ever *Playboy* centerfold and reading her turn-ons: "Walks on the beach, beautiful sunsets, a man with a sense of humor . . ." So it may be a double standard, but it's a standard defined . . . by women. Women set the bar, men make up the story about the two Jews who walk into it.

But gentlemen, here's the bad news for the rest of us. Despite what she says, being funny won't cut it. *Funny* may satisfy her "number-one criterion," but it won't satisfy the criterion that really counts. In fact, while *funny* is supposedly expected in a man (hence, his responsibility), for any man who believes that women truly want a funny guy above all else, the joke is on you. In the real world, women don't fall for a man because of his sense of humor. Oh sure, a sense of humor can *help,* I suppose, because often humor indicates a degree of intelligence, and intelligence implies good job prospects, and good job prospects correlates with an ability to put food on the table and purchase nice things like Kate Spade bags and Alaskan king crab. But it's not, in point of fact, the quality a woman it attracted to in a man—despite what *Cosmo* tells you, and despite what you hear from the horse's mouth.

Because when a woman says that a sense of humor is her number-one criterion, she's indicating to you what she thinks of herself, not what she thinks of you. She's announcing that she is mature and sophisticated, that her tastes are more refined than superficial; after all, looking for a solid sense of humor in a man, we can all agree, seems more evolved than looking for, say, a rock-hard stomach. If you're Mel Brooks, they can be Anne Bancroft.

And yet, women essentially desire a pretty face, if not a rock-hard stomach—a fact they don't want to admit to themselves, let alone to *Cosmo*. So what they do next is a genius bit of self-delusion: They'll somehow convince themselves that the guy with the rock-hardest stomach is also the guy with the best sense of humor. Oh, he may not have said a single witty thing all night, but they'll go home chuckling at the half-baked sentence he muttered about hair product. "If I don't use any, my hair looks like SpongeBob!"

SpongeBob? SpongeBob becomes funny, because SpongeBob is what they need to feel better about their choice in men.

I guarantee you, Reese Witherspoon thinks that Ryan Phillippe is *hilarious*. But has he ever made America laugh?

Jennifer Aniston didn't marry Brad Pitt because of his rapier wit. And yet, Jen likely told herself that she married Brad because late at night, no one—no one!—could make her laugh quite like Brad could. "I don't know," she probably said to Courteney, Lisa, David, Matthew, and Matthew after that first glorious date. "I guess you just had to be there. It was the *way* he said it . . ." (I bet she didn't think it was very funny when he asked for a divorce.)

Men, I mention all this because sooner or later, you'll feel the temptation, either during that first date or sometime between then and the honeymoon, either out of inspiration or desperation, to make your date laugh ("Be my wife, please!"). You'll feel it's your responsibility, even, because somewhere along the way you read, or were told, that women really dig a sense of humor. And you'll want to show her you can yuk it up with the best of them. Well . . . be my guest. Go right ahead. It won't affect her impression of you, but it may affect your impression of you.

Ladies, ask yourselves, are you truly hot for a funny guy? I remember a particular episode of *Politically Incorrect* in which a beautiful actress/model from some forgettable sitcom—likely the one where the guy was funny/fat and the woman was gorgeous—insisted that what she looked for in a man was someone who could make her laugh. Unfortunately, Jon Lovitz was seated nearby, and he quickly dismissed her.

"I hear that all the time," Jon said, rolling his eyes. "Women always say they want a guy with a sense of humor."

"And we do, we do!" she insisted.

"No you don't, you don't! And I can prove it," Jon pointed out. "I'm pretty funny."

Now *that* was pretty funny.

She Said . . .

I try not to date comedy writers. It's not that I don't want to date someone in a similar field, or that I don't want to date funny men. I'll happily date a writer, and if you ask me what I'm looking for in a guy, one of the first things I'll say is "funny."

But I avoid dating comedy writers for the same reason I avoid watching network sitcoms: the laugh track. As annoying as that canned laugh track can be to listen to—imagine a guy who expects you to *become* one.

That's right. Go on a date with a comedy writer, and he'll make you into his personal, one-woman laugh track. While you're innocently trying to enjoy your fried mozzarella appetizer, your date will deliver one-liner after one-liner, in that same monotonous three-jokes-per-page sitcom rhythm you heard on *Everybody Loves Raymond*. And you, in turn, will be required to laugh heartily at every single joke.

Even if a joke is directed at the waitress (trust me, it will be—but at least *she* gets a tip for laughing), you'll be expected to giggle appreciatively. It's like watching TV, except there's no changing the channel, no TiVo-ing out the bad parts, no talking on the phone with the volume muted in the background. In fact, don't even *try* to talk—because your date will interrupt every fifth word of yours with a joke. For two solid hours, you'll be pelted incessantly with witticisms like bullets from a fully loaded AK-47, and there's no escaping his one-liner of fire.

Maybe you don't see why this experience is so brutal. You might even think it's easy to sit there, eat your free dinner (see chapter 10), hear a few jokes, and not get a word in edgewise.

Well, let me tell you, it can really test your gag reflex.

You can snort, cackle, and double over at twenty of his jokes in a row, but if *one time* you merely chuckle (or simply smile, or God forbid show no reaction at all), he'll sulk for hours. He might even express his anger by making mean-spirited wisecracks, first about the busboy, then your fellow diners, and finally—if you accidentally miss your laughter cue again—*you*. ("Is that a bandana or a blouse you're wearing? Just kidding!")

It would be great if women could avoid this situation simply by avoiding comedy writers. But even men with no professional comedy ambitions may treat your date like open mike night at the local club. And in that case, so should you: Remember the two-drink minimum and the evening will go by much quicker.

When women say we're looking for funny men, we simply mean we don't like dull men. If we're thinking about eating breakfast with someone for the next fifty years, we want to know that he won't put us back to sleep. We're looking for wit, not Coney Island schtick.

But no matter how patiently we try to explain this, some men refuse to give up their comedy routines on dates. They'll even resort to silly puns in moments of panic. ("Sure, I'll look at the *whine* list . . . but I don't have any complaints.") Men feel that being funny is part of their masculinity. It's how they court us. It's their role in the mating dance. The unstated punch line of their joke is, "Do you like me?" and if you laugh, they think you've said yes.

Which explains why when a guy—professional comedian or orthodontist alike—says, "I want a woman with a sense of humor," what he really means is, "I want a woman who appreciates *my* sense of humor." Only the most confident men feel comfortable dating women who might be equally entertaining. Perhaps it's because women have traditionally used their beauty to attract men (hence, the pressure to be thin), while men, to compensate for not looking like Orlando Bloom, have attracted women with their personality and charisma (hence, the pressure to be funny). Steal their thunder, and they'll feel castrated.

Meanwhile, guys argue that we're sending mixed messages by saying we want men with a sense of humor, then giving them grief for cracking a few jokes in order to woo us. They feel that if we want funny men, we shouldn't fault them for occasionally being too clever (or not clever enough). I suppose the good news is, at least we're clear about some things. Like, when we say we want a man with ripped abs or a real job or a heart of gold—we really do want a man with ripped abs or a real job or a heart of gold.

As long as he's funny, of course.

9

I'll Drink to That

He Said . . .

To drink or not to drink. That is the question. (Whether 'tis nobler to suffer the samarai slings and arrows of outrageous bar tabs, or by opposing, cut 'em off.)

Alcohol is dangerous. It lowers inhibitions. It slurs speech. True, it can also disinfect a gaping flesh wound, but if you're using alcohol for that purpose, you should be in a hospital, not a wine bar.

For that reason alone, *whether* to order alcohol on a date is a calculation best made, fittingly, with a sober mind.

What to drink is also fraught. One summer night I drank two glasses of merlot, leaving my entire mouth stained red for the rest of the evening. Later, I ordered two mojitos and managed to plaster specks of green mint atop my ruby red bicuspids. It looked like my teeth were celebrating Christmas.

How much to drink is possibly the toughest calculation. I, for one, drink in what's called "Irish moderation"—just enough to enjoy the evening, but not enough to accidentally fly to Ireland.

There's a reason they call alcohol the "social lubricant." Fact is, there was a time—presumably before drunk driving laws—when many men would pour themselves a drink before heading out for the night, to put them in the right mood. That first snifter even acquired a nifty name: "the psychological," because it gets a gentleman's head in the right place before an evening of being charming.

Ultimately, that's the purpose alcohol ostensibly serves for those of you who choose "to drink": It lets you become the gregarious version of you—the you that speaks your mind, the you that goes for the joke, the you that isn't intimidated when your date puts her hand on your knee under the table. With alcohol, all those tentative, timid yous disappear, and you're left with only the you that kicks ass.

Alcohol is date steroids.

I don't deny that when I drink, I get marginally more entertaining/charming/confident. I also get chattier; for me, an open bar leads to an open mouth. But I've always wondered what the ratio is between a bona fide change in my personality and simply an imagined one. Am I truly becoming more charming, or merely less discriminating about what it means to *be* charming? After the third gin and tonic, is my personality spiked, or watered down? If I were a drink, what would be the recipe—three parts vodka, one part water, two parts delusion?

And why the hell am I TALKING SO LOUDLY?

In college, frat boys were always accusing each other of getting "beer goggles." After a few drinks, the popular beer-goggle theory went, even the plain sorority girl started to look like a supermodel when seen through the haze that aged hops and barley provided. I was never in a frat, and in college I didn't like beer. Which is why, I suppose, I've never gotten beer goggles. But what alcohol provides me now is a "wine mirror": My date stays just as attractive, but I'm suddenly irresistible.

Mirror, mirror, on the wall, who's the fairest of them all? *You are! But any fairer and I'm going to have to call you a taxi.*

She Said . . .

I'm all for drinking on first dates. Even though I don't, generally, drink. But drinking on a first date makes the evening go more smoothly. It gives your mouth something to do during awkward silences, makes your date's wiry black nose hair seem like a mere floater in your eye, allows you to peek discreetly at your watch while reaching for your glass, and camouflages the involuntary rolling of your eyes as a sign not of disgust but of mild inebriation. Depending on your date's level of sophistication, you may even discover a nice wine to order on your next agonizing first date.

Even if the evening begins splendidly, I still recommend a tasty mojito to keep the conversation flowing. Or at least, to avoid the inevitable conversation about *why* you're not drinking. For some reason, ordering a nonalcoholic beverage makes a man suspicious. He wants to know the *reason* behind what seems to him like nothing short of deviant behavior.

"What, are you in AA?" he'll joke. (Except he's not joking.)

"No," I'll say. "I'm not in Alcoholics Anonymous." (Besides, isn't AA supposed to be, um, "anonymous"?) Actually, I'll tell him, I just don't like the taste of alcohol, which explains both why I'm not in AA and why I didn't order a drink.

But logic doesn't appease him, because not ordering a drink casts an emotional pall over the evening. Here's an area where women are less judgmental than men: If my date doesn't order dessert, I don't say, "What, are you in Overeaters Anonymous?" If we're at a Japanese restaurant and he doesn't like sushi, I won't say loudly, in earshot of our fellow sushi bar patrons, "What, you're just getting a cucumber roll? That's not real sushi!" It takes a lot more before a woman will write off her date as a dud. (For instance, he'll have to pick at his dinner and say things like, "Don't let me touch this. I'm watching my carbs.")

But for men, it seems, there's nothing less sexy than watching his date order a Pellegrino, a Diet Coke, or a "virgin" anything. (As my friend Andy put it, "She might as well be saying, 'I'd like a Platonic Juice, please.'") It's not that most men believe they'll get some action off a glass of chardonnay—it just allows for the fantasy (which often it is) to exist. Just as women realize that a guy saying "I'll call you" doesn't mean he'll call—it just allows for the fantasy (which often it is) to exist. So as a gesture of goodwill, order a drink. You can always pretend to sip.

Of course, not all women recommend this tack. Everyone from your mother to *Glamour*'s advice columnist shares cautionary tales of tipsy women being "taken advantage of" on first dates. Like if you order a margarita, you'll end up starring in your own personal episode of *Girls Gone Wild*. Maybe they had a point when we were in college. But there's a big difference between being encircled by a half-naked crowd of hormonal twenty-year-old frat boys counting to ten and squirting cheap beer down your throat at a keg party, and enjoying a citrus vodka at a Westside happy hour.

To me, the *real* danger of drinking on a first date is what happens once you get home safely. Because your safety is an illusion. Here's why: Chances are, you're far lonelier after the date than you were before it. Prior to setting eyes on Bob or Steve or Nose Hair Guy, you'd taken that dangerous drug we call Hope. You were, in fact, slightly high on Hope. And since the Hope buzz wore off as soon as your date said, "I think anyone who takes showers longer than three minutes is wonderful," you survived the meal through a combination of sheer willpower and the miasma of a martini.

But now you're home. When you go to undress, you notice how good you look and think, "What a waste." You admire the clarity of your complexion, the hairlessness of your moisturized legs, and the padding of your Wonderbra. You're too wired to sleep, so you decide to check your e-mail. And that's when you'll chase your last drink with a shot of humiliation.

Do not, under any circumstances, log on to your computer after the potentially lethal mix of Hope with a half liter of wine and a bad date. In fact, before leaving for the date, change your computer password to something you'll never remember at midnight, unplug your phones, and surround all other electronic communication devices with blinking orange cones. Otherwise, you put yourself at risk for drunk dialing, typing under the influence, and leaving a record of this mortifying alcohol-and-loneliness-induced behavior in the voice mail boxes and e-mail accounts of your mother, coworker, and most recent ex-boyfriend.

You'll e-mail your mother with the news flash that: "Guess what, Mom! I'm too depressed to masturbate." You'll send your coworker a priority e-mail: "I've just had an epiphany, let's fire Sue!"—and copy Sue. You'll write pathetic poems to your ex-boyfriend—or worse, leave a detailed account on his voice mail of your last encounter in order to prove that *you* broke up with *him:* "Okay, so maybe you said, 'I think we should break up,' but I was *thinking* that we should break up long before you said it!"

And when you wake up the next morning with a hangover and that gnawing feeling in your gut that what you pray had been a nightmare was, instead, the night before—you'll wish you hadn't had so much to drink on that very first date.

10

The Fake Purse-Grab

He Said . . .

Experts tell us money is the single most common topic couples argue about. It's also the *first*.

Let's say you're at the end of your first date, and by and large, a good time was had by two. No argument here. Yet.

Then . . . the check comes.

And with it, the beginning of an elaborate ballet that is repeated hundreds of thousands of times in restaurants all over the world. It has been performed more often than baptisms, end zone dances, and *Cats* combined. We'll call it "The Fake Purse-Grab."

> **HIM:** I'll get this.
> **HER:** Oh. Are you sure?
> **HIM:** Yes, of course—
> **HER:** Really? Because I can—
> **HIM:** No, I insist.

Or, to translate:

HIM: I'm a big boy.

HER: Hmm. Are you really a big boy?

HIM: Yes, I'm really a big boy.

HER: I'm not so sure you're a big boy.

HIM: I'm a big boy, dammit! I'm a big boy!

And there it is: Your first fight. Of course, that moment when she turns to her side and pretends to look for her wallet only to pretend to struggle valiantly while pretending to tug at the zipper on her purse (Damn you, confounded contraption! You have bested me yet again!) is only the climax. The curtain had come up on this particular performance much earlier. There was even a supporting cast. Enter Waiter #1.

Act I

The waiter drops off the check. He places it in a neutral position on the table and, while staring vaguely into space, or turning his head to and fro as if your meal had suddenly became a tennis match with no balls (she's playing the part of "Anna Kournikova," you're playing the part of "no balls"), says, "I'll take care of this whenever you're ready." The "you," purposefully, is indeterminate. He might as well be talking to the saltshaker for all the eye contact he offers.

Act II

The check sits there. No one notices it. As far as you and your date are concerned, it doesn't exist. (If a check arrives at the table, and no one is there to pay it, does it make a sound? And is gratuity included?) This stage is, of course, both practical—you were in the middle of your can't-miss anecdote about how you spend your weekends caring for disadvantaged children, so why interrupt that?—and political— acknowledge something as petty and trifling as money? *Please.* You're *made* of it. (You're also *full* of it, but it's too soon for her to know that for sure.)

Act III

There's a lull in the conversation. This lull, however, is different from the previous lulls, because the previous lulls were alleviated by merely thinking of something new to talk about, while this lull is likely a more profound lull, simply because it comes after the arrival of the check that, it turns out, you *did* notice after all. (What's this? A check?! Doesn't this restaurant realize I'm not made of money? How insulting! Didn't you hear—I spend my weekends caring for disadvantaged children, for crissake!)

Act IV

You reach for the check. She turns to her side and reaches for her purse. And then: The aforementioned "big boy" conversation.

By the way, ladies, we're not even convinced there's anything *in* that purse besides a mirror and a can of Mace. And since we know you don't really intend on paying, and since there's no reason to use the mirror when all evening the back of the butter knife has worked just fine (yes, we noticed), we'd rather just wave you off and pay the damn bill than face the last remaining alternative: The one where you blind us with chemicals and run off with the dinner rolls.

We men have other options, of course. We could let her pay her half. You know, "go dutch." (What is it with the Dutch? Am I supposed to believe that if I go on a date in Holland, she'll eagerly split the bill and I'll still have a snowball's chance of seeing her tulips? Doubt it. Definite clog in that theory.) But if we let her pay, we're no longer on a date. We're two single people who happened to share a table at a restaurant.

No. Men should pay. And we want to. And so we do.

But here's where the argument really gets interesting.

Women want to pay too. Only they don't. Pay. Or even want to.

They want to *think* of themselves as *wanting* to pay, but they don't actually want to do it. Or think about it.

Because if they think about it too much, they won't be able to perform the absurd mental gymnastics required to make the impossible connection that *wanting* to pay and actually paying? Pretty much the same thing.

If, later, we foolishly point out that we did, in fact, pay for the lovely dinner, you ladies can say, "Hey, I offered." Thing is, you didn't. You pantomimed an offer. At best, you offered to offer. Your body semaphore said "I WILL PAY NOW," only your body semaphore was lying. Fact is, Israelis and Palestinians have put deals on the table more sincere than yours.

But women desperately need to fool themselves into believing that, if they had their way, they would have paid. Because such delusion is an imperative step in the feminist calculus:

If I pay, then I'm not obligated to have sex with him.

If I later *choose* to have sex with him, it won't be because he paid for me.

Therefore, I am not a prostitute.

Quod erat demonstrandum.

And simply turning to her side and pawing feebly at her purse is, apparently, enough proof for most women. Because it reminds them of a time when they actually, you know, *paid*. Athletes call it "muscle memory." Bill Maher calls it "convenient feminism." My guess is even prostitutes would call it "prostitution."

Which is not to say that we men aren't complicit. We are. As we sit across the table from this lovely, progressive, sophisticated woman, we're unconsciously clinging to the delusion that there is still a part of her—a Cro-Magnon part, a Neanderthal part, a pre–Steinem part—that remains beholden to her unspoken cavewoman bargain. If we bring home the bacon, she'll show us her pan. Men know better, yet clutch at the hope that she's in touch with her vestigial prostitute.

So we argue.

> **HIM:** I'm a big boy.
> **HER:** No, I'm *not* a prostitute.
> **HIM:** Really, I'm a big boy.
> **HER:** Really, I'm *not* a prostitute.
> **HIM:** I'm a big boy, dammit! I'm a big boy!

Therein lies your first argument. The Big Boy vs. the Prostitute. At least we got the last word.

She Said . . .

Most women are terrible actresses. Much as we try, we can't fake loving a gift we despise. We can't pretend receding hairlines are hot. We can't pull off excitement over going to a "hole-in-the-wall" restaurant instead of a "hole-in-the-wallet" one.

But no matter how bad an actress a woman might be, there are two things she's genetically programmed to fake quite convincingly: 1. Multiple orgasms. 2. Offering to pay on a date.

When it comes to the latter, I'm not talking about a half-hearted performance, or merely an Oscar-winning one. No. I'm talking about a Lifetime Achievement Award in the art of making the Purse-Grab seem genuine.

The Fake Purse-Grab, of course, is that moment on a date when the check gets plunked down exactly midway between the couple. The guy quickly reaches into his pocket. The woman slowly reaches for her purse. The guy says, "No, no—I'll get it." The woman makes a big show of rifling through her purse (how hard is it to find a wallet in a bag the size of a doughnut?). The guy places his credit card down. The woman kinda sorta pulls out the corner of her wallet. The guy says, "No, I insist." The woman says, "Really, are you sure?" The guy hands the check to the passing waiter, and the woman lets go of her purse, adding, "Thanks . . . I'll get it next time."

Believe me, she won't.

Because next time, she'll also do the Fake Purse-Grab. And why not? The Fake Purse-Grab is easy, it's economical, and most important, it makes us feel good about ourselves for (faux) offering. After all, doing the Fake Purse-Grab makes it *seem* like we're paying (or would) even when we're not (and wouldn't). Where else can you get that kind of deal? Certainly not at Bloomingdales.

More important, though, the Fake Purse-Grab can politely convey information to our date about our romantic interest. Even men know that the entire subtext of "to grab or not to grab" is "Does she or does she not desire me?" The Fake Purse-Grab is a win-win: Sure, we get a free meal, but the guy gets spared potential humiliation. Except when we're the ones humiliated.

Consider these scenarios:

1. *You're both interested.* Check comes, he reaches for it, she does the Fake Purse-Grab, he insists, she says she'll get it next time. She won't. But she *will* go out with him again.

2. *He's interested, she's not.* Check comes, he reaches for it, she does the Fake Purse-Grab, he insists, she insists more vigorously, he brushes her hand under the guise of pushing her credit card away, she pulls her arm back and says, "Thanks." Then instead of replacing her wallet, she pulls out her cell phone. And starts dialing. (The message being: You are so excruciatingly boring that I should be fiscally compensated for my pain and suffering. It's like a fine for having been a bad date.)

3. *She's interested, he's not.* Check comes, he reaches for it, she does the Fake Purse-Grab . . . and continues to do the Fake Purse-

Grab . . . and continues to do the Fake Purse-Grab (where *is* that pesky wallet?) . . . while he watches patiently, leaving the check in the middle of the table, his credit card waiting for hers to join it. His hand does not brush hers.

4. *Neither person is interested.* Check comes, nobody reaches for it, nobody acknowledges it, and you both avoid it, like kryptonite. Finally, you both pull out your credit cards and place them on the check. Your hands never touch.

Admittedly, it's not a perfect system. Some guys complain when women allow them to pay but say, "I'll get it next time"—even though there won't *be* a next time (which he learns only after his calls aren't returned). And if there is a next time, he'll end up paying then, too. Because when she says, "The next one's on me," it means the next, oh, half dozen will be on him. A more honest dialogue might be:

HIM: I've got it.

HER: Are you sure?

HIM: Yes.

HER: Thanks, I'll get it next time.

HIM: No, that's okay, I'll take care of the next five meals, too.

HER: Are you sure?

HIM: Yes.

HER: Well, okay, but maybe I'll pay once after that, and still expect you to pay for 70 percent of our future meals.

HIM: Deal. So, how's next Saturday?

The truth is, for many women, having a guy pay makes us feel safe. In some hard-wired part of our brains, a man's credit card signals that we'll be fed and clothed even if we're perfectly capable of feeding and clothing ourselves *and* him. Men may be genetically programmed to respond to a certain type of female body, while women may be programmed to respond to a certain type of male bank account. I'm ashamed to admit it, but if a guy doesn't pay on the first few dates, I'll probably lose interest.

My friend Mike says he doesn't mind the Fake Purse-Grab. To him, treating the woman on early dates is like a "guy tax." To be sure, it's a pretty high tax bracket, but maybe that's where the equality comes in: The guy foots the dinner bill, but the woman had to shell out for the fashionable handbag in order to hide the wallet she has no intention of removing.

Now if a guy makes an offer (fake or not) to split *that* bill with us, we're happy to take him up on it. Because a girl can never have too many doughnut-sized purses.

11

Eup*him*isms and Eup*her*isms

CAN TRYING TO BE NICE BITE YOU IN THE ASS?

He Said . . .

Right now you're just figuring out how to let me down easy. It's our first date (or our second, or our tenth) and you've determined I'm not worthy of another. How do you tell me? In other words, how do you break up with me before we've even gotten together?

Simple: by not actually doing it.

By avoiding the situation.

It's a method with which men are quite familiar. Instead of a woman suffering the awkwardness of telling us she's not interested, she'll just lie. Or what many women call, "being nice." She'll say something that sounds vaguely complimentary, but is really a veiled insult to our manhood. For some reason, women think they should be kind to be cruel.

It's odd that men are often accused of being poor communicators, given that *women* conveniently choose to undercommunicate at one of the most important moments in the dating ritual. As we seek clarity, they trade in euphemisms: Those turns of phrase that sound like one thing, but mean another—usually something much more sinister and offensive. That's what a euphemism is: An insult wrapped in a compliment.

Euphemisms abound in my dating life. Jessica and I had—by the most objective standards—a great first date: a private tour through a museum, wonderful Cuban food, a lovely walk through Old Town Pasadena, many laughs, even an occasional furtive glance. Another date seemed in order. I asked; she said yes.

Our second date went horribly. No fireworks, no fizzle, no connection. At the end of the night, after I walked her to her front door (yes!), leaned in to kiss her (yes!), she turned her head to the side (no!), and offered me her cheek (NOOOOO!). But instead of giving up hope, I put my heart on my sleeve—presumably so that it would be closer to my dignity, which by then was gasping for life somewhere on the ground near my feet.

"J-J-Jessica," I stammered, "I know we were on different planets tonight, but I just wanted to say that I find you delightful and . . . and I'd like to . . . see you . . . again . . . soon."

Silence.

Pause.

Pause.

Pause pause.

Nothing.

Silence.

Pause.

Then: "Oh, you're sweet."

Ouch.

You're sweet. That's what she said.

My face fell so far, so obviously, the motion-sensitive security light above her garage popped on. Okay, maybe that's not the real explanation for why the light came on, but it did, and suddenly my pitch-red embarrassment was on display, spotlighted by a night sun aimed directly at me from above. Hard to say what the light meant, but at the time I thought it may have been God telling me to join a monastery.

And of course it wasn't just *what* she said—it was *how* she said it. She said "You're sweet," as if I had collected stones, painted them different colors, begged for my mom's permission to sell them in the neighborhood, knocked on Jessica's door, asked if she wanted to buy a "pet rock," and offered her two for the price of one.

"Pet rocks? For me? Oh, you're sweet."

Not as if I was trying to ask for a third date.

You're sweet. Now, in almost any other situation, you would consider "you're sweet" a compliment. If you were, say, a lollipop. Or even better: if you were artificial sweetener. If you were artificial sweetener, and a woman said to you, "You're sweet"—why, that's the best compliment you could imagine! You tried to be sweet, and you were!

But if you're a hopeful suitor desperate to be evaluated as sexy, strapping, and significant, "You're sweet" sounds an awful lot like "You're pathetic." It's the oral version of a pat on the head. Which is itself the euphemistic version of a kick in the stomach.

So again . . . *ouch.*

Later, she even employed technology to help with her euphemisms. A few days after that second date, I received the following e-mail, which I shall reprint verbatim and interpret in full in the interest of romantic science. Her actual words will be represented by the flowery *Apple Chancery* font, to appropriately represent its flowery euphemistic connotation, and its translation will be represented by the utilitarian courier font, to accurately express its true meaning:

Dear Kevin,

Or, to translate:

Kevin,

This is an inexcusably late thank you for the delicious dinner last week and an apology of sorts for not being as lively as one ought when being so kindly squired about.

Again, to translate:

I'm sorry I didn't kiss you, especially considering you did all that driving.

I am truly sorry for being such a disappointing date.

Again, I'm sorry I didn't kiss you (which you wanted), despite the dinner (which you paid for).

By way of explanation, I offer up my extreme fatigue on the night in question as well as, I confess, a certain carefulness on my part.

I just couldn't fake it.

Perhaps I explain and presume too far, but you seem the kind of gent ready and deserving of the most unabashed and unrestrained affection—and for reasons I am still in the process of figuring out (generally speaking), I feel I am not quite up to the measure…please forgive me.

It's not you (generally speaking), it's me. And by that I mean: *I* don't like *you*.

You are a dear and generous person and eminently deserving of a far less confused and far more engaged lady.

Don't hate yourself too much. You're not your fault.

And if you never wish to speak to me again, I'd understand, though I'd be heartily disappointed…

I'd be heartily disappointed if you ever spoke to me again. I wish you wouldn't.

Jessica

```
Don't look for a "love," or a "yours," or a
"best," or a "sincerely," or even a "take care."
You won't find it.
```

I'd love to see euphemisms become extinct, much like the Euphemium writing style that relied on them in the sixteenth century (it's true—you could look it up), because in dating, euphemisms can be uniquely painful. Unlike the `cold hard truth` (which men often employ), *euphemisms* don't inflict clear pain that can be immediately triaged and healed. The *indirect vagueness* of euphemisms makes it too difficult to diagnose our actual status. Imagine if you asked your doctor, "Am I okay?" and he shot back, "You're sweet."

So don't euphemize around the bush. `Go ahead and put us out of our misery.`

She Said . . .

I hate endings. Good-byes of any kind make me sad. I cry at airports, bookstore closings, and during movie credits. But there's nothing I dread more than the end of a first date. In fact, dating would seem tolerable if only we could skip the part where we say good-bye. The date may be irritating, but the ending is excruciating. No matter how badly you'd like the stranger sitting across from you to magically evaporate into a cloud of hydrogen gas, deep down the panic of how to reject this person hangs over your head from the minute you have your first murder fantasy to the final awkward, "Wow, well, uh, great meeting you . . . take care!"

The end of a first date isn't fun for anyone. Last week, my friend Michael called me to complain about a woman who ended the evening with, "You seem like a really nice guy, but I'm just not feeling that spark."

"I'm not even nice!" Michael told me—which seemed like an odd thing to get upset about.

Granted, I'd rather be the rejector than the rejectee, but not by much. I've tried—and failed—at honesty:

> HIM: (LEANING IN FOR A KISS) I had a really nice time. I haven't felt such a connection on a first date in months! When can I see you again?
>
> ME: (LEANING AWAY FROM KISS) I had a really nice time, too. (Not the honest part.) But, the truth is, I just don't feel a romantic connection here.
>
> HIM: (TAKEN ABACK) Well, what makes you think I do?
>
> ME: (TAKEN ABACK) Um, that thing you said about the connection and wanting to see me again?
>
> HIM: I didn't mean that. I was just trying to be polite!

I've tried—and failed—at neutrality:

> ME: So, thanks for the coffee. But I have to get to a . . . thing.
>
> HIM: Oh, so soon? Wow, this was fun. Let's do this again.
>
> ME: I'm going to be late for my . . . thing.
>
> HIM: (WHIPPING OUT HIS PALM PILOT, QUICKLY) Are you free on Saturday night?

After realizing that honesty is too harsh and neutrality makes men think, "Hey, she likes me!", I decided to employ euphemisms for men, or eup*him*isms.

And why not be nice? No matter how disappointed we might be that a date didn't work out, there's no need to take that stinky bile brewing in our bellies and barf it out on the other person. Is it really his fault if he's conceited, boring, stupid, bald, fat, cheap, immature, awkward, or smells bad? Isn't throwing a few euphemisms his way the gracious thing to do?

Of course not! Nice, shmice: it's still rejection.

Put yourself in his position. When a guy tosses out a eupherism—"I think you're really cool, but I'm preparing for this big trial at work" instead of "I find you flat-chested and unattractive"—does it make you think, "What a sweetheart," or "What a bastard"? It pisses us off when guys make an effort to be nice. In fact, we hate them for it. It's hard to get mad at them for good intentions, but at the same time it feels condescending, like they're trying to pull the wool over our eyes. (Well, obviously—they're trying to be nice.)

Besides, you'd think for credibility's sake, a guy might bother to come up with original eupherisms. Not so. Often he'll simply spout a cliché from a *Maxim* "How to talk to women" article: He met someone else before you and he needs to see where that goes; he'll be out of the country for the next month; or the perennial standby—family illness.

But even original eupherisms can lack a certain panache. One guy told me that he had to go watch *Joey* because he and his sister have a ritual of quoting lines from the show. ("I was jilted for a sitcom starring the dumb guy from *Friends*!" I complained to my friend Sara the next day. "How boring must I be?")

Then there's the queen of all eupherisms: "I think we both know this won't go anywhere, but we could still see each other." What he means is, we could still see each other . . . naked. Or as one guy put it, not just "let's be friends," but "let's be friends-plus." (The "plus" being no-strings-attached sex.) I replied to this offer with, "Or instead, we could be friends-minus." (Mathematically, friends-plus and dating-minus are equivalent. Both make us feel like a zero.)

The most confusing eupherisms are those that offer false hope. In order to appease his guilt over rejecting us, a guy will say, "Let's do this again after my big project ends next month," or "You're someone I could see falling for, but the timing is wrong. Maybe after the holidays . . ." I ask men everywhere: How, exactly, are you rejecting us by giving us the impression that you like us and want to be with us? Is creating a stalker out of a perfectly decent human being accomplishing your goal?

Then again, I'm not one to talk. Once I blew off a guy by saying I'd give him a call "when things calmed down at work." But being a girl, I actually called. Which pissed him off. "Why are you calling me just to say you won't be calling me anymore?" he asked. "Why didn't you just *not call*?" The answer: Because if the situation were reversed, I'd rather have a guy call to say he's not interested than sit by the phone waiting for him to call. This way I can leave the house and stop checking my messages every twenty minutes. In fact, I'd respect him for it.

At least I wasn't as clumsy as the guy who ended our very pleasant four-hour date with, "So, I'd love to see you again, but I should tell you that I'm just getting out of a relationship." Then, as I gave him the hairy eyeball, he added, "Actually, it's not really a relationship. It's just a sexual thing"—as if *that* disclaimer made it better.

"So, can I call you?" he asked. I was no longer interested, but the sick thing is, I still hoped he'd call.

Because for women, that's the hardest part of ending a date. The second you say good-bye, our mental stopwatches turn on, counting the days—nay, hours—until you call. We need you to call to confirm our belief that you found us alluring, that we're worthy of a second date, that you weren't just tossing out an empty eupherism. Of course, don't be surprised if we tell you over the phone that our "plate is full" or we "just got back together with an ex-boyfriend." I mean, we may have "enjoyed meeting you," but unfortunately, "it's a bad time" and "things are crazy-busy right now."

12

Zeroing In

HOW DO YOU NARROW IT DOWN WITHOUT SCREWING IT UP?

He Said . . .

I once resolved that instead of deciding for myself what to do when it comes to women, I would give up my dating fates to the dating gods. Or at least, to the women themselves. I'd date as many women as possible for as long as possible, inevitably some of them would stop returning my calls, and the last one standing would become my girlfriend. It was, I thought, a novel idea: dating by attrition. The theory was simple: Perhaps the best way to find "the one" is to learn which of the twos, threes, fours, and fives just plain got tired of me.

Unfortunately, it is a method that remains untested. Who are we kidding—I've never asked five women out at a time, let alone five women who said yes. Besides, dating multiple partners is not only tacky in this day and age, it's dangerous (so says the checklist during my annual physical) and immature (so says my mother). Instead, there comes a time in every dating chronology when you have to zero in or check out. You can't leave it up to fate.

How does one decide?

The criteria for when it's time to zero in can be different for different people. On reality television shows, the test seems to be whether the man and the woman "felt a connection." As in, "I really felt a connection with Tiffany, and I'm looking forward to spending some quality private time with her when Angela, Tykesha, Natalie, Cindy, Shanequa, Kimberly, Caitlin, Tina, Ursula, Monica, Pearl, Arianna, Lindy, Gina, Georgia, and Gigi aren't around."

Could the signal that it's time to "zero in" simply be a vague feeling of "connection"? Perhaps. On the golf course one weekend, my friend Ross told me that he knew it was time to zero in on his girlfriend when the thought of spending an entire weekend with her (and her alone) gave him a "warm fuzzy feeling inside." When I pointed out that he was on the golf course with *me,* and that it was the weekend, and that he wasn't with her (and, I added, that his current "warm fuzzy feeling" better have nothing to do with me), he conceded that maybe he wasn't there yet—but he was close. Maybe he could convince her to take golf lessons . . .

Cameron felt that "connection" as well, although his was far less subtle. Only one woman had said yes in a year's worth of asking women out. He didn't exactly have to do much zeroing in. It's quite easy to go from one to zero.

And then there's me. I am, I've come to realize, a special case. Unlike others who zero in after a relationship has matured, I zero in before I even ask a woman out. This is because, like all men, I'm phenomenally afraid of rejection. Unlike most men, however, it affects my dating life. I have to be confident that a woman is interested in me before I risk the monumental blow to my ego that comes from learning that she isn't. I do most of my zeroing in before date number one.

Then again, I'm the exception.

Ladies, this may not be what you want to hear, but it isn't the rare man for whom the motivation to zero in on you is whether he's bothered by the thought that you're not zeroing in on him. Cruel irony, yes, but such is romance sometimes: a zero-sum game. Healthier is the relationship that develops in its early stages because both interested parties are entirely on board, but very common is the relationship that gets its boost merely because one interested party (us) was upset that the other interested party (you) was interested in going to interesting parties with other interested parties. So we rely on these feelings of white-hot jealousy to tell us how much we care about you.

Isn't dating fun?

Sorry, ladies, but it's in our nature. Someone once did a study about mall parking lots and male psychology. Turns out that if a man knows that there's a car waiting to take his spot, instead of being considerate and vacating the spot more quickly, he will, on average, take longer to pull out. Economically speaking, that makes sense: Anything in demand becomes more valuable, so we milk it for all its value. Yes, it's immature and a little abhorrent, but so are men. And sociologically speaking, it's perfectly logical.

So, ladies, don't be surprised when men apply it to dating: Sometimes we zero in merely because we can't stand the thought of someone else parking in you.

She Said . . .

A first date is like a big "whatever." The potential for connection on a first date is so slim, you might as well walk down the street, grab a random guy, and drag him to the corner Starbucks to see if you have anything to talk about over a half-caf-no-foam latte. You'll probably never see this person again and if you do, you'll pretend not to recognize each other.

But if, by chance, you're asked on a second date by a guy who neither bored nor repulsed you, you figure, why not? You lied your way through that first date (see chapter 7) so why not sign up for another?

When you agree to a third date, though, watch out. Because now you've entered into an unspoken contractual agreement: you're "dating."

Not officially, obviously, and not exclusively. But you both, on some level, *want* to be there. You can't simply disappear at the end of the night and never again take his calls (totally acceptable after first or second dates). If you decide to stop seeing each other, it will have to be communicated (and not on voice mail or in a "nice" e-mail). So before you accept that third date, think long and hard about your level of potential commitment.

Now, let's say by some miracle, you get through a first date with Guy A and you also get through one with Guy B. Then, at your second dinners with both Guy A and Guy B, you start thinking, "Hey, I kind of like Guy A/Guy B." So both A and B ask you on that key third date, and maybe—I realize this is verging on science fiction—there's even a Guy C or Guy D involved with whom you also had decent first and second dates.

How do you zero in?

Naturally, you may be wondering, "But why do I *have* to zero in this early?" A valid question. The answer, like most things, has to do with sex.

In this age of BlackBerries, Instant Messaging, and Instant Gratification, busy single people don't want to waste time. Which means that if at the end of a third date, the only bodily fluids you've exchanged have been from sharing the olive oil in which he dipped the bread he slobbered on, you'll both leave thinking, "Hmm, this just doesn't feel like it's 'happening.' It's not 'going anywhere.' There's no 'momentum.'" Rather than enjoying the process of getting to know each other gradually, you'll think that he's not attracted to you, and he'll think that you're not interested in him.

Back on Planet Sanity, though, you know something's wrong in a world where if you've only known somebody for a maximum of *eight hours,* not fooling around together on a third date is interpreted as lack of interest. Does it occur to any of us that holding off until you've known each other for, oh, I don't know, at least fifteen or twenty hours, might actually be a sign of a more substantial kind of interest? Instead, midway through the third date, you're trying to decide whether to fool around after dessert. And since there's no rational way to assess how you truly feel about this virtual stranger, you probably will—just to keep your options open.

Which only complicates things further. What if, after date three, you *still* don't know whether to reserve Saturday nights at the movies for this particular guy? And what if you've been on three dates with Guy B, too? And you've been intimate with one, or both. Is there an implied commitment? Somehow you're expected to figure out if you can deal with the way Guy A whistles through your silences, or the fact that Guy B wears cologne to the gym—and make a choice.

Note: Never, under any circumstances, mention to Guy A or B that you're dating two guys. Granted, Guys A and B will pretend to be blasé. They'll say that it's still early, that they're cool with you "exploring" multiple people. But what they really mean is, they're cool with *them* exploring multiple people, even though they're insanely jealous of the competition and will therefore call back two hours later and dump you.

Note to the above note: Even if you do the healthy thing and keep your mouth shut, the men you're juggling will still find out. Like the time Guy A left my apartment after our third date, only to call an hour later. Instead of saying, "I had such a nice time," he dumped me with: "I just got home and noticed that you've already logged on to Match.com. I'm not really comfortable with that." (He claims that he logged on simply to see whether *I* logged on. Frankly, I'm not really comfortable with *that*.)

And then there's the problem of keeping their stories straight. Was Guy A the one who loves jazz, or was that Guy B? Is Guy B's stepsister adopted, or was that Guy A's? When you ask Guy A "So, where in Santa Monica do you live?" and he responds with, "You asked me that last night—I haven't moved" you'll remember that's a question you meant to ask Guy B. You might even say something to Guy B flirtatiously in French, forgetting that Guy A, not Guy B, spent a semester of college in France.

So I try not to juggle, but it's tricky to know which guy to pick. Guy A is more attractive but Guy B is more accomplished. Guy A is more sensitive but Guy B is more charming. (To be fair, men also go through a cost-benefit analysis in deciding whether to pursue another date with us. They ask themselves, "Is the cost worth the benefit of pursuing her?" If you're not asked out, the guy determined that you weren't worth the cost. You were too expensive, which sounds like a compliment, but isn't.)

Eventually, you've got to choose one guy or lose them all. If you can't rely on either your head or your heart (after all, you barely know these guys), I suggest writing their names on index cards and picking one from a hat. (Just remember to save the other cards for when this relationship goes south.) Meantime, go ahead and take the plunge. Because once you get over your buyer's remorse, the best part of the dating ritual—the hallucinatory infatuation part—is about to begin.

PART

TWO

THE EXCLUSIVE ON BEING EXCLUSIVE

13

Love, at First, Bites

DEEP BREATH. REALLY, IS IT WORTH IT?

He Said . . .

Consider this your dating intermission. Your chance to get up, stretch your legs, and put a little perspective on what you've experienced so far. And really, your last chance to ask yourself a vital question: Holy crap, is it even worth it?

I mean . . . *really?*

I mean . . .

. . . *really?*

It's not a rhetorical question. It needs to be answered. And soon. Like, before she calls back. Does it make sense to expose the most vulnerable parts of yourself to someone who—let's face it—you barely know, especially when he or she is the exact someone who, if experience is any guide, may one day leave you in worse emotional shape than you are now? Forget the aphorisms. Is it truly, utterly, clearly, sincerely, genuinely, frankly, honestly, indisputably better to have loved and lost than to never have loved at all?

Think about it. You're about to put your hand on the stove, even though it's burned you before. You're about to sidle back up to the bar even though you had one too many last time around. Even though the horse threw you flat on your back, you're contemplating getting right back on. Despite it all, you're actually considering . . . an exclusive relationship. In fact, the thought of spending your entire life with just this one person doesn't even make you throw up in your mouth a little. Something about it feels right this time.

Just like last time.

Because that's what love does to you: It deludes, it makes you irrationally optimistic, it wipes away your previous wounds and current fears. So desperate are we to find some kind of durable companionship, we think, *yes, it's better to have loved and lost, because this time just maybe, I can love and win.*

Love, when you think about it, is the emotion who cried wolf and gets away with it. All the townspeople come running, somehow forgetting the dozen previous times the wolf wasn't a wolf at all, but just an immature narcissistic sheep with overripe fear of abandonment and a low-grade obsessive-compulsive disorder. Show me a person who falls in love easily and I'll show you a person with a short memory. (Hello, my name is Kevin, and I have a short memory.)

I'm not alone in my suspicions about love. Essayist Andrew Sullivan has come to a very pessimistic conclusion about the emotion. To paraphrase, love is a big crock. Love, says Sullivan, isn't the glorious transcendent communion of two complementary souls we're told it is; rather, love is, at best, an effective distraction from reality and self-awareness. Useful, perhaps, but not worth getting all googly-eyed about. Frankly, he contends, love stinks.

So, as a public service, allow me to be the boy who didn't cry wolf. Allow me to be the boy who helped pull the wool from over your eyes.

How do I *hate* love? Let me count the ways . . .

For starters, despite the refrain, *love doesn't lift us up* where we belong. Love can bring us down. We *fall* in love. We don't *climb* into love. In life's game of chutes and ladders, love is as often a chute.

Love lies to you. And love justifies the means. Ladies, hate to break it to you, but if a guy is putting you up on a pedestal, it may be so he can see up your skirt. A man will do and say almost anything to get a woman to fall in love with him.

Love isn't surprising, special, or rare. Case in point: Valentine's Day. Valentine's Day is the antithesis of romance. Anyone who has ever been in a relationship knows that it's a fraudulent holiday women exploit simply to get their minimum yearly requirement of roses and chocolate.

Love doesn't last. Tom Cruise called it quits with Nicole Kidman. Alec Baldwin broke up with Kim Basinger. Jennifer Aniston left Brad Pitt, after Pitt cheated on her. Meg Ryan tossed Dennis Quaid. Meg Ryan tossed Russell Crowe. In other words, even the people who get to see *themselves* having Romantic Love onscreen can't find it in real life. So neither will you. So go ahead and put extra butter on that popcorn. *The idea of love is always better than the reality of love.* Don't believe me? Videotape yourself making love sometime. You'll quickly notice that love is awkward and just a little ugly. Why is this? We're told Romantic Love, at its best, should be beautiful, aren't we? But in our experience, the difference between Romantic Love and real love is like the difference between a boudoir portrait and a *Penthouse* pictorial. One is impossible to attain without special filters and artificial lighting, the other just requires a donkey, a vat of mud, and a devil costume. Try as we might, there's nothing pretty about the way most of us show our love.

Of course, Sullivan was simply rephrasing the French philosopher Rousseau, who wrote that Romantic Love is the ultimate con game: It fools people into thinking that their lives have meaning, thereby keeping them from actually *finding* or *creating* real meaning in their lives. At least that's what I think he was getting at. I was too busy watching *The Bachelor* to pay close attention.

So take it from me, and the gay guy, and the Frenchman. There may be only one way to make sure that this relationship won't make you cynical, and it's this: start cynical. Open your eyes to the true hideous beauty that is love. Smell love's rancid fragrance. Taste love's bittersweet ripeness, listen to love's sinister siren song, and just for good measure, slap love's copious ass and watch the thing wiggle. That may be the only way to give this relationship your best—assume the worst.

Now, do I believe any of this? Not really. Because like you, despite having loved and lost, I haven't learned my own lesson. I still think I can love and win.

Just like last time.

She Said . . .

It doesn't take a blow to the head to fall into a love coma. It takes a combination of proximity, timing, hormones, and the suspension of reality. In the beginning, he is perfect, you are perfect, and you can't believe it took this long to find each other.

"Where *were* you?" you'll ask him, moon-eyed, while feeding him pot stickers in bed.

"Where were *you*?" he'll reply, kissing you lovingly in that spot between your carefully tweezed eyebrows.

If you weren't in the love coma, not only would you stop obsessively tweezing your eyebrows, but you might remember where you *actually* were before "he" came into your life. You were at work, actually doing your work. You were at parties and movies and art openings. You hung out with your friends. In short, you had a life. And when you come out of your coma, you'll realize that instead of telling him "I miss you" fifteen times a day, a part of you also misses, well, *you*.

It's not that you want to be alone-alone. It's just that certain things you took for granted as a single person are now off-limits to you: changing the sheets or cleaning the bathroom only when you feel like it; talking to your friends about your love life whenever you feel like it (now he always seems to *be there*); eating pastrami dipped in mustard with your bare hands, if you feel like it.

You're neither single nor married, and have the perks of neither.

But at the beginning of a relationship, you lose both sleep and perspective. You idealize the other person, put him on a pedestal, and overlook his foibles—which is surprising, given how much trouble you have overlooking your own. You spend an entire forty-five minutes daydreaming about his smile, the way he pours his cereal, the way his face looks when he's reading.

You become impatient when listening to the play-by-plays of your friends' dates, assuring them that soon they'll find someone just like you did, while secretly thinking, *Nobody out there is as great as* my *guy.* You gush about your new boyfriend so nauseatingly that these same friends begin to avoid you.

Then one night, watching your boyfriend pick his nose with a toothpick, you'll realize that the object of your affection is just another person—not the godly creature you made him out to be. The more you see how normal he is (as opposed to "sent from the heavens"), the more disillusioned you'll become. You may even wonder what you saw in him in the first place. And then you'll start to wonder whether he's wondering what he saw in you in the first place.

Don't panic. This is only a problem if one of you regains consciousness earlier than the other.

Meanwhile, there's something amazing about getting a new lease on life simply by spending every waking hour with a virtual stranger. So what if four months later this virtual stranger will be referred to as Fuckface?

Right now, you both believe in love . . . or at least, the initial head trip of falling into it.

14

"Hi, It's Me"

He Said . . .

I'm not a big fan of voice mail.

First of all, I'm tired of the computerized voices on voice mail talking to us as if we were children: "At the sound of the tone, leave a message. When you are finished speaking, hang up, or dial one for more options." Is there a single person on the face of the planet who doesn't know what to do when the beep beeps? Has anyone finished leaving a message, only to stand there dumbfounded with the receiver in his or her hand, unsure how to proceed?

Yet I'm even more perturbed by the *human* voices on voice mail; specifically, those of girlfriends, who I may have known for just a few weeks, leaving voice mails that imply I've known them in twelve past lives.

"Hi, *it's me.* Call me."

I'm sorry, it's who? Call who?

That's all I get: "It's me." No name. No phone number. Nothing else to go on. How odd that the computerized voice provided by

Sprint offers me far more information than I ever need, and the voice who ostensibly wants me to buy her gifts at Christmas can't be bothered to identify herself.

Give me something. Anything. Initials would help. I once got a phone message from my scatterbrained assistant at work: "Mike or Eric called." Even that narrows it down a bit.

Tell me, are you too busy to be bothered with all those extra syllables? I doubt it. I've seen you take two-hour bubble baths—you're not exactly pressed for time. Even the Knights of the Round Table, who I'd venture didn't have the luxury to attend power yoga, found space in their schedule to say, "It is I, Lancelot, come to win your fair heart." They never left it at, "It is I. Call me."

Now I'll admit, usually I do know exactly who is saying "It's me" on my voice mail. I'm not a hound who juggles fourteen women, all of whom think we're on exclusive "it's me" terms. But when a girlfriend leaves "it's me" on my voice mail, the first thing I identify, especially the first time she says it, is how strange it sounds. Is she being wary, in case the phone is tapped? Certainly she's not expecting me to call back and say, "Hello, *you*," is she? The last time a fledgling girlfriend said, "Hi, it's me" on my voice mail, I was tempted to call back and leave my own message on hers: "Honey, you'll never guess who called . . ."

I know, I know, the act of withholding her name is simply an attempt to simultaneously test our current status and force premature intimacy by claiming exclusive ownership of the first person pronoun. (Didn't follow that? Read it again.) Hers is a calculated move; by saying "it's me," she's secretly implying there's only one "me," while hoping that even if there *isn't* only one "me," perhaps by *saying* "It's me," she'll soon be thought of as the *only* me by *me*. (It's the *way* she says it that really sells it: always casually, yet, paradoxically, with absolute certainty. As in: Who else *could* it be?)

"It's me" can become a very dangerous game. Saying "it's me" as a tool of intimacy early in the relationship merely starts the clock ticking to the moment when you *stop* saying "It's me" as the relationship fizzles.

Divorced couples, I'd wager, can measure their relationship between the first time they heard "Hi, it's me" from their future spouses to the last time they read "Dear Mr. So-and-so" from their former spouses' lawyers.

I knew my relationship with Katrina was in real trouble when she called someone on the phone and said, "Hi, it's me. I need you to bring Ralph to the vet." I soon learned the someone wasn't just anyone. It was her ex-boyfriend Peter, to whom she was once engaged, and with whom she shared custody of Ralph. Ralph gets named, but Katrina does not. I explained that I found her choice of words inappropriately intimate when speaking to a former fiancé, especially when she hadn't said it to me in a while.

"There's only one 'it's me,'" I told her, "and it's *me*."

It's me—just a scant five letters and a single speck of punctuation, but possibly one of the most loaded sentences in the English language. Wield it carefully. And, ladies, as our relationship develops, hold off as long as possible with the "it's me" when leaving a voice mail message. Name, rank, and phone number. That's all we're asking.

Now hang up, or dial one for more options.

She Said . . .

A group of women sitting around listening to replays of answering machine messages may seem silly. But we're no sillier than a group of men sitting around watching instant replays of touchdowns on ESPN. You saw the touchdown the first time, and we heard the message the first time. Yet we both have a need to replay them incessantly with friends.

Men, be warned: No syllable is too small for our voice mail analysis. Pretty much anything you say can and will be used against you in a court of women.

A few years ago, I started dating an investment banker who often traveled between New York and LA. A few weeks into the relationship, he left me a message that went like this:

*"Hey, it's me. I'm at the airport and was just thinking about you. The weather sucks, it's fucking freezing and I've got that **** meeting tonight. I just want to go back to the hotel and **** with you. Wish you were here. Okay, well, I **** you."*

The **** is where his cell phone went out. Of the nine women who heard this message, nobody could agree on what the third **** was. (The first **** was "dinner" or "business" or "fucking"; the second **** was "cuddle" or "make love" or "watch *The Sopranos*.")

"It's 'love,'" said Sara of the third ****. "He said 'I love you.'" Her theory was that when he spontaneously said it on the phone, he freaked out and hung up. "Did you hear how quickly he clicked off?" she asked. "He didn't even throw in a 'bye.'"

"No," Linda said. "He said, 'I miss you.'" That made the most sense, but secretly I hoped Sara was right.

My friend Annie, who had just gotten out of a relationship and wasn't feeling particularly romantic, said the missing words—not word—were "will talk to." "There's no good-bye because he was signing off with 'I'll talk to you.' That was his good-bye." We all rolled our eyes.

After much discussion about the *is* sound versus the *uv* sound (my friend Kate majored in linguistics), it was four for "love," four for "miss," and one undecided. (Nobody voted for "will talk to"—not even Annie.)

I had to find out what he'd said—partly out of curiosity, and partly because if he did say "love" and I didn't say it back on our next phone call, he'd feel rejected. After much strategizing, we all agreed that I should tell him I got his message, then casually mention that "certain parts" didn't come through clearly.

"Oh," he said on the phone back in New York. "I was at the airport and just wanted to say hi."

"Yeah," I replied. "But your phone kept going out. Was there any-thing I missed?"

"Maybe the weather report?" he said, laughing. "Why, what do you think you missed?"

The proper response here would have been, "Nothing." Ordinarily, women are great at saying "nothing," especially when a guy asks, "What's wrong?" But instead (I'm not proud of this) I played him the message—and asked what the missing words were.

"Huh," he said. "I can't tell. Maybe 'I'll call you'?"

We broke up two months later, and nobody ever said, "I love you."

In this way, voice mail analysis helps us assess how a guy views us. Our outgoing messages should really say: *After the tone, please leave a message . . . and spell out your feelings for us slowly and clearly.* We even chart the time/date stamps with the exactitude of our menstrual cycles, all in the service of finding out how much we mean to him.

My friend Sara, for instance, got this message from a guy who'd re-cently broken up with his girlfriend.

"Hey, baby. A bunch of us are hanging out at Sky Bar later. I miss you so much. Come join us."

We all knew that while Sara focused on the "I miss you" part, the "bunch of us are hanging out" part (not to mention the slick, "Hey, baby") meant that they might become, at most, sex buddies. Which they did—for the next six months.

Tone matters just as much as content. My friend Nicole played us this message:

"Hey, it's Evan. I had a really nice time last night. Let's get together soon. When are you free? I hope you're well. Call me."

The content was flawless. But Evan sounded like he'd taken an over-dose of Valium. Clearly he wanted to give Nicole another chance, but the zing wasn't there for him. The verdict: great script, poor delivery.

Of course, sometimes poor delivery is a good thing. Like when a guy left this on my machine:

"*Hey, it's Jake . . . Rothman. You know, Jake. Just calling to, you know, say hi and wondering what you're up to. And if you want to do something. Or something. I mean, not just something, but something . . . with me. Sometime. Soon. Unless you're busy. It doesn't have to be soon. But sometime. Whenever. Call me. Bye. Oh, wait, did I say this is Jake? If not, this is Jake. Rothman. Okay, bye.*"

It wasn't the smoothest message, but I was thrilled. Not only had Jake asked me out, but he sounded nervous. Really nervous. Which could only mean one thing: He was excited. And so was I.

Message received.

15

I'll Show You Mine, If You Show Me How

IS THERE ANY CIVILIZED WAY TO GET NAKED?

He Said . . .

*I*n previous chapters I have chosen to speak on behalf of all men. Issues of sex, however, are so personal, so unique, and so delicate that it seems only appropriate I continue to do the same.

Hypothetically speaking, we lost our virginity to a lovely Englishwoman named Emma who we had met while on an overseas study program at Oxford. You know, hypothetically.

We're not saying it didn't happen. We're just not certain it did. All we really remember is feeling nervous, being sweaty, and experiencing the odd sensation of floating over the bed and watching us as if we weren't a part of the proceedings. (Leave it to us to make sharing our body with a woman an out-of-body experience. Silly us.)

To complicate matters more, it was our second attempt. Or more accurately, *hers*. The night before, as we lay naked in bed together, she cozied up to our ear. "I want you," she whispered.

"To what?" we asked.

We honestly didn't know what she was aiming at. The next night she didn't leave any room for misunderstanding, and to this day we know that nothing would have happened had she not taken us by the, um, hand. Which she most definitely did. We think.

Hypothetically.

Sex has only gotten marginally easier since. But at least now we know when we're having it.

First there's foreplay. We tend to be very chatty in the moments leading up to sex. Once the lights go off, so do we. Sports, politics, current events—we'll weigh in on any topic. It's the opposite of smooth or suave, and we don't think the woman in our bed appreciates it. "Hey there, naked lady, did you see it topped one hundred degrees in the valley today?" is hardly setting the mood.

We're not exactly sure why we become such a motor mouth—perhaps it's because we got tongue-tied before our hypothetical first time.

Or possibly—and we've given this far too much thought—we get chatty before sex as a preemptive maneuver. If we talk long enough before we get undressed, we might manage to get around to a topic we find it imperative she be made aware of: our gargantuan penis (penises?).

Whoa, whoa, whoa. We're not saying our penis is gargantuan. We're just not certain it's not. All we know is that, as most men, we're a little obsessed with the question. It is, after all, the first unknown that makes getting naked in front of a woman so fraught: Despite everything every woman has ever said to us about and before sex (that is, when we let her get a word in edgewise), and despite the politically correct insistence on the contrary . . . size matters.

Which is why, if we had our druthers, we'd always have first-time sex in a car, because depending on the tilt of her head, the recline of the passenger seat, and the angle of our side door reflectors, we might convince our date that objects in mirror are closer than they appear.

What's our point? Our point is this: When we get naked, we all like to make a grand entrance, even when we're not so grand. And since our penises aren't accompanied by a trumpet blast, or a herald proclaiming their arrival (*"Madames et monsieurs, please welcome the gentleman from Los Angeles, California"*), or a ringside announcer hyping the impending bout (". . . hailing from Tinseltown, CA! . . . weighing in at seven ounces! . . . and measuring a staggering but still manageable 5.75 inches!"), we'll do anything we can to convince ourselves that we're huge.

Personally, I measure my penis diagonally, like a television.

Whatever the method, right from the outset, we want to stack the dick in our favor, because we know it just gets more difficult from here.

The sex act, the actual *doing* of the doing, is a prolonged series of tricky obstacles, beginning with the navigation of far too many throw pillows (ladies, what is it with you and throw pillows? Half the time we're afraid to get in bed for fear of upsetting the delicate throw-pillow Jenga that you mistakenly believe to be so inviting), *and* ending with the miraculous transportation, via a complicated Rube Goldbergian sequence of events, of our date from mildly amused to somewhat aroused to absolutely ecstatic.

Yet, despite all those *Cosmo* "how-to"s, sex should come naturally, because sex is best in its natural state. Sex is simple. It's all the ways we fiddle with sex—our sure-fire tricks, our patented moves, our go-to gestures—that inevitably ruin a good thing.

Don't pretend you don't know what we're talking about: Instead of just enjoying the way our bodies respond to each other, we try a complicated move, maybe groaning just a little, so she moans a little, so we moan a little to encourage her moaning, which she takes as bona fide moaning, so she moans a little to encourage *our* moaning, which we interpret as ecstasy, which she interprets as abandon, which we're certain is imminence, and soon we're both hollering at each other in a continuous self-sustaining preorgasmic feedback loop, completely unaware that neither of us is even close to anything resembling satisfaction.

"I'm close!" she might be screaming.

"To what?" is not the right response. We know that now.

She Said . . .

A common complaint among my married friends is that they wish their sex lives were more exciting. Despite the fact that these women are having regular sex and I'm, well, not, they'll call me up to wax nostalgic about their single days in a speech that invariably ends with, "I wish *I* could have first-time sex with a new guy again!"

All I can say back is: *Are you insane?*

The first kiss, you bet. The first kiss is romantic, sexy, and most important, there's no nudity involved. It fuels the fantasy of what comes next, the anticipation of sultry, steamy, *Red Shoe Diaries* sex. But who can live up to that when you're standing buck naked with dimpled skin and cellulite before a brand-new body that belongs to the man you think you're falling in love with? The novelty may be exciting, but the novelty is also the problem.

We've all learned the *Sex for Dummies* mechanics, but with each new person, we're mere amateurs. A certain "thing" might have been a huge hit with your last three lovers, but this new guy might say "Ouch!" instead of "Mmmm." Then what?

If you don't click that first time, you may start to question your compatibility, as if compatibility were even possible in a state of abject terror. When a woman sees a naked man for the first time, her immediate thought is, "Will he call?" When a man sees a naked woman for the first time, his immediate thought is, "Will she come?" It's surprising anyone gets through sex without having a full-fledged panic attack. (In fact, first-time sex follows a distinctive pattern: anticipation beforehand, anxiety during, and airbrushed memories after.)

I used to think the anxiety would go away if I waited longer before having sex. I reasoned that if my boyfriend and I became good friends first, then even if my diaphragm went flying across the room and injured his dog, it would be okay.

But when I did wait . . . and wait . . . and wait, it was no more romantic. The pent-up lust was incredible, so incredible that we knew the sex, when we finally had it, would feel, well, anticlimactic.

And it was.

Worse yet, because we were so used to listening to one another, no matter what I whispered during sex, he'd actually pause and whisper back, "What?" (Me: *You're making me so wet.* Him: *What?*) Nobody should ever say "What?" during first-time sex. It's always better to guess or ignore it than to say, "What?" If a woman really needs you to hear what she's saying, she'll raise her voice. This is the one time a woman doesn't really care how well you're listening. Take advantage of it.

A woman, on the other hand, will hear everything you say and memorize it. Even while cuddling, women forget that there is absolutely no correlation between what a guy says naked in the dark *(I've never met anyone I've felt this connected to)* and what he says fully clothed in broad daylight *(I need some space).* In fact, there may be an inverse relationship. After revealing vulnerable feelings he didn't even know he had, he'll probably break up with her the very next day in a fit of intimacy panic. (And men say women are emotionally fragile?)

Even nonverbal communication can get first-timers in trouble. Have you ever opened your eyes during sex and seen the other person's face all puckered and squished half an inch from your own? It's not a flattering angle or distance. And then there's the risk that you'll both open your eyes at the same time.

"What?" you'll say accusingly, like you caught him spying on you.

"What *what?*" he'll reply like a counteraccusation.

But the question that throws me off most during first-time sex isn't "What?" it's "What do you like?" Do men actually expect women to *think* at this moment? (Later in the relationship, we'll be thinking about how to ask our boss for a promotion, whether to get our highlights done before our stylist goes out of town, and what our mother said earlier on the phone, but in the beginning, we're too nervous to think.) I can't list my favorite sexual acts off the top of my head, *High Fidelity*–style, like my top-ten albums or movies or TV shows. Everything loses its flow. Besides, the one time I managed to give a quick rundown, the guy apparently felt he had to get through the *entire* list our first time out.

Then there are the dirty talkers. "What are you gonna do to me?" they ask. I never know what to say. I mean, I'm *already doing it.* I'll probably finish rubbing here, then maybe put my lips there. But I can't enjoy what I'm doing if I have to consult my mental activity schedule to see what I'm about to do next.

Maybe women have a greater capacity to stay in the moment. When women say, "There, there, exactly there, *don't stop*"—men often have the urge to attempt to improve on the matter by going harder or faster. (What didn't you understand about *don't stop?*) Also, insisting on your repertoire of "slick moves" usually does less to make us quiver and more to get you stuck in auto-pleasure mode (kiss here, touch there, suck a little here, rub rub rub). You may think that following your nooky flow chart is fail-proof, but if we take you out of order, please don't insist on getting back on plan. And if we yell out, "Ouch, you're on my hair!" don't keep pumping like you didn't hear us when our neighbors two doors down probably did. Get the fuck off our hair, okay?

By far the biggest turnoff is men getting power trippy with their penises. We don't want to dress up as a biker chick, a maid, a schoolgirl, a cheerleader, or a nun. Once, a guy asked me to dress up as a cop.

"How?" I asked. "Do you have a uniform, or a badge I can pin to my bra?"

"No," he grinned, reaching behind his headboard for shiny pair of handcuffs with large restraints attached. "Just these."

"Pretend you're a virgin," another guy whispered during sex. I tried acting timid and coy and scared and excited all at once.

"No, no," he directed, "act *innocent.* You're a *virgin.*" Short of stitching up my hymen, I didn't know how to play that role.

"Okay," he finally sighed in frustration. "Pretend you're a slut instead."

Even if we make it through the sex unscathed, there's always the awkwardness that follows. After so much physical proximity, we often feel the need for distance. We pull away, take our time returning calls, reschedule dates for half a week away, wonder what we saw in the person anyway—all in the name of self-protection. If we thought the actual sex was anxiety-provoking, just wait until it's over.

So take heart, my monogamous married friends: No matter how routine the sex becomes, it's always better than that very first time.

16

I Love You, Nice to Meet You

DO YOU SUFFER FROM
"PREMATURE EXCLAMATION"?

He Said . . .

It's said that the mass of men lead lives of quiet desperation—that we're desperate for enlightenment, happiness, and love, but that we often keep it to ourselves. Not me. When I'm at my most desperate, I'm rarely quiet about it. I usually say things like "I think I love you." Truth is, I fall in love pretty damn fast. When I ask a woman for a date, half the time I mean a date for the wedding. I hear June is nice.

Bad move, I tell myself. *Play it cool. Don't be in such a hurry.* But sometimes I can't help it. I jump right in. *Nice to meet you. So, what are you doing the rest of your life?* That kind of thing.

Yet, every time I make that move—whether it be a premature "I miss you" or a romantic gesture that in retrospect is a bit overzealous, like, say, shopping for a baby stroller on a third date—I regret it. It's at those moments I wish dating were more like chess—my king could move to capture her queen, but as long as I kept my finger on my king's head while analyzing the new layout of the board, I could look the queen in the eye, and if she's not responding the way I hoped, I could withdraw my king and pretend the whole thing never happened. I could regroup, reconsider my options. I could, instead, decide to use my bishop. Bishops aren't in such a hurry. Bishops are nonchalant. Bishops play it cool. Heck, when they make a move, they only move diagonally.

Unlike me, they aren't so damn *eager.*

I should know better. Over the years, I've dated a few women who have themselves been rather eager in their declarations of love for me, who have put me on the receiving end of a premature exclamation, who have themselves proven that the mass of men aren't the only ones who could benefit from a little *quiet* desperation. And I know how it feels.

Not long after I started dating Katrina, we were driving back from the grocery store when she mentioned, apropos of nothing, "My sister says you're husband material."

"Huh," I said, noncommittally.

I kept my eyes on the road, but I couldn't shake the thought that with a single six-word sentence Katrina had revealed precisely how much thought she's given to our impending nuptials. Consider: She had already a) wondered whether I was husband material; b) consulted her sister about whether I was husband material; c) provided her sister sufficient evidence of my husbandly qualities (when she insisted her sister join us on our third date, I thought it was a bad sign—turns out I was merely facing a jury); and d) received a conclusive report determining whether my husbandly qualities passed muster. *All before date four.*

Clearly I *was* "husband material." I was merely hoping to be "fifth-date material."

Another woman taught me that when it comes to premature exclamations, sometimes actions speak louder than words. *Civil* actions, for example. While attending the Republican National Convention in 2000, I had a short but PG13-rated affair with the Republican vice mayor (no, not a mayor in charge of vice, I was sad to learn) of a well-known East Coast city. To protect her identity (after all, she is an elected public official), let's just say the city rhymes with "Aimingham, Assachusetts." I don't remember doing so, but at some point during the week I must have mentioned that my mother's birthday was coming up.

After returning home, I received a large envelope in the mail. It was addressed to my mother, c/o me. It was very official. It was embossed. It was on authentic city stationery. I'm pretty sure John Hancock signed it. And it read:

WHEREAS:	*It has come to the attention of this City Council that Maureen Bleyer shares the birthday of August 5th; and*
WHEREAS:	*Maureen married the love of her life, Dr. Archie Bleyer, and their marriage was blessed with two fine sons, Kevin and Keith; and*
WHEREAS:	*Maureen Bleyer has a standing invitation to visit our fair city of [Aimingham, Assachusetts] where she will be an honored guest; now therefore be it*
RESOLVED:	*That the City Council go on record wishing Mrs. Bleyer a Very Happy Birthday and Many Happy Returns.*

The resolution went on, explaining that copies of the declaration would be sent to my mother, as well as kept in the official city record.

By mayoral fiat, she had strong-armed the entire council into wishing my mom a happy birthday. As far as I know, they put on party hats and blew out some candles. Really, it's enough to go to a guy's head. Within two weeks of meeting a woman, she had practically named a town after me.

To be sure, it was an incredibly touching gesture. I'll never forget it—heck, if I were a vice mayor of a city, I'd probably be sending out fourteen resolutions a day—but from a relationship standpoint, it was undeniably early. I generally expect to be given a key to an apartment before I'm given the key to the city.

It scared me just a little. Premature exclamations can make even a mayor seem desperate.

While I'm still tempted to wear my heart on my sleeve like it's going out of style, these women have taught me a thing or two about restraint. So here's my new resolution:

WHEREAS: *Only a homeless person should want to move in with someone after a first date; therefore be it*

RESOLVED: *That sometimes it's better to be quiet about my desperation.*

She Said . . .

It's possible that premature exclamation is a woman's way of getting back at men for premature ejaculation. ("Did you come?" men ask, cluelessly—as though it were physiologically possible for us to reach orgasm in under three minutes while being banged, jackhammer-style, like Jenna Jameson.) But whatever the reason, women tend to talk about the "relationship" (itself a premature exclamation) earlier than men do.

Fortunately, most women aren't careless enough to let an "I love you" slip out accidentally. A more common premature exclamation (or PE) is an innocuous offense, like running into some mutual friends at the movies and introducing your date with, "This is my boyfriend, Rob." Often, Rob reflexively will look behind him for this so-called boyfriend, seconds before it hits him that *he*, in fact, is "boyfriend, Rob." Then, during the movie, Rob will let the term roll around in his head: *boyfriend, boyfriend, boyfriend.* He may even begin sweating, or insist on getting separate popcorns.

Even though, technically, you've done nothing wrong.

According to *The American Heritage Dictionary*, "boyfriend" is defined as 1. a male friend; 2. a favored male companion or sweetheart. So Rob is indeed your boyfriend. (Note, however, that using "sweetheart" is another potential PE offense.) Yes, you're dating him exclusively, by mutual consent, but Rob hasn't quite put two and two together. Which sometimes leads to a reverse PE, or LE (Lack of Exclamation). As when my friend Jenny went to the movies with her new boyfriend Sean, who in private confessed that he thought she was "The One," but who introduced her as, "This is my friend Jenny." Did he not realize that The One would lose sleep over the omission of the prefix "girl" to "friend" in that introduction?

Men may pretend that we're getting ahead of ourselves, but we're actually calling it like it is. And this disconnect between the boyfriend we know in private ("You're The One") and the one in public named, simply, Rob ("Me, a boyfriend?") can lead to icy silences, heated arguments, and unreturned phone calls.

Even more frustrating are the "Me, too" guys. You know, the ones who reply to "I love you" or "I miss you" or "I think you're adorable" with "Me, too." *You too, what? You love me, too? You love yourself, too? You think I'm adorable, too? You think you're adorable, too?* It's bad enough that he can't initiate the endearment but, at the very least, he should be able to return it.

Personally, I've never said "boyfriend" before the guy said "girlfriend." But that's only because I have a massive fear of rejection. So in my experience, it's the guy who gets ahead of the game. Not just with "girlfriend" or even "I love you" (which once made me laugh—I mean, how can a person love somebody whose apartment they've seen maybe twice?), but with those insidious nonverbal PE substitutes: gifts.

Early in a relationship (oops—don't call it a "relationship"), men will start coming over with not just wine and condoms, but teddy bears. What is it with men and teddy bears? Do they actually think a grown woman wants a teddy bear? Sometimes, the teddy bear is carrying chocolates. Other times, though, the teddy bear is delivering the PE by proxy: YOU'RE CUTE! the bear will have written on its tiny stuffed-animal T-shirt. Or YOU'RE MY HONEY! Or even, I ♥ YOU! (If you point this out, the guy will pretend that he "didn't notice.")

Of course, sometimes gifts *must* be given prematurely—say, when we start dating right before our "new friend's" birthday. As long as a guy doesn't give jewelry (premature jewelrification) we're not in the least put off by grand materialistic gestures early on. An iPod? So what if he's only known us for three weeks! Premature, shremature! If a woman likes him, she'll be flattered. (But if she doesn't, she'll pity him *and* keep the gift.)

Still, it's hard not to empathize with the person who commits a PE. We've all said, "I love you" back to a guy simply because we felt sorry for him—or didn't want to have to get dressed at 2:00 A.M. to go home (and if we sat there mutely, he wouldn't want to sleep next to us that night). It's hard not to cringe on behalf of the guy who says he wants to date exclusively, only to hear you stammer, "Ooh, you know, I just can't make a big decision right now—I can't even decide which phone plan to get."

Even if we haven't committed a PE ourselves, we've all wanted to at one time or another. We've agonized for days or weeks over whether to share our feelings. *Do I really love him? Yeah. Does he love me? I think so. Will this freak him out? Maybe. Hmm, maybe I don't really love him. Maybe he doesn't really love me. Maybe I should keep my mouth shut. But . . . I love him! Do I really? Yeah. Does he love me? I don't know.* This plays over and over until we're stuck in mind-lock, too paralyzed to speak.

So instead of running away from the person who exclaims prematurely, cut your new lover (oops, I mean "friend") some slack. At the very least, be grateful that he made a big fool of himself before you did. And if all else fails, go ahead and get him a teddy bear. The message on its T-shirt?

I ♥ silence.

17

The Straight and Narrow About the Short and Curlies

SHOULD YOU CARE ABOUT YOUR HAIR DOWN THERE?

He Said . . .

Like the hair on my body, I'll keep this short.

Aside from trimming nose hair and plucking ear hair and, on rare occasions, keeping the hair sprouting from his toes shorter than the toes themselves, the only hair that a man should pay any significant attention to is the amount of hair on his face. Growing scruff, after all, is man's way of applying makeup without being gay.

'Nuff said.

She Said . . .

I always felt that one of the great joys of a committed relationship is that I don't have to be so obsessive about hair removal. After all, the guy loves me, he's seen me when I wake up in the morning, he's seen me on the can—what's a little leg stubble to him at this point?

Then, a few years ago, I interviewed an actress for a women's magazine. I asked about her biggest beauty insecurity and instead of the usual Hollywood celebrity reply about imaginary fat cells and wrinkles, she said: "Oh my God, I am so hairy! If my husband knew how much hair I actually have on my body, he'd divorce me!"

Wow, I thought. I was surprised not just by her unusual answer, but by the fact that she could sleep next to the same man for ten years and hide how much body hair she has.

How did she do this?

And why?

Maybe this actress has both the ample free time and ample bank account with which to remove every square millimeter of body hair that grows below the scalp. Men have no idea how much money and effort go into making a woman appear hairless. (Most don't even know what the word "depilatory" *means.*) I have a friend who keeps tweezers in her car so she can pluck an errant leg hair should the need arise. And who hasn't seen a woman tweezing her upper lip, chin, or eyebrows in the rearview mirror? We're so terrified of having excess hair that we'll voluntarily place a sharp metal object in front of our *eyes* while driving on the freeway at sixty miles per hour.

Even the razor companies (owned by men, naturally) play up our fears. They're always marketing some "new triple-action technology" just when we thought the "double-action" was working just fine. (And by the way, what's with the Venus razors? Was Venus hairless? Is hairlessness next to godliness?)

I understand the concept of neatness but we still have to be women. You'd never know it from a *Playboy* centerfold, but sexually mature adult women have pubic hair, and it doesn't happen to grow in the shape of a Mohawk or a tiny, wispy triangle. Who, exactly, came up with this idea of shaving, waxing, or taking a laser to one's pelvis? We'd like this man's name and address so that we can put *him* on a cold table, bend his knees to his chin, apply hot wax to his genital area, and rip off his delicate pubic and ass hair with a strip of cloth that will leave *him* red and sore for three days.

If guys had to get the equivalent of bikini waxes (Speedo waxes?), they'd likely change their attitude. Instead, boys are taught at an early age that their pubic hair is manly, but that a hairless vagina is sexy. Incidentally, boys learn this at an age when the girls they know really *do* have hairless vaginas. But by the time these boys are old enough to see a real naked woman (as opposed to the clean-shaven, airbrushed, Internet porn versions), their female counterparts have sprouted what looks to them like an unseemly dark forest of hair.

Oh, the horror! After they've recovered from the shock, they'll tell us we should shave it *for our own pleasure.* They'll even say this in a compassionate tone and with a straight face: "It'll feel so much better when I go down on you." Oh, sure. We love the feel of itchy ingrown pubic hairs and infected waxing rashes. Why don't they just come out and say it: "We've been conditioned to find prepubescent vaginas attractive. We're a society of pedophiles, but in order to avoid imprisonment and the 'sexual offender' label in our neighborhood of choice, we make grown women feel ugly unless they transform themselves to look like little girls." (And by the way, nipple hairs are perfectly natural. Try plucking a few nipple hairs from *your* chest and get back to us, will you?)

Guy hair doesn't trip our triggers either, but we put up with it. We don't tell you to shave your sensitive genitals (and yes, we get hair stuck in our throats, too); or your legs, which on hot summer nights feel like an extra blanket of wiry, itchy wool; or your thick unibrows; or your apelike chests that drip waterfalls of perspiration onto us during sex. We pretend not to notice those dark things sprouting from your ears or those Bozo-like masses of hair on each side of your shoulder blades. We don't even laugh at you when you're bald on top but insist on growing one of those pathetic, skinny, long ponytails *and* a beard to compensate for your insecurity (okay, we laugh, but never in front of you).

Still, I asked that actress I interviewed why, after a decade of marriage, she's still so mortified by her body hair. After ten years, wouldn't her husband accept her as she is, hair and all?

"It's too late," she said. "I've given him the impression that I'm hairless, and if I change now, he'll feel deceived." The moral? Throw away the razor early on or be imprisoned by it forever.

18

Prozac Notion

ARE YOU OVER THE MOON,
OR OVER THE COUNTER?

He Said . . .

My girlfriend thought I was diseased. Katrina wasn't an M.D., or a doctor of any kind, and would likely faint at the sight of blood, but she was 100 percent certain that I needed a prescription. She had heard about the antidepressant Paxil, seen it on *Oprah,* read about it in a women's magazine, and was convinced that I was the perfect candidate for it. I wondered why.

"It's not that you're depressed," she said. Good, I wasn't depressed.

"It's not that you're manic," she said. Glad to hear it. I wasn't manic.

"It's not that you're anxious," she said. Frankly, I thought I *was* anxious, but I wasn't about to argue with my own doctor.

"Then what is it?" I asked.

And she answered. "You argue with me."

You argue with me. So you need to be medicated. I want to say that was the beginning of the end of our relationship. But we had gone through so much by then, and would go through so much more, that it was really the beginning of the end of the middle of the end of the beginning of the middle of the end.

But the end was near. Katrina had come to the conclusion that arguing with her was a clear symptom of a neurological disorder worthy of medical attention. And she had a quick fix. *A Paxil a day keeps the asshole away.*

After discussions with my male friends, I've come to realize that what happened to me is not an uncommon phenomenon: Women used to try to "fix" their boyfriends, but now they try to medicate them. Instead of nudging and nagging, it's Nardil.

I suppose it's no surprise. Over the years love has become a rather quantifiable entity. And even if there's still an art to love, we certainly speak of it in scientific terms: if there's great *chemistry,* you might answer the call of your *biology,* get a little *physical,* perhaps leading, with a little luck and some mood lighting, to a late-night *anatomy* lesson. (Okay, nobody really says that last part, but you get my point.)

With all that science, I understand if women think of their boyfriends as *experiments.* I just hated being a test case.

I imagine the conversations that women have when they speak openly with their female friends: "I finally got Charlie on Paxil, and I'll tell you, he's so much more relaxed around me." "Jim's on his third selective serotonin reuptake inhibitor, and it's working beautifully this time. There's nothing the least bit masculine about him at all anymore." "Bill's Zoloft had an unexpected contraindication with his Viagra last night and—get this—he *exploded!* No shit—there are bits of him clinging to the ceiling of my bedroom."

How did we get here? No longer can a man liquor up a woman in the hopes she'll sleep with him, but a woman can anesthetize a man in the hopes that he'll be a more subservient boyfriend.

Think I'm kidding? A book called *The Irritable Male Syndrome* just appeared on my desk last week. It's written by an expert in male emotional dysfunction—the author of *Male Menopause*—and it maintains that more than 30 percent of men suffer from the male version of PMS. The expert writes: "Just as PMS has become a recognized problem in women, IMS will soon be acknowledged as a genuine affliction among men." (Never mind that if you tell a woman *her* PMS is an "affliction," she'll punch you in your sexist nose.) Luckily, the author offers "a program for prevention, diagnosis, and treatment." Not a moment too soon, because apparently being irritated by, say, your girlfriend's behavior ("You argue with me," she'll protest) is merely one stop on the road toward antisocial psychotic behavior and, if left untreated, may result in violence.

There it was in print: "male" is no longer a gender, it's a syndrome. A dangerous one.

But back to my personal disease.

My girlfriend Katrina wanted me to see a doctor. Like a gentleman, I made an appointment I didn't need with a psychiatrist I didn't know and I admitted I had a problem I didn't have. I told the doctor exactly where it hurts: *My girlfriend thinks I argue with her too much.* He rolled his eyes in a way that implied he's heard that a thousand times before, but instead of telling me how ridiculous she was being, he pulled out his prescription pad.

It was then that I realized how ridiculous *I* was being, told him how ridiculous *he* was being, and politely excused myself—although not before making an appointment for the following Thursday. (I needed to argue with *someone,* even if I had to pay for the privilege.)

There was a time when men could be unapologetically male: angry, tempestuous, grouchy, intimidating. To borrow one of Dennis Miller's best lines, the emancipated man used to be one of the most loved, hated, feared, and respected beings on the face of the planet. We were all Frank Sinatra, and women loved us for it. Now, I can't help but think, we're not even Woody Allen. We're just, well, wood. Women have liberated themselves from being Stepford wives, and ushered in the Stepford boyfriends. But I wonder, is this really what women are looking for? "I've got just the man for you. He's handsome, sensitive, comatose . . ."

I doubt it. But I'm not about to argue.

She Said . . .

Dating may be a contact sport, but without a National Dating League, there's no mandatory drug screening before the games begin. Heck, there's not even FDA oversight. This is unfortunate, because if you're ingesting somebody's bodily fluids, you should at least know what's in them. You should have access to the ingredients, like the nutritional information labels on pasta sauce and soy milk.

But until Congress gets on the case, all we can do is check out our boyfriends' medicine cabinets. (And since we're already rummaging through the bathroom, we might as well do a full sweep.) Here's what I've discovered in men's bathrooms, from least to most disturbing:

1. **The entire Clinique skincare line.** Taking care of oneself is nice, but a guy who uses exfoliant must be vain, self-involved, or George Hamilton.

2. **Diet pills.** Disturbing because I assume they belonged to his last girlfriend, which means not only does he still keep her stuff around (*He must still love her! How romantic, he kept her diet pills!*), but also that he dated someone who takes diet pills. I don't question his choice of pills. I question his taste in women.

3. **Lactaid.** This must be how men feel when they find out we're on the Pill. They're thrilled, as long as they know we take it each day. If I know a guy is lactose intolerant, should I sleep in his bed after sharing a double cheese pizza? Can I trust him to take his meds, or will I suffocate in a noxious gas cloud in the middle of the night?

4. **Athlete's foot medication.** I can deal with a guy who has a foot fetish. But fungus is never sexy.

5. **Prescription hydrocortisone cream.** Whenever the label says "Apply to affected area twice daily," you can't help but wonder: Just where *is* this affected area, exactly? Maybe I'm being a bit rash about his rash, but in my experience, these situations rarely turn out well.

6. **Condom-mania.** Birth control is good. The massive Costco-sized box, now almost empty, makes my mind wander to scary places—like wondering where his penis has wandered.

7. **Viagra.** While the point of going through someone's bathroom is to find answers, often what I find are more questions. For instance, why is a healthy 32-year-old taking Viagra? And do I bring this up with him? If I do, he might lose his erection. But meanwhile, I'm left wondering: Is he gay or am I ugly?

8. **Antidepressants.** Sure, Prozac, Paxil, and Celexa come up in casual conversation these days, but they take on new meaning when they're on a shelf next to the dental floss in your lover's medicine cabinet. The good news: This is a guy who uses dental floss *and* has feelings. The bad news: He wants to medicate them all away. Hopefully, you can quickly get past that demented line of thinking, and move on to: Why is he depressed? Or even the enlightened: At least he'll be sympathetic to my down moods. Until you consider the prescription date: Did he begin taking the medication before or after he met you? Maybe he's only dating you because he's depressed and once he gets better, he'll trade you in for someone better. On the other hand, maybe he's less depressed because he's dating you, and he's tapering off the meds due to the unfathomable joy you've brought into his life. (At least now you know why he's taking Viagra—to offset the sexual side effects of the Prozac. Finally, an answer!)

9. **Diarrhea medication.** Perhaps he ate bad fish once. But if a guy stocks all kinds of over-the-counter remedies—NyQuil,

Claritin, Nexium—watch out. You're looking at someone with either a damaged immune system or a damaged sense of reality (read: hypochondriac).

10. **Ritalin.** I can barely get a normal guy to focus during a relationship conversation. Most guys seem like they have attention deficit disorder. But one who *really* does?

11. **Valtrex.** The slick soft-focus TV commercials for this herpes medication may look like Calvin Klein ads, but we're talking about oozing pustules of contagious mucus, not the sultry-smelling Obsession. The ads say that one fourth of adults in America are infected with herpes, so go ahead and admit that you found his Valtrex. Don't worry, he'll be far more embarrassed than you are.

12. **Lithium.** Some men can make manic-depression and psychosis seem sexy. Take Richard Gere in *Prince of Tides,* or Russell Crowe in *A Beautiful Mind.* But remember, these are *movies.* In real life, lithium makes you fat. Besides, you should never date anyone more mentally ill than you are, no matter how low that bar is.

Admittedly, women tend to snoop more, but we're also much more tolerant of what we find. When my friend Michael discovered Prozac and yeast infection cream in his date's bathroom, he decided to stop sleeping with her, then he decided to stop returning her calls (never mind that he probably *gave* her the yeast infection from their twice-a-day sex). But my friend Jenna married a guy who had both lithium *and* herpes pills in his medicine cabinet. For men, Prozac + Masengill = break up. For women, lithium + Valtrex = get married.

Even so, we should be able to ask about any items we find in our boyfriends' bathrooms. When I found a bottle of penicillin in a boyfriend's medicine cabinet, I wondered what it was for. I figured he either had the flu (which I didn't want to get because I was on a tight work deadline) or syphilis (which I didn't want to get because I like having vision and not dying a horrible, painful death). Turns out it was an antibiotic for his dog. (On closer inspection, the label said it was prescribed to "Scout.")

I was relieved, but he was angry. He thought I was being invasive.

In hindsight, maybe I was. Because when it comes to arming yourself with the right information, in order to win the war, you've got to pick your bottles.

19

Quantity, Not Quality

IS THERE SUCH A THING AS TOO MUCH OF A GOOD THING?

He Said . . .

I'm not in the least embarrassed to admit that in the eighties, I loved Huey Lewis and the News. *Loved* 'em. Couldn't get enough. I bought their album and played it for three weeks straight. I had every lyric memorized. I knew which choruses Huey snapped his fingers to, and for which he preferred to grip the mike with both hands.

Okay, maybe I'm a little embarrassed.

But one day, in the second chorus of the umpteeth listening of "The Power of Love," I'd suddenly had enough. For Huey, the news was bad: I was Huey-ed out. (Of course, as a sentimental fool, I can't bear to dispose of any of these albums. I now have the world's largest collection of music I can't stand anymore.)

Point is, nothing spoils a good thing like too damn much of it. Same with relationships. I can't tell you how many times I've tried to tell girlfriends that I can only stand so much of them, that they were cramping my style, that it's important that she back off and give me some space before we—

Wait a minute. I'm lying. Frankly, I can't think of a single relation-ship where *I* haven't been the one insisting we see more of each other—at least, once it's clear that we're going down the road to exclu-sivity. It dawns on me: The problem isn't Huey Lewis. The problem is me. It's possible that I now have the world's largest collection of ex-girlfriends who, even while dating me, couldn't stand *me* anymore.

Come to think of it, I smothered. Occasionally, my girlfriends ac-tively advocated for healthy buffers between our idyllic togetherness, and I didn't listen. I now remember Katrina even once told me, "I'll understand if you need a night out with the guys." I didn't ask; she of-fered. *How thoughtful,* I remember thinking. *Let's snuggle.*

More often, girlfriends would say nothing, no doubt because they feared that I'd take it wrong; that I'd interpret their need for space as merely the prelude to a breakup.

"Don't you love me?" I'd ask.

"Sure I do," she'd say. "Just not this often."

There's the rub. How often is too often? Hard to say. It's not like we can have a conversation with our girlfriends and determine the ex-act proportion of our week we need to spend with each other to en-sure the greatest chance of long-term success. But the amount of time we spend together speaks volumes about the fidelity of our fidelity. It's one of the barometers we have to determine any real compatibility. *How do I love thee? Let me count the days . . .*

One night a week? Not good. If there's a there there, she should see you more often than she sees her therapist.

Seven nights a week? Worse. Nobody wants to date a loser.

Aside from those extremes, it's hard to know. To a degree, frequency is vital. A relationship has to build some momentum if it's going to take hold. I learned that lesson with Jeannie, a television director I found quite attractive. For no good reason I waited two months each time be-tween asking her out for our second, third, and fourth dates. As much as she may have liked me, I'm certain she was suspicious of where I disap-peared to between dates. In her mind, no doubt I was retreating to a cave in Afghanistan for intensive six-week terrorism training sessions and that soon I'd be outed as an American Taliban. I mean, what else could I be doing?

If a love is going to grow, it needs to be nurtured, although it's naive to think that we'll spend every waking hour together. We're adults, with adult agendas, schedules, and jobs. Only back in high school did we get to spend most of our weekday hanging around the hallways with our girl-friend. I even remember picking classes so that I could sit next to Elyse; and when conflicting class schedules made it difficult, I found various ways to be with her (she was captain of the cheerleading squad, and I was no fool). I'd employ clever surrogates that made sure she was thinking of me even in my absence. I'll never forget the feeling I had when Elyse insisted on wearing my letterman's jacket through the halls, out to the movies, pretty much everywhere she went. She looked good in my jacket; hell, it was an ego stroke that stands unrivaled even in my adulthood (did I mention she was captain of the cheerleading squad?). So overwhelming was my charisma, it implied, so reassuring was my presence, she wanted to take a piece of me with her. (*That's* the power of love. Can you feel it?)

Many years later, my girlfriend Katrina absentmindedly put on my watch one morning, but decided to wear it around for the first few weeks of our relationship. I was late for a few appointments, but I didn't care. I had an appointment with destiny.

Frequency implies commitment, particularly when it becomes ca-sual. My relationship with Katrina galvanized its momentum when I began sleeping over at her place *as a default*. Every relationship gets to that stage: When it's simply expected that either you or she will sleep at either your or her place, with the understanding that at the end of the evening, even if you spent it separately, you'll rendezvous together without having to propose it. (Malcolm Gladwell calls that instant the "tipping point"—the moment at which a phenomenon truly takes hold—but of course he was writing about important things like crime waves and virus outbreaks, not my love life.)

Problem is, even if we don't subscribe to the idea that absence makes the heart grow fonder, too much damn presence *can* make the heart grow really annoyed. Just like movie stars who suddenly appear in every film at the local multiplex, relationships too can suffer from over-exposure. Yes, you love each other—*just not this often.*

Truthfully, I'm not even sure we're programmed to love someone 24/7. I'd say the best we can expect from each other is about 14/4. Or maybe 11/6. Love is hard, tiring work. It takes careful attention and an unwavering focus that most of us men can only muster when we're playing Game Boy.

Knowing when to clock out is key, because no matter how pure your devotion, no matter how heaven-sent you are for each other, no matter how divine your relationship, a week of uninterrupted physical presence isn't a sign of love. It's a stakeout.

Remember—on the seventh day, even God gave it a rest.

She Said . . .

You know you've been spending too much time with your boyfriend when your message machine is full, the cable's been turned off, and your boss starts questioning those early-morning "doctor appointments." Soon, you've lost not just your favorite pair of panties, a dozen hair clips, four pairs of earrings, and a big project at work—you've also lost yourself.

Which begs the question: When does bonding turn into bondage?

It's natural to want to see your boyfriend in the beginning. He's funny, smart, sexy, and highly entertaining. Most seductive of all, he thinks the same of you. Is there any drug on earth more addictive than that? Forget the twelve-step approach of taking it "one day at a time"—you want to see him several times a day. You need your fix.

But since a tiny part of the person you used to be remains intact, occasionally you take the love needle out of your arm and spend time apart.

You go to work, for instance, even if you IM mushy I-miss-yous during every single conference call. You sneak out of meetings to report your breaking news on the half hour—how the guy at Baja Fresh gave you a chicken instead of vegetarian fajita; how you lost your Palm Pilot again; how you bruised your foot when you tripped over your computer cord. (Making our lover into our own personal biographer helps us to feel like we exist—if we haven't told him about these things, did they really happen?) You think about him all the time because everything reminds you of him and your inside jokes (nobody has funnier inside jokes than you two!). And when you aren't around him, you wonder, dreamily, what he *does* in the hours you don't see him. You want to know *everything* about him.

Then, suddenly, it hits you: You've been hanging around him so often that you've pretty much solved that mystery. You've seen what he does with every spare second of his non-work time—and it's not that fascinating. In fact, secretly you wish you could send him off somewhere else to do those now not-so-mysterious things that he currently does in your apartment: listening to loud music, throwing a Hacky Sack at the ceiling, reading magazines while monopolizing your bathroom. (This is particularly unfortunate, because the only place you find any solitude is in the bathroom, where you can shut the door and be alone with your candles and loofahs. But spend too much time there, and he'll think you have constipation, not claustrophobia.)

You start to become weary and realize you're not just tired, you're tired of him. But oddly, the more you feel stifled, the more your boyfriend feels a sense of comfort. He'll throw his stuff into your closet, eat your food, and stop wearing clothes in your apartment altogether. He'll watch TV naked, eat naked, work on his laptop naked. He's not just exposing himself to you (what you always wanted); he's overexposing himself to you (what you quickly begin to lament). Even worse, he thinks it's a compliment that he feels comfortable enough to be a nudist around you (and nobody but you).

Before long, the pent-up need to surgically remove your Siamese twin will be channeled into the art of sabotage. Say, for instance, that he's singing along to a car commercial on TV when you're trying to relax after a tough day at work.

"Hey, honey—hear that sound?" you'll ask sweetly, pushing MUTE on the remote control.

"What sound?" he'll reply.

"The sound of silence," you'll say with barely concealed venom in your voice. "Isn't it beautiful?"

He'll get his revenge, of course, when he interrupts your story about your unreasonable coworker with, "Shh, I'm trying to watch this"—"this" being a Bally Total Fitness commercial. You'll fight about trivial things, like the way you leave the juice bottle slightly opened, or the way he makes restaurant reservations with the pretentious "party of two" instead of just saying "two people."

All your time together will be spent bickering, but as soon as he says, "You know, maybe we need a night apart," instead of screaming "You betcha, brother!" you'll feel abandoned and whimper, "OH MY GOD, ARE YOU BREAKING UP WITH ME?!"

He wasn't breaking up with you, but if you're not careful, you may force him to. You'll get paranoid, decide that he hates you, and cling to him for dear life. It's amazing how quickly you can go from loathing to loving him. You'll forget that a mere twenty-four hours earlier, you prayed for just a couple days of solitude. You desperately needed to be alone, but since your boyfriend said it first, you desperately need to be together.

Normally you believe in aphorisms like "absence makes the heart grow fonder," but suddenly you're worried that your boyfriend goes by "out of sight, out of mind."

The good news is, you've just hit bottom. Because that's the first step to overcoming an addiction. You may go through withdrawal at first, but stay off the IM. Just remember to take it one day at a time—or, rather, every *few* days at a time—and you'll be mooning over each other again before either of you can say, "Ooooh, I miss you! Come over!"

20

If I Have to Explain It, Never Mind

CAN YOU READ MY MIND,
OR DO I HAVE TO READ IT TO YOU?

He Said . . .

Men are boring. When a man knows what he wants, he asks for it. *Boring.*

Women aren't so simple. When a woman knows what she wants, she often doesn't ask for it. Instead, she asks herself why she's wasting time with a guy who didn't figure out what she wanted before she even knew what she wanted, and who should have quickly provided it without her ever expressing what she wanted because, after all, a real man who really understood her would know what she wanted long before she even knew what she wanted and certainly before it became, you know, a *thing.* And now it's a *thing* and even if he provides what she wants, it's too late because the moment has passed and, gosh, I don't know, it's like we're on different planets. Should we break up? I think we should break up.

Not boring. *Insane*, but not boring.

For all the lip service women pay to the idea that all they want in a man is a "good listener," what they really want is a "good mind reader." Forgetting, of course, that it's hard for us men to be a good listener when there's nothing to listen to—that is, when a woman stays silent in the hopes that we'll miraculously intuit her thoughts. (Further, when you think about it, someone who is a "good listener" to complete silence isn't a good listener—he might be a good candidate for a padded room in Bellevue. He's hearing voices that aren't there.)

Withholding information is the new *withholding sex*. Whereas withholding sex is a test—*If he's truly into me, he won't just be into my body*—withholding information is also a test: *If he's truly right for me, he'll be inside my head at all times.* Women cling to the irrational notion that a man who truly understands them should understand them without actually having to understand them. That is, without having to converse with them. It has become a common refrain: "Honey, you should know what I want without me having to tell you."

Who decided this? What patron saint of effortless romance decided the best relationships are the ones with the least communication? Why do women think it's unnecessary to tell us what is bothering them? Just because we know them intimately, and they let us poke and prod their bodies, we're supposed to have a hotline to their unspoken thoughts? Do they have the same relationship with their ob-gyns? "So what's bothering you today, Ms. Lindman?" "Gosh, Dr. Saperstein, it's like you don't even know me anymore . . ."

Personally, I can't imagine that this is where we'd prefer relationships to have progressed. What happened to good ol' conversation? What happened to give and take? What happened to the ability to make irrational demands of each other merely with passive-aggressive sarcastic comments? Isn't that what separates us from the apes?

My girlfriend Katrina certainly subscribed to the theory that if a boyfriend can't read a girlfriend's mind, he's no boyfriend at all. Which is why, I suppose, I ultimately became no boyfriend at all. By the fourth month of our relationship, she already expected me to read her mind as if I were snuggled up inside her head with an Itty Bitty Book Light.

On occasion, she would drop a subtle nonverbal hint. When she leaned in and tipped her head forward just a little, I knew she wanted me to hug her. When she adopted a voice that sounded slightly more immature—just shy of baby talk—I knew she wanted me to make whatever decision was on the table. When she lit a candle before bed, I knew she wanted me to light *her* candle before bed.

I can follow clues. I can't read minds.

Frankly, six months in, I thought I had done both. Christmas was coming, and all December she had been complaining she couldn't find her favorite wool socks. In the great tradition of the holidays, and since both of our families subscribed to the practice, we had decided to exchange one present on Christmas Eve, and would do so at "our restaurant," Vincente's on Montana. Yes, we had "our restaurant," just as we had "our song"[1] and "our joke."[2] We were pathetic that way.

As it happens, on our way to "our restaurant," we got caught in a freak Christmas Eve rainstorm. It was a flash flood to rival Noah's, and in the two blocks between the car and the restaurant we both proceeded to get thoroughly soaked. It could have been a miserable meal as we sloshed around in the puddles that had formed inside our shoes. But after we sat down, I reached under the table, removed her shoes and socks, and slipped brand new wool socks—surprise!—onto her waterlogged feet. For the rest of the night, I massaged her grateful toes while we drank red wine and talked of our futures together. Perhaps you had to be there, but it was, up to that point, possibly the most low-impact romantic thing I've ever done (and I've rented *Notting Hill*). As serendipity, I couldn't have designed it more perfectly. For once, God

---

1. Rufus Wainright's "Cigarettes and Chocolate Milk."
2. A duck walks into a bar. Asks the bartender, "Got any grapes?" Bartender says, "No, this is a bar. We don't serve grapes." Duck leaves, comes back the next day. Asks the bartender, "Got any grapes?" Bartender says, "No, I told you yesterday, this a bar. We don't serve grapes!" Duck leaves, comes back the next day. Asks the bartender, "Got any grapes?" Bartender, really pissed now, says, "No, dammit. I told you already, this is a bar! And if you ask for grapes one more time, I'm going to nail your feet the floor!" Duck leaves, comes back the next day. Asks the bartender, "Got any nails?" Bartender says no. "Got any grapes?"

had decided to give me an assist, a holy hookup for which I'm grateful to this day.

I thought I'd read her mind: She never asked for wool socks, but she needed wool socks, and I gave her wool socks.

Only she didn't want wool socks. She wanted a Christmas Eve marriage proposal. I hadn't read her mind, after all. Two weeks after Christmas she broke up with me because I hadn't asked her to spend the rest of her life with me. Of course, two months after *that,* she came knocking on my door on a similarly rainy night, soaked, wearing her wool socks, asking me to take her back. So I took her back. We stayed together for six more months until she realized she didn't want a boyfriend who could read her mind. She wanted a husband who could read her mind, just like she did on that Christmas Eve. And I was the fool who gave her wool socks instead of a wedding ring.

Women say men are incapable of reading a woman's mind because we're not trying hard enough, or we're distracted, or we simply have other priorities. Instead of perfecting our ESP, we're perfecting our ESPN. That's bogus logic. First off, if we could read your mind, don't you think we'd be doing it all the time? I assure you, we would. We've seen *Sex and the City,* we know that you ladies have dirtier thoughts beyond our most fantastical male imaginings. Hell, if we could read your dirty minds, we wouldn't be just clairvoyants, we'd be clairvoyeurs.

Second of all, don't we still have to *talk,* even if boyfriends and girlfriends are supposed to be two separate parts of the same whole working toward a shared goal? So are the CIA and the FBI, and we've all seen what can happen when they don't communicate.

Women think keeping their mouths shut about what they really want makes things more intimate: "You complete me" only if "You complete my sentences." Personally, I don't want someone who finishes my sentences. I want someone who hears my sentences, parses them, and parries back with a few sentences of her own. I like conversation— I'm old-fashioned that way. And besides, her demand that I constantly read her mind reinforces an unfair double standard: Why is it that men are supposed to be "great listeners" while women aren't supposed to be "great talkers"?

I'm tempted to ask. But I guess I should *just know.*

She Said . . .

Midway through the psychotically blissed-out part of a relationship, you'll realize that not only are you and your lover not the same person (Shocking! You seemed so well-suited!), but that you don't—despite what you've gushed to your friends—"have that freaky mind-reading thing going on." Whereas you used to interrupt each other with, "That's amazing! I was just thinking the exact same thing!" nowadays you look at each other with creased foreheads of incomprehension. You still finish each other's sentences, but you finish them with the wrong words, prompting your lover to say, "Um, no, I was about to say Chinese, not Italian." You're oddly out of sync, like Mad Libs gone awry.

This wake-up call might be something as simple as your lover bringing over a large mushroom pizza after work.

"Why didn't you get pepperoni?" you'll ask, peering into the box.

"You didn't say pepperoni," he'll reply.

"I did, too," you'll insist. "I said get pizza."

"How was I supposed to know 'pizza' meant 'pepperoni'?"

At this point, you'll think of all the reasons he should have known (you had pepperoni on your first date; he knows you've been craving protein lately). But instead you'll just sigh and say, "If I have to explain it, never mind."

For women, "If I have to explain it, never mind," translates to, "If we were right for each other, you'd be able to read my mind." To which your boyfriend might reply, "Since when do you believe in telepathy? You don't even believe in horoscopes." Which you won't answer, because he should *just know.*

Take this conversation I had once (or twice) with a boyfriend (or boyfriends):

ME:	I'm so upset, my mother just called.
BOYFRIEND:	Oh no, is she okay?
ME:	Yeah, she's fine.
BOYFRIEND:	Well, what happened?
ME:	Nothing "happened."
BOYFRIEND:	Then why are you so upset?
ME:	Forget it. If I have to explain it, never mind.

Then I'd call up a girlfriend who would understand.

ME:	I'm so upset, my mother just called.
FRIEND:	Ooh.
ME:	Yeah.
FRIEND:	Did she . . . ?
ME:	Uh-huh.
FRIEND:	And she . . .
ME:	Yup.
FRIEND:	Wow!
ME:	I know!
FRIEND:	So how's Alec?
ME:	Awful. He doesn't get me at all.

The point is, my boyfriend should *just know* that if I'm upset when my mom calls, it's simply because she can drive me nuts, not because something "happened." He should be able to tell *by my tone alone* whether "I'm so upset" indicates a chipped fingernail, maternal annoyance, or major family illness.

Basically, anything a woman *doesn't* say can be used against men, because for women, merely having a *thought* counts as communication. Let's say that your girlfriend yells at you for something trivial, like putting your shoes on her sofa. You may think she's upset about her slip-covers, but really, she's upset about the fact that you had lunch with an attractive female coworker. How would you know this? If she has to explain it, never mind.

Books, magazines, and relationship seminars offer ways to cope with the gender communication gap. The bestseller *He's Just Not That into You* told women that men who don't communicate just aren't that into us. But since there's no companion book for men called, *She's Just Not That Into You, Unless You Have ESP,* let me offer some tips.

1. *If you can't read her mind, read her journal.* I know, it's unethical, and if she finds out, she'll dump you. But why take a cheesy mind-reading class at the local community college when the Rosetta Stone to her brain is right there in her underwear drawer?

2. *Earthlink is the link to her heart.* She doesn't keep a journal? Hack into her e-mail account. You'll be sure to find counterintelligence like, "If Steve doesn't get me the Billie Holiday box set for my birthday, he doesn't understand me at all."

3. *Don't ask, don't tell.* Never ask what she's thinking, because, God knows, she won't tell. And for merely asking, you'll be tried, convicted, then sentenced to your own bed. "Why?" you ask. Again, don't ask. Because if she has to explain it, never mind.

Also take note of the following common recurring themes:

WARDROBE:

GIRL: Are you sure you want to meet my family tonight?
GUY: Yeah, why?
GIRL: Because of what you're wearing.
GUY: What am I wearing?
GIRL: Jeans.

GUY: And that means I don't want to meet your parents?

GIRL: If I have to explain it, never mind.

JEALOUSY:

GIRL: How was your day?

GUY: Great! We've got this amazing new set designer. I've never worked with anyone so talented.

GIRL: Wow.

GUY: Yeah, and she's only twenty-eight! And she's already won an Emmy! You should come by and meet her.

GIRL: Why?

GUY: What? Why not?

GIRL: If I have to explain it, never mind.

INTIMACY:

GUY: Do you think you could take some of your stuff back to your apartment? I don't have much room here.

GIRL: Okay, sure.

GUY: Thanks.

GIRL: I mean, if my panties take up so much room, maybe I should just leave them *on me*. And if my three-ounce jar of moisturizer takes up too much space, from now on I'll just sleep at home—where I'm allowed to wash my face!

GUY: Why are you so upset? I'm just trying to clean stuff up.

GIRL: If I have to explain it, don't bother.

CONSIDERATION:

GUY: (WALKING INTO ROOM AND CHANGING THE TV CHANNEL) Hey.

GIRL: (ICY STARE)

GUY: What? Were you watching something?

GIRL: (GETTING UP AND LEAVING THE ROOM) If I have to explain it, don't bother.

And yet, men *do* bother. They *do* mind. Because despite our demented expectations, our boyfriends stay and love us anyway. And really, isn't that all we can ask (without actually asking, of course)?

21

What Your Lover "Forgot" to Mention

WHO'S THIS STRANGER INSIDE ME?

He said . . .

After making *loooove* one night, my ex-girlfriend Katrina and I started a rather dangerous game of pillow talk (I should explain, she wasn't my ex-girlfriend *at the time*). You know, the way couples do. It started playfully enough. *Was it good for you? Isn't it scary how compatible we are sexually?* That kind of thing.

Then she went off script. I didn't mind. I was having fun.

"If you could have sex with any movie star, living or dead," she asked me, "who would it be?"

It wasn't a question I had considered before, but I didn't blink. Not for a second.

"Neve Campbell," I blurted out.

"Why?" she asked.

Still no blinking. "Simple," I said. "Because she reminds me of you."

Katrina kissed me deeply, touched by my answer. Now it was my turn.

"How 'bout you?" I asked.

"That's a tough one," she said.

In my mind, she would pick either Kenneth Branagh or Timothy Busfield, two actors with whom I've been told I share a passing resemblance. I offered to help her out. "Do you need some sugg—"

"No, I just can't decide between the two."

"You mean between Kenneth Branagh or Timothy Busfield?" I asked.

"No," she replied. "Rupert Everett or Jet Li."

Rupert Everett or Jet Li?

Keep in mind, I'm 5'6". I'm American. I employ no discernable accent of any kind, unless I'm telling a joke. What I'm *not* is either a six-foot-tall gay Brit who speaks the Queen's English, or a brooding Asian karate master who speaks English as a second language.

I don't have a black belt in anything. I'm not even sure I have a black belt.

Why, oh why, couldn't Katrina have substituted Jet Li with Timothy Busfield? If Jet Li and Rupert are her prototypes for her ideal sexual partner, what am I? What competition did she lose to win me as a consolation prize? I felt deflated. It was a good thing we had just had sex, because I wasn't sure I'd be able to reflate again. Even for Neve Campbell.

My point is, you think you know what—and who—you're dealing with. You think that after a few months of regular meals and intimate conversation, you've got her figured out. But I've yet to enjoy a relationship that hasn't confounded that theory. Suddenly, out of nowhere, she's hot for Pat Morita.

Granted, I too have a few secrets that I don't disclose right away. I have mild OCD (self-diagnosed). I lost part of my big toe when I got my foot stuck in an escalator accident while traveling with my soccer team in East Berlin (I tried not to take it personally when Katrina didn't notice my missing appendage until I pointed it out to her *many months* into our intimate relationship). Still, my secrets are either trivial, or in keeping with the general theme of me: picky, self-obsessed, athletic, flawed.

But women's secrets throw me for a loop. Often a few months in, I'll uncover some blip, some anomaly, some does-not-compute bit of new data that is not just merely inconsistent with the pattern already established, but is a revelation so astounding it permanently warps the way all new information is incorporated. In politics, they call it "reframing the debate." In relationships, they call it "fucking a stranger." Or at least they should.

What, you don't think a hidden Jet Li fetish is that shocking? Okay, fair enough. Try this one on for size.

Over pizza Katrina told me she was a thief. She had stolen a leather jacket. Mind you, not when she was a kid who didn't know any better. Not when she was a cash-strapped teenager who couldn't afford the finer things. Not when she was an ambitious college student who was being hazed by her sorority. But when she was deep into her twenties and just decided *it was the kind of thing Katrina-in-her-twenties would do.*

I was sleeping with a felon. Somehow that made me an accomplice, I was sure of it.

What was even more troubling than her rap sheet (I had immediately, probably unfairly, jumped to the hasty conclusion that she had a closet full of stolen leather jackets) was her complete lack of shame. It's not just that her stealing bothered me—it's that her stealing didn't bother *her.* The woman I had fallen for would have some scruples about taking something that didn't belong to her. So I asked myself, who was this woman I had become intimately acquainted with all this time? She was no longer the Katrina I knew and loved. She was the Winona I had seen on television.

It's tempting to overlook surprising revelations like these when the relationship is chugging along nicely and everything else about it feels right. It's natural to want to cling to the person you thought she was, rather than the person she's proving herself to be, bit by bit. But it may be a mistake to think that she's anything but what her secrets reveal her to be.

Scientists talk about fractal geometry. In fractal geometry, all of the information about the larger entity, the larger shape, is contained in every smaller section of it. Well, to put it bluntly, some girlfriends are fractal girlfriends. That little glimpse of her personality she reveals to you during pillow talk—that she's an Asian/English fetishist thief, for example—tells you everything you need to know.

In retrospect, Katrina was a fractal girlfriend. So it only figures that this thief who I loved dearly, but who secretly obsessed about Rupert Everett and Jet Li, would eventually steal my heart and marry a tall man with an English accent who was much more Rupert Everett than I could ever be. I just pity the poor bastard should the happy couple ever take a trip to Asia.

She Said . . .

After going out with men who'd spill their sordid personal histories in the first thirty minutes of a date, I had dinner with a guy who told me virtually nothing. Not just on our first date, but on the half dozen or so that followed. It's not that he was shy or inhibited—he was actually quite charming (always a red flag—see chapter 3). But when it came to self-revelation, he had what my therapist initially called "good boundaries" then, as weeks went by, "a possible fear of intimacy."

Still, there was something refreshing about his reserved nature. As opposed to the men who'd say on our third dinner, "I don't want to hide anything from you—I want us to be closer than I've been with anyone else"—this guy seemed stable and solid and manly, but not incapable of feeling. He was an attentive listener, and he knew just what to say in response to *my* stories. As my friend Sara put it: no need to be concerned about there being a giant void hiding behind those big blue eyes.

"Still waters run deep," she said. "I'll bet he has a lot going on under the surface."

Sara was right. This guy's emotional waters contained an ocean full of killer sharks. And once I put on the scuba suit and dove below eighty feet, I couldn't come back to dry land without suffering from a bad case of the bends. (My therapist's new conclusion: "Well, he certainly has a dark side.")

Here are a few things I eventually learned about this boyfriend: He didn't graduate from college, due to a "technicality." He was sexually attracted to his mother. The child of his married next-door neighbor with whom he once had an affair may, in fact, be *his* child. He broke up with his last girlfriend because she used a fork instead of chopsticks in Japanese restaurants.

As two people get to know each other, there's going to be a massive information exchange. But what's strange about some revelations, especially major revelations, is how casually your new lover drops them into the conversation.

A few years ago, I went out with an architect named Adam who talked about his father constantly—his father the brilliant businessman, his father the family man, his father with the corny sense of humor. One day he mentioned that his mother was coming to town for a visit.

"What about your father?" I asked. "Is he coming, too?"

"No," Adam said. "He's stuck in New York."

A week later, Adam, his mother, and I were chatting over dinner when I said that I'd like to meet her husband, maybe when we go east to visit.

His mother looked at me oddly. "You mean, you'd like to visit the prison?"

Confused, I turned to Adam, who said matter-of-factly, "Oh, my father did some illegal trading—you didn't know?"

I don't understand friends who, hoping to avoid the boredom that comes from learning everything about their lovers early on, wish they could extend the process of getting to know them. To me, there's a feeling of security in recognizing which story my boyfriend is about to tell for the millionth time rather than being disappointed that there are "no surprises." It would be great if lovers came without a past (or if they must, a past that we micro-engineered), but since they don't, I'd rather get the highlight reel sometime after the first date and before the first "I love you."

For instance, there are times you may stumble across something—say, an old photo album in your boyfriend's apartment—and you'll ask of the woman who looks like Natalie Portman and has her arm around your boyfriend in every picture, "Who's this?"

> HIM: Oh, that's Sophia.
> YOU: Wait, Sophia-your-friend, Sophia?
> HIM: Yeah. Why?
> YOU: Well, uh, I didn't know you two dated.
> HIM: It was a long time ago. Before she became a model.
> YOU: You didn't tell me she was a model.
> HIM: I didn't? Oh, well—she's a model.
> YOU: And she's the one who calls all the time?
> HIM: Yeah, so?
> YOU: Nothing, it's just—I didn't realize that Sophia-your-platonic-friend-who-calls-all-the-time is also Sophia-the-model-whom-you-used-to-date.
> HIM: Oh, you didn't know? I thought you did.

Of course, sometimes you do know, but choose to ignore it. One friend dated an older, divorced man, got pregnant, and had a shotgun wedding, only to learn that he wanted out six months after the baby was born. "I didn't know he was such an asshole!" my friend said, while I looked at her and thought: *This is a guy twenty years older than you with three kids he never sees and a wife to whom he's constantly late paying child support. And you didn't know he was an asshole?*

More commonly, though, there's something jarring about dating someone for a while, believing you know him, then hearing him toss out some detail that makes you recalibrate everything. How are you supposed to respond? Do you take it in stride when he says he was the only boy in his tenth grade class who got a nose job? Do you break up with him when he mentions that he hasn't paid taxes for years? Do you change your locks when he says that his all-time favorite movie was *American Psycho*? I still haven't figured out the best plan of reaction at these moments.

Even worse are the guys who reinvent themselves just before meeting you. They've gotten a new lease on life, and the old them, the one you may have liked better, has been discarded. They'll share this, of course, the minute you profess your love.

"I used to take the trash out for my girlfriends," one guy told me. "But I realized that's sexist so now I let my girlfriends do it instead." Another guy told my friend, whenever she asked for something reasonable, "I used to say 'yes' to things all the time, but now I'm going to say 'no' instead. No, no, no." Another said, "I used to bring my girlfriend flowers, but now I've decided that's silly." And yet another: "I used to care how I looked in public, but now I don't give a crap."

It's at times like these that we wish we knew not just about the guy's past—but the actual guy in the past. We want to date the man he was, not the man he's become. Even if the man he was has a father at Sing Sing. Because the only thing worse than knowing is not having a clue.

22

We Interrupt This Lovemaking for a Word from Across the Bed

ARE YOU READY FOR "THE TALK"?

He Said . . .

I knew it was merely a matter of time before my girlfriend Katrina popped the big question. Not the one about marriage. Rather, the one about whether I was gonna ask the one about marriage.

I just didn't know what angle she'd take.

"What color will our children's hair be?" she eventually asked me through her doe eyes, as nonchalantly as she might have inquired, "What movie do you want to see?" Babies were on her mind, and she wanted to know if they were on mine. And if they were, given my red hair and her light brown hair, what color hair would they have? We hadn't even gotten engaged yet, let alone gotten married, and she was already gauging what color to paint the rec room. (That's the problem with being a redhead. Your offspring may clash with stuff.)

For the record, I like children. In fact, children seem to dig me. I hope to have children someday, and likely someday soon. But Katrina and I hadn't yet discussed children, so her question was a preemptive strike, clearly designed to see if I bristled at the very idea of children, and by extension the prospect of she and I having them.

At the time, I didn't like the sly game she was playing, so I didn't play along. I wish I could claim to have said something clever in response, but what I said, from the standpoint of her potential husband, was much worse: *nothing at all.* I let the question hang in the air as if it had nothing to do with me. As if I just happened to be in the vicinity when the question was asked of someone else, and any minute now that someone else would show up and relieve me of my obligation to answer. An obligation I abdicated wholeheartedly.

So while I may not have played along with her game, I still lost.

I should have seen this coming. I should have been prepared. I should have consulted an encyclopedia or something. Because, as any relationship progresses, there are a number of "talks" we should expect to have. The one about exclusivity. The one about any diseases that warrant mentioning. The one about spending the holidays together. And then, inevitably, there's the one about "What exactly are we doing here?" Which, more often than not, when it concerns women of a certain age, implies "Are we going to have babies?"

And if we are, "What color will our children's hair be?"

With Katrina, there were valid reasons for my hesitance. First, I felt like Katrina and I still had milestones to pass as a couple before the one marked "baby discussion." I subscribed to the rules of engagement: First comes love, then comes marriage, *then* comes baby in a baby carriage, and I was still happily entrenched in the love stage. In other words, before we had babies together and confronted all the diaper-changing obligations that came with, I still wanted to honor my duty as a boyfriend; not be a boyfriend to someone who had doody on her.

And, okay, I was scared. Not of commitment—the usual accusation tossed a man's way. Rather, I was afraid of being used. I was, it pains me to admit, suspicious of Katrina's intentions. Call me paranoid, but to paraphrase what is often said about paranoia, *just because I'm paranoid doesn't mean they're not out to get pregnant.* The secret fear we men share is that a woman is with us merely because we're a necessary ingredient in the baby-making process, that perhaps our only real worth to a woman lies in our magical ability to put our *gazinta* into her *thingama-jiggy* and nine months later, out will pop a cute-as-a-button *whipper-snapper.* We're David Copperfields of procreation.

It's not an irrational phobia; it's a fear grounded in reality and expe-rience, because we've all too often seen women of a certain age be-come obsessed with the idea of motherhood. Dreams of their wedding day and of being a blushing bride are supplanted by fantasies of their first delivery and of being a proud mother. At times it seems everything a woman does at that point is in service of getting pregnant.[1] Some call it "entering the zone." Others call it "answering the call." Men call it "freaking us out." Call us paranoid (again), but we worry that a woman has agreed to spend New Year's Eve with us not because she loves us, but only because she wants to have kids by Labor Day. She has, we worry, become a child-seeking missile, singularly devoted to zeroing in on the man who will not only entertain, protect, and provide, but also father, diaper, and coach youth soccer. (All of which we want to do, side by side and hand in hand with the woman who loves us equally as a husband *and* father.)

We recognize the forces of biology—that there's a primitive com-pulsion for women to copulate that has nothing to do with indulgence,

---

1. Scientists at the University of Chicago have even determined that the smell of a nursing mother's breast milk makes women horny. They asked ninety childless women to sniff the breast pads of nursing mothers several times a day for two months straight. The results? The women reported a 24 percent increase in sexual desire, and a 17 per-cent increase in sexual fantasies. Their conclusion was that the presence of nursing women in the area sends a signal to the childless woman that this particular location might be good for child-rearing, kicking a woman's sex drive into higher gear. Simple survival of the tittest. It's all about motherhood for these women. You can practically smell it in the air.

and has everything to do with mere existence. As good as sex feels, anthropologists and televangelists will argue that, in fact, sex is so darn pleasurable solely because that pleasure will entice us to do it more often and therefore increase the chance that we won't go extinct. Sex feels good, because sex does good. It propagates the species.

So, frankly, we wonder why you're really with us. Forgive us—we're insecure. We want you to tell us that we're worthwhile on our own merits. We want you to reassure us that the man is as cherished and vital as the child. That's "the talk" we'd like to have. Then we'll happily have "the talk" we'd love to have, the talk we can't escape, the talk we don't want to escape, about the children we'd love to have together.

She Said . . .

Okay, so you've got his work phone, home phone, cell phone, *and* pager, but still, that's not reassurance enough. You need to know, with the precision of a *Times*/CNN poll, how serious your relationship is. In other words, you're ready for the dreaded "Where are we?" talk.

I've never understood why couples voluntarily embark on this conversation when they could be out enjoying themselves at the multiplex. Or, more accurately, why women insist on having it. I mean, you know where you are. Overall, you've been relatively happy. But then you start to wonder—*Is he as happy as I am? Because if not, I'm moving on.*

So you have The Conversation. And despite your neurotic fears, your boyfriend will tell you that he *is* happy. He'll say that he's "massively excited" about you and "lucky" to have found you. He might even add, with heartfelt sincerity, that he can "see a future" with you. You got the reassurance you wanted.

That's when all hell breaks loose.

Instead of calming you down, The Conversation makes you engage in one of your own. "Just how 'massively excited' am *I* about him?" you ask yourself. "Do *I* associate the word 'lucky' with him and can *I* 'see a future' with him?"

It's the flip side of being single. When you were single, you lowered your standards to ridiculous levels. "Oh, he's separated and just out of rehab?" you'd think to yourself. "Well, maybe he understands himself better after all that group therapy, and besides, I'll bet his soon-to-be ex-wife drove him to drugs, the bitch."

But now, after dating a guy who's been to neither Betty Ford nor the altar, you've gotten cocky. And who wouldn't? For the past few months, someone has been telling you several times a day how fabulous you are, so it's natural to think, "Yeah, I am pretty great."

Which logically leads to this next thought: "Hey, wait a minute! If I'm so great, maybe I can do *better.*"

Whereas before The Conversation you looked at your boyfriend with a combination of lust and affection, now you look at him and think: That yellow rain slicker you wear? *I'm not so sure about that.* And the way you snort when you laugh too hard? *Not crazy about that either.* You used to tell your friends, "I think I might be falling in love," but now you say things like, "He's kind of awkward at parties."

So your friends try to talk some sense into you, and if they get really sick of your whining, might add, "What, you think *you're* flawless?"

This only fuels the irrational fire burning in your brain. Yes, you'll agree, yes I have flaws. So maybe I don't even deserve him! You'll ping-pong between *I don't deserve him* and *He doesn't deserve me* with a few *We're not right for each others* thrown in for good measure.

After The Conversation, you'll be haunted by an internal monologue that can be summed up by the following mathematical equations:

1. Nobody is good enough for me + nobody could ever love me = premature breakup.

2. I'm unlovable + my boyfriend seems to love me = my boyfriend must be screwed up for loving me.

You may even have a hallucination in which there are tons of eligible, attractive, interesting single guys out there. Or you'll reason that all the good guys are taken, and the fact that your guy was available when you met him means he's damaged goods (never mind that you were available, too). You'll consider this theory perfectly rational: If all the available people (i.e., your single boyfriend) were so fantastic, they'd be unavailable (i.e., married). You'll wonder whether you should start dating married men.

Clearly, it would be so much easier to forgo The Conversation and let the relationship progress naturally. But then our friends start to butt in. And when the question, "How's Rob doing?" is always followed by, "What's *going on* with you two?" you fall into the trap. What's "going on" is that you and Rob are happy together, but that doesn't satisfy all the relationship gawkers.

So in order to provide an articulate answer and some concrete news, you run home and ask Rob what's "going on." At least that's how you justify doing such a stupid thing in the first place. It's your friends' fault—and don't ever let them forget it. Play this to the hilt, making them feel so guilty for disturbing your peaceful romance that they feel they owe you, big time. Remind them that they should take your frantic calls at 3:00 A.M. as penance. Because assuming you make it past The Conversation, you'll need all the support you can get as you enter the next phase of your relationship—the serious part.

PART
THREE

SERIOUS BUSINESS

The "Friends & Family" Plan

HOW IMPORTANT IS IT TO BE LOVED BY YOUR LOVED ONE'S LOVED ONES?

He Said . . .

My friend Danny has a theory about how relationships work. I have a theory about how I should be allowed to steal theories from Danny. So here goes:

Just like the government, a relationship between a man and a woman has a delicate distribution of power and depends upon on a series of checks and balances. In fact, it has three distinct branches.

- ◆ *The Executive Branch, which keeps the relationship moving. That's usually the man. We're the President of the Relationship (largely—we've come to realize, a figurehead position. Ultimately powerless).*

- ◆ *The Legislative Branch, which makes all of the truly important decisions. That's her. She makes the laws that we have to live by if we want domestic peace (the Speaker of the House of the house, if you will).*

And finally,

◆ *The Judicial Branch, which judges everything we've done and decides if it's acceptable. That's her friends.*

Gentlemen, like it or not, we are at their mercy. Our girlfriend's friends are the Supreme Court of the Relationship, sitting in judgment on our every move. Our *every* move. She relies on them to keep close watch and weigh in when they see an injustice.

Like that time we accidentally called her by our *ex*-girlfriend's name. *Verdict? Guilty.*

Unfair, we say. *My relationship with my girlfriend is private,* we say. *It's between her and me,* we say. But even as we say these things, we know we're wasting our breath. We fool only ourselves when we think that just because we're the President and we sleep with the Legislative Branch, whisper sweet nothings into the Legislative Branch's ear, and buy the Legislative Branch flowers on Valentine's Day, we are immune to the judgment of the Supremes.

On the contrary, this is where the metaphor falls apart. There is no executive privilege. The President's behavior isn't above the law; it's below the law. In fact, simply being male, or sometimes simply being human, can be an impeachable offense. Be the slightest bit moody or mercurial, and we're only innocent until proven grouchy. Steal the slightest glimpse at an attractive woman, and we've taken too many liberties with our liberties (she noticed, and she told them; justice isn't blind).

Worse, it's no surprise that her friends aren't impartial or nonpartisan. If they had been relied upon to determine the 2000 presidential election, for example, Oprah would be commander-in-chief today. They are, in the current parlance, "activist judges" who only have a very self-serving agenda: to protect their friend's social calendar. And, perhaps, her heart.

At some point, our girlfriend will insist we meet her friends (no sense objecting; hostile witnesses don't have girlfriends). She'll suggest it casually, flippantly, almost as an afterthought, but make no mistake: The date of our trial is set. The subpoena will arrive in the form of a proposed brunch with her friends Tracy and Julie at the place that makes the omelets to order.

Our appearance is mandatory because our girlfriend wants approval from her friends that she's made the right choice. So on the day in question, we should be charming. We should be nice. We should avoid stating our case. We should demur from saying anything too provocative. We should ride the line between boring and overbearing.

May we please the court.

Then, if her friends like us, we'll next be expected to appear before a different kind of judge and jury: her family. These introductions are rarely, if ever, comfortable. They are always, however, memorable. I met Heather's parents when they suggested that the four of us rent a houseboat during our senior year in high school. Heather and I, having only dated a few times, were nervous, but game. I brought my swim trunks, Heather brought her new bikini, and Heather's father brought his . . . gun. Which he proceeded to shoot at various targets on the beach as we scooted by at a (blistering) one knot. Think he was sending me a message? I do.

You can have my daughter when you pry her from my cold, dead hands.

Naturally, some men to try to avoid these "Meet the Fockers" moments in the first place. To evade the potential in-laws: Be out of town when they're in town. Engineer our schedules such that we never have to bring our girlfriend near our girlfriend's parents. Take her on a vacation to a spa across the country.

But that's not a relationship; that's a kidnapping.

So we'll meet. Probably over the holidays, because holidays are made for family, and because on any other nonholiday day there's not enough joy to spoil.

Now, because so many families are dysfunctional, it's difficult to know how to behave around them. Do we match their lunacy and imply we're just part of the gang, or do we come across as the lone sentry of sanity amid an onslaught of dysfunction? That is, are we our girlfriend's other half, or her rescuer? Is she a daddy's girl or a rebel daughter? Should we complete her, or save her? It's a pickle.

We need to do our due diligence here, because ultimately, any true gentleman seeks her parents' blessing.

Of course, if they rule against us, we can always try to appeal to a higher court. The honorable Tracy and Julie presiding.

She Said . . .

It's finally happened: He wants you to meet his friends and family. Enjoy the adrenaline rush. Because soon you'll discover that what you thought was an excited feeling in your gut is actually a potent combination of nausea and terror.

No wonder. You've spent so much energy getting to a place where you could relax and feel secure in the relationship, but then the real test begins. You're like a political candidate who works tirelessly to get her party's nomination, only to realize that she'll have to campaign for the job. Your boyfriend has nominated you for the position of girlfriend, and now you'll have to get voted into office. Friends, family, coworkers—you'll be vetted by all.

The problem is, no matter how great you are (and, of course, you are), your boyfriend's friends are a special interest group. They're supposed to be judging your suitability as their friend's lover, but secretly, they're judging your suitability as a new addition in *their* lives. If they'll have to socialize with you, chat on the phone with you, spend holidays with you—how will your presence affect them? (They may even feel obligated to add you to their Friendster page—so make sure to pad it with extra "testimonials.")

It's all about their self-interest. If, for instance, your boyfriend's mother is envious of your youth and success, she'll say something cutting, but in a sweet tone. ("You're so beautiful and accomplished—it's odd, isn't it, how young women like this often end up alone?") If his best friend is still single and fears losing his buddy, he'll say that you seemed "clingy." If his closest female friend is secretly in love with him, she'll tell him he can "do better." If his sister has always wanted a sister-in-law with whom she can go white-water rafting, she'll insist that he bring you on the next family vacation.

And your boyfriend is just as guilty. He doesn't want to introduce you to his inner circle as a way of announcing, "Look how lucky I am to have met this amazing woman!" Sadly, he doesn't trust himself enough to decide whether you're the woman he wants to wake up with every day—in his insecure mind, that should be the decision of *other* people. (Never mind that the only impression these people have of you may be formed after two hours in a noisy bar.)

I know this because I've had my male friends brief me before introducing their new girlfriend: "Tell me if you think her haircut is weird or cool." "She went to Princeton, but see if you think she sounds like a Valley girl." "Tell me if you find her laugh embarrassing."

Really, the only way to get through this is to turn the tables. No one wants to feel judged, so why not do the judging instead? Just as you might be viewed as a reflection on your boyfriend, his friends are a reflection on him. If his friends are juvenile, dull, or sport weird facial hair patterns, consider that you'll have to spend time with these yo-yos as long as you're with your boyfriend. I once dated a guy whose best friends were a tight-ass couple named Chris and Sarah. While my boyfriend was quirky and spontaneous, these two showed emotion only when I forgot to put my Snapple on a coaster—by the pool! Did I really want to sign on to that for the next fifty years?

Another advantage to meeting the friends is that you learn information about your boyfriend he'd never tell you himself. When I was dating Ben, his friend Jody said she could tell that Ben liked me because, "He's not freaking out the way he did when he asked Emily to live with him."

"He and Emily lived together?" I asked.

"No, they never moved in," Jody said, then, registering my confusion, added, "Oh, oops."

But if you really want the scoop on your boyfriend, agree to meet his family in all their dysfunctional glory. The mother who sings her grown son lullabies in French, the father who calls the family dog "son"—these folks explain a lot about why your lover periodically goes AWOL. Occasionally, he will confuse you with one or both of his parents, despite the fact that you look and act nothing alike. So pay attention. In the heat of an argument, you and his sixty-year-old, 220-pound father will be indistinguishable in his mind.

Just make sure never to tell your boyfriend how nuts his family really is. Your boyfriend can make fun of his own family and friends, but you should never make fun of them—unless he makes fun of them first (then heartily agree, even if you don't). If you think it's obnoxious that his mother's first words upon meeting you are, "My gosh, you're so tiny, you could get into movies for the child's price!" don't complain to your boyfriend. If he thinks his best friend who's trying to be a comedian is hilarious but you think he's bone-chillingly annoying, readily agree that it's a bummer his friend hasn't been "discovered" for his comic genius.

Why? Partly to keep the peace, and partly to keep his confidants on your side. Because the second you and your boyfriend get into a major argument, he'll go straight to his cronies and sell you out.

"Lori's so judgmental," he'll tell his mom. "In fact, she didn't even understand that you were being endearing when you said she looked like a child."

"You know what Lori did?" he'll say to his best friend. "Oh, and by the way, she thinks you suck as a comedian."

It's nothing short of a smear campaign. So be a shrewd politician and form strong alliances with the other side. Work that bipartisan angle from the very first meeting. And pick the right venue for the stump.

If you can, avoid meeting his clan at a wedding. Weddings are awkward. Single people hate them (we feel pathetic); married people hate them ("Were we ever in love like that?"); and couples hate them (encounters with nosy relatives who ask loudly, "So, when are you two getting up there to do this?"). Complete strangers will handicap your odds of marriage; sloshed sixty-year-olds will look down your dress and say, "You've got quite a beauty there, champ"; and one or more of his exes, newly broken up with a long-term boyfriend, will try to steal him away. Let's just say it's not the best photo op.

Eventually, you may feel comfortable enough with his friends and family to let down your guard and be yourself. Don't. Remember, this is getting serious. Which means you're no longer dating just your boyfriend. You're also dating his family, his coworkers, and pretty much everyone on his Friendster page. And every six months or so, you'll have to run for romantic reelection. So manage your campaign wisely.

24

Terms of Adorement

SHOULD YOU SAVE THE PET NAMES FOR YOUR DOG?

He Said . . .

I've never been given a nickname by any of my girlfriends. Not by Dawntana, not by Katrina-ballerina, not by Kelly-Girl, not by Meinie-mo, not by Blossom, not by Ladybug, not by Yahoo!, not even by Princess Goebbels. Clearly, *I've* been forthcoming with a few creative entries, but the fact remains none of my girlfriends have ever taken it upon themselves to return the favor.

Some friends have. For a while my Asian friend Greg, embracing the stereotype of his own people, thought it was hilarious to transpose the "r"s and the "l"s in my last name and call me "Breyel."

Coworkers have, too. A few of the guys at *Politically Incorrect* called me "Blur" because it's slightly homonymic with "Bleyer" and for the first few years on the job I was a blur of activity.

Even bosses have. From day one, Dennis Miller took it upon himself to call me "Kevvers," and I took it upon myself to be cool with it. It was a term of endearment I embraced. But when I screwed up somehow, I knew I was about to be chewed out the moment he called me "Kevin"—even if, in inimitable Dennis style, he said, "Kevin, babe,

I haven't seen writing this shitty since Aleksandr Solzhenitsyn scratched his memoirs on the walls of the Gulag Archipelago with a used prison-issue Q-tip and an inkwell of his own feces."

Family members have. My grandmother, for reasons I assume have something to do with her Bavarian heritage, called me "Keh-win" right up until the day she dwied. May she west in pweace. (I called her "Nana," by the way. Because I woved her.)

But never girlfriends. The conclusion I draw, understandably, is that none of my girlfriends has ever really loved me. They have shown a complete lack of imagination in the nickname department. Oh, there may be other explanations, I suppose. Perhaps because my name isn't particularly difficult to pronounce (it's Kevin, by the way, nice to meet you), girlfriends haven't felt compelled to shorten it, or bastardize it, or make it sound childish. What can I say—I fall trippingly off the tongue.

So I should be okay with it. But I'm not. The problem is that nicknames imply intimacy. If a woman chooses to assign you a nickname, you know she's enjoying your company. Shortening a name says, *We're so simpatico I don't have to go through the trouble of finishing all those annoying syllables.* "Kevin," it turns out, has only two syllables. Say what you will about his music, I bet Engelbert Humperdinck always knew where he stood with a chick.

I would have accepted a whole range of monickers: K-dog, Killa, the Governor. I've even offered up some: K-dog, Killa, the Governor. None stuck. Dawn once called me "Kevy-Wevy," but she was drunk. That doesn't count. A nickname isn't valid unless it's delivered a) sober, and b) nonironically. The giver of the nickname has to a) remember she said it, and b) own it.

Don't I deserve to be reduced to some cloying vernacular shortcut that will only embarrass me when uttered in mixed company? Have I done something to offend these women who might otherwise be forthcoming with a term of endearment? I'll bet even Eva Braun called Hitler something cute.

E-mail has been some consolation. E-mail is designed for this kind of shortcut language. My heart swelled when Miranda wrote me an e-mail that was rife with romantic possibilities:

> K—
>> *Call me.*
>> *XO*
> M

"K" is close to a nickname, I told myself. And then there's the way she signed off—with two nonchalant keystrokes that suggest anything but nonchalance. "X" and "O"! A kiss and a hug! "X"s and "O"s are nicknames for kisses and hugs, if you think about it.

I spent three days thinking about it.

Only later did I come to the likelier conclusion that M hadn't come down with a case of Kevy-Wevy fever; she was stricken with Black-Berry Disease. The fewer keystokes the better. E-mail out-shortcuts nicknames, and as such, they are notoriously untrustworthy indicators of intimacy in a relationship.

There is one attempt at a nickname I could have done without. Af-ter we had made out once—scratch that, *twice*—Gloria immediately took it upon herself to call me her "lover." Every time she'd use it casually—and always in public—I'd cringe. I wouldn't have minded *be-ing* her lover, I suppose, but I definitely minded being stuck in a bad Harlequin romance. Not only was it embarrassing, it was premature: It seems to me that moving past heavy petting is a prereq for assigning a pet name. Besides, when you really think about it, "lover" isn't a nickname—nicknames have to be unique and specific, and, from what I could tell, she called all her lovers "lover."

Cringe.

But still, I can't help think that I'm missing something. I'd like to pre-tend I don't envy those couples that use nicknames for each other out in public, but I do. I envy them the way I envy those couples who liberally embrace public displays of affection. I'm both disgusted and covetous.

But maybe it's okay that I've escaped nickname-dom. After all, I hear from my guy friends, Geoff, Brian, and Gil (Geoffy-Juice, Bri-guy, and McGillicutty), that nicknames are a double-edged sword. Why? Because while men use nicknames with women to get them to be something ("my love," "my darling," "my honey"), women use nicknames with men to get them to *do* something ("Sweetie, will you . . . ?", "Darling, could you . . . ?", "McGillicutty, can't you just . . . ?").

So I may not have a nickname. But I've also had very little to do. Which leaves a lot more time to write essays about why none of my girlfriends—not Dawntana, not Katrina-ballerina, not Kelly-Girl, not Meinie-mo, not Ladybug, not Yahoo!, not Blossom, not even Princess Goebbels—have ever taken it upon themselves to return the favor.

She Said . . .

My friends and I have so many nicknames for our exes (The Toxin, Derwood, Clambake, Cockroach, Boy Genius, the Kennedy, Leather Boy, Club Med Guy) that sometimes we forget their real names (Greg, Alec, Scott, Josh, Bruce, Tom, Rob, Todd). And no wonder: While dating them, we rarely used their real names, even to their faces. Instead we called them by sappy terms of endearment (Schmealy, Nelly) that years later, we're still reluctant to share with our friends. (Do I really want them to know that the boyfriend I called Foonsterinio called me Bunster Vindaloo?)

It makes no sense: Why would we want to call our lover a name to which even a Chihuahua would refuse to answer? Because it's cute? Intimate? Funny? No, we use pet names, as we do with an actual pet, to establish ownership. It's like putting a heart-shaped collar around your significant other. By naming him, you're claiming him. His coworkers, friends, and parents (who actually *did* name him) may address him as "Jonathan," but now that he's yours, he answers to "Stanley the Great."

The nickname a boyfriend chooses for you is very telling. I immediately lose interest in guys who name me after a generic food (Cookie, Peanut, Sugar) or animal (Bunny, Monkey, Mouse).

Then there are boyfriends who use pet names to project their fantasies onto you. One boyfriend called me the name of a famous ballet dancer he was obsessed with, because he thought I resembled her physically. Never mind that I don't know a plié from an arabesque. I've also had a guy call me "Tara"—not after the estate in *Gone with the Wind,* but after the Olympic figure skater Tara Lipinski— supposedly because, like her, I'm tiny.

"She's my type," he explained, to which I replied, "*She? Or me?*"

I also dated a guy named Jeff Kaplan who would call me up and say, "Gottlieb, it's Kaplan. I'm thinking about you." I haven't been on a last-name basis with anyone since I was ten and imitating the way my thirteen-year-old brother addressed his thirteen-year-old friends. Jeff never called me "Lori," only "Gottlieb." "Gottlieb, it's Kaplan. I'm out by the pool. Call me." "Gottlieb, it's Kaplan. I'm on the cell. Call me."

What are we, I wondered, Starsky and Hutch? Soon I realized that to him, we *were* Starsky and Hutch. Our mission: to fuck. I was his fuck buddy, Gottlieb. His nickname for me said it all.

Most often, though, pet names are like baby talk in a relationship. Once you both engage in mutually mortifying behavior, you've formed a bond. A dysfunctional, codependent bond, but a bond nonetheless. You might be having screaming fights over dinner, but you're still his "Ellsworth" and he's still your "Attila the Honey."

The magic of pet names wears off when you realize that your boyfriend had pet names for all his girlfriends before you, and they had pet names for him. You, too, should beware of continuing to call your ex by his pet name. He should not be referred to by his previous title when his term is up, unlike the way we still call former presidents "Mr. President."

Oh, and one last thing: Please don't ask us girlfriends to nickname your genitals. Never make us utter a sentence like: "Hey, Poodle, can you put Mr. Rattlesnake back in your pants when the FedEx guy comes to the door?" Because a girl has to retain a little dignity, even if she answers to the name "Boobie Doll."

25

The Ghosts of Sexcapades Past

ARE THEY HARMLESS EXES, OR IS THIS RELATIONSHIP GETTING A LITTLE...CROWDED?

He Said . . .

Never talk about exes on a date. That's one of those inviolable rules, isn't it? Talking about exes—or so say the rule's oft-cited bylaws—puts our date on the defensive, indicates we have unresolved emotional baggage, and invites fool's comparisons between the mammoth intimacy we once shared with our ex and the fledgling intimacy we're trying to nurture over coffee with this relative stranger. It is, by all accounts, a bad idea.[1]

But when we're knee-deep into a serious relationship—when she ostensibly knows everything else about us and has seen us naked a few times—are we still supposed to keep mum? Certainly, if she's suffering you for the long haul, she deserves to know everything, doesn't she?

At some point, full disclosure is inevitable. The more successful a

---

1. And yet, I often do it. I've even considered drawing a caricature of one of my exes (the tall one) on a cocktail napkin to prove a point I was making about "irreconcilable genital placement." I can be quite forthcoming.

relationship is, the longer it is, and the longer it is, the more we run out of tedious drivel to say to each other. So everything, especially anything remotely interesting, becomes fair game. "Did you know that I once— Oh, you did? Okay. [Beat] Hey, did I ever tell you about Elizabeth?"

No, we didn't ever tell her about Elizabeth, but at some point we will.

She understands this, too, and she knows she could be hurt by it. So it's a man's job to make certain that the confidence she has in our love for her eclipses the threat she'll feel when we start talking about our previous romantic conquests. If she trusts us implicitly, she may even enjoy cataloguing the many romances we've had—after all, they made us the complex, dimensional, emotionally available man we are today. If, alternatively, she mistrusts us for any reason (especially if we've given her reason to), well then, she needs to believe that she's the only woman we've ever met.

In my experience, men are the more fragile sex when it comes to being pelted by our girlfriend's sexual past. A few details about her ex's great taste in music, or savvy with tools, and we're shattered. Worse yet, should our girlfriend ever mention any physical description of her ex—his eyes, his skin color, his smile—we've quickly built him up like a studly Mr. Potato Head. Even without any further allusion to Mr. Potato Head, we're plagued by the image of our girlfriend and Mr. Potato Head, naked, doing naked things. When we note a faraway look in her eyes, we're certain that she's reliving the Potato Head experience in her mind, and loving every minute.

Ohh, Mr. Potato Head. I miss you.

Far more worrying for us men are the Mr. Potato Heads who live not only in her mental Rolodex, but in the neighborhood. The ones who still call, still drop by, still send birthday gifts. These are the dangerous ones. Fear not the exes from her past. Dread the exes in her presence.

Long after she had begun dating me, for example, Katrina stayed in touch with her ex-fiancé Peter. There were lingering complications:

He owned a house with her. Shared custody of a dog with her. And was still in love with her.

At first I wasn't threatened by Katrina's ties with Peter, until I came home from a business trip (which, I realize, already makes this sentence sound ominous) to find that in my absence Peter had built a doggy door in Katrina's house for her beagle, Ralph. "It's his dog too, remember," Katrina said before I so much as raised an eyebrow. Someone had a guilty conscience, and it wasn't the dog.

Granted, Katrina wasn't cheating on me, not in any conventional sense. And to be honest, I wasn't about to cut a hole in her door on my own without taking some classes in doggy carpentry. So I appreciated Peter's handiwork. But a doggy door isn't a cup of sugar. It isn't something you drop off while you're in the neighborhood. Building a doggy door is tantamount to a neighborhood improvement project. There are measurements to be taken, wood to be sawed, possibly sex to be had. There may even be permits to be filed. I don't know.

But I do know this: Beware of exes who stay too long at the fair. They're hoping for one more ride. Building a doggy door together is a lot of time to devote to an ex when there are at least a dozen people in the local Yellow Pages who a) could get the job done perfectly well, and b) haven't seen my girlfriend naked.

Every Katrina has a Peter. The sad truth is that women often want to keep someone (their ex) on deck, just in case the current batter (you) strikes out.[2] For our part, we men, as a rule, don't hang around our exes for the sparkling conversation or to keep up our carpentry skills. We hang around our exes only if we're still—at least a little bit—attracted to them (and for men that's plenty attracted enough). We continue to be drawn in, like a moth to an old flame.

---

2. Less obvious is why exactly they want to keep tabs on the guy they just sent to the showers. It's certainly not my style. The only time I've ever stayed in touch with an ex is when I accidentally sat on my cell phone and left a message on her voice mail that apparently consisted of the last eight minutes of *CSI: Miami*.

Women know this, and at the same time refuse to acknowledge it. For ego's sake, they enjoy the power they have to seduce their exes into building doggy doors for them, but they would never admit to being so manipulative. Much better to have plausible deniability, to be deliberately ignorant of his intentions. *What? We're just friends now. It's his dog too, remember.*

Is that so? Then why is he the one doing the heavy panting?

She Said . . .

If you're older than fourteen, finding a lover with no exes is unavoidable. The country is teeming with exes. They're everywhere, like ants. If there were a spray to keep them away, "ex-terminators" would make more money than investment bankers.

Like ants, exes supposedly serve some useful purpose in the food chain, but we have no idea what. To us, they're just pests. Sure, our boyfriends need to have had other relationships in order to "grow" and "become capable of intimacy." But once these relationships end, their exes should gracefully ex-it. Instead they stick around, either figuratively or literally. They never simply disappear. I'm not saying I'd want them to die (mostly because then my boyfriends would idealize their dead ex-girlfriends to the point of sainthood and I'd hear about them even more than I already do). But moving to Europe would be the considerate, thoughtful thing to do.

Quite simply, no good can come of bringing an ex into a new relationship. *Hey wait,* a guy may say, *my ex and I dated more than five years ago and my girlfriend and I trust each other.* Baloney. This is a rule with no ex-ceptions. Your girlfriend may insist that she's "cool" with the fact that you and your ex, Jill, are still friends, but believe me, she has not only Googled Jill repeatedly, but forwarded the link with Jill's photo to ten people with the note: "Is she prettier than me?"

You and your girlfriend might be out with Jill and her current boyfriend, talking about their romantic trip to Italy and how her boyfriend proposed on a gondola in Venice. Even so, your girlfriend won't be able to stop this thought from playing in the background of her mind, like bad Muzak: *Jill has had sex with my boyfriend.* Your girlfriend will try to say something about how lovely Venice is in May, but instead she'll be thinking, *What a sleazy top Jill's wearing. And my boyfriend is trying so hard not to look.* Then she'll angrily excuse herself to the restroom because you didn't even *notice* she was angry since you were too busy trying not to stare at your ex-girlfriend's cleavage.

During the fight in the car (even the valet knows there will be a fight), you'll tell your girlfriend, "But Jill's engaged!" to which she'll reply, "So? You're still attracted to her." To which you'll reply, "I am not!" But your girlfriend will shake her head and roll her eyes and make that *pffft* sound that shoots saliva onto the dashboard. It's not very flattering. Still, she knows she's right.

Why does she know this?

Because she's still attracted to *her* exes—even the one who turned out to be gay. (Forget the fact that he's not interested in having sex with her—after all, apparently he didn't want to have sex with her when he *was* having sex with her.) The physical attraction doesn't go away. She may not want to marry the guy, but he probably still turns her on. You can't just "ex" the exes.

Case in point: my last boyfriend. His ex-girlfriend Erin was married with a kid, but while she and my boyfriend were dating, he thought they'd get married. So after my boyfriend made the fatal mistake of saying, "You know, Erin still looks good, even after having a baby," I asked whether he ever wondered about what might have been. And you know what the idiot said? He said, "Not really. I mean, maybe it would have worked out, you never know."

Maybe it would have worked out?! This is not what you say to your girlfriend about an ex with whom you're still friends. When it comes to exes, lie, lie, lie! Say you never *really* had good sex with your ex. Say you never *really* fell in love, it was just a confusing time in your life. We know that you're lying, and we'll still make that sourpuss face at you, but at least we'll feel respected.

It's disrespectful to bring the exes into the picture because they're inherently threatening to our self-esteem. You may have loved other women, but we want you to love us the *most*. And we want to be the person who knows you best (how can we compete with the woman you lived with for three years when we've known you for three months?). We prefer not to think about the women who came before us.

Men, on the other hand, seem overly curious about a woman's exes. In particular, they want to know how many men we've slept with. It seems masochistic. Why would a new boyfriend want to hear about our former lovers?

I finally figured it out. It's not to determine whether we're promiscuous. It's to make sure that *they've* had more lovers than we have. They'll deny it, of course, but if our number (which we'll subtract five from anyway) is bigger than his number (which he'll add five to anyway), he'll feel emasculated. (Forget the fact that a woman may have had fewer lovers but more actual sex because she was in a series of long-term relationships. Guys don't count that as "winning.")

But back to the issue: Since there are so many people on earth to choose from, why do you have to be friends with those you've seen naked? Why do you have to have hushed, private conversations with your ex-girlfriends at 2:00 A.M.?

"Katie really needs to talk to me about her problems with her new boyfriend, Ed," you'll say, while we're thinking, "Why doesn't Katie talk to *Ed* about her problems with *Ed*?" When you say, "Great news! Katie and Ed are solid again and they're having a party Friday night," we do not consider this news "great." Socializing with a boyfriend's ex presents all kinds of problems. Not to mention the fact that we'll be wearing plunging necklines and strappy sandals for *her* benefit—not yours. It's just not right to make us crazy enough to do this.

If you absolutely must be friends with an ex, never come back from lunch with her and say you had a great time. Don't even smile like you're in a particularly good mood. Don't laugh at old inside jokes—or worse, try to explain them to us. Better yet, don't admit that you and your ex ever had any inside jokes. If you have your ex's old love letters and other memorabilia, hide them in a closet, preferably at your parents' house. There's no need to keep framed pictures of exes in your apartment. (And don't display a photo with your ex cut out and when we give you the evil eye, explain, "But it's a flattering picture of me. She's not in it anymore, so what's the problem?")

The irony is, if all this effort is worth it to you—if you do everything you can to eliminate your exes from our lives—then we'll tolerate having your exes in our lives. It's perplexing, I know, but if you're willing to jump through this many hoops for us, well, golly, maybe you really *do* love us the most.

26

Get Misty for Me

BOYS DON'T CRY, BUT SHOULD MEN?

He Said . . .

I assume you turned to this chapter in an emergency. You found yourself getting caught up in the emotion—hers or yours, doesn't matter—felt your eyes watering, the tears welling up, and you consulted your trusty "He Said . . ." to determine if you should open the floodgates. An emotional 911.

Good. I've caught you just in time. FOR FUCK'S SAKE, DON'T DO IT.

You must be in an emergency situation here, because not only am I absolutely certain that you should never, ever cry in front of your girlfriend, I'm convinced it's dangerous even to be *reading* about it.

So suck it up, crybaby.

A little self-disclosure: I'm a crier. I cried when I got my first B on a history test; I cried the first time I beat my father in tennis; I cried giving the best man speech at my brother's wedding (thereafter referred to as the "best girl speech"). Hell, odds are I'm crying right now. But that's okay, because there are no girls around.

Except for, of course, me.

Point is, I know from whence I cry.

Women often make me cry. A few have quite literally asked me to cry. In an intimate moment—not *that* kind of intimate, not *intimate* intimate; I mean, I don't cry during *intimate* intimate moments, at least not yet—a few have told me that they feel much closer to a man if he lets them see him at his weakest. And I've foolishly taken the bait.

Wah. Wah wah wah wah.

You see, we men are told that you women want a complex guy. Strong but weak. Determined but flexible. Macho but sensitive. The kind of guy who'd rope a steer but won't order meat if you're feeling a little vegan today. Who'd kill a cockroach, but feel real bad about it. Who'd defend your honor, but honor your ability to defend your own.

But none of this has *anything* to do with crying. Over the years, I've learned the hard way (or "the soft way," really), that crying is never a good idea, unless you've just been sprayed in the eyes with a toxic household cleaner.

One simply cannot alter this inalienable truth of the male–female relationship: aside from the moments after your birth (when crying is allowed only because it proves you're, you know, *alive*), you are allowed to cry in front of a woman once—*once*—and still keep her respect. And even then, it had better be about your mother dying. And even then, it had better be recently. And even then, it had better be *one* tear, like you're Iron Eyes Cody lamenting the rape and pillage of your native land. And even then, you had better wipe it away quickly, and make damn sure she knows you're embarrassed.

And even *then.*

This is no joke, gentlemen. One of my ex-girlfriends broke up with her former fiancé because he was taking too long getting over the death of his mother. He was coming home too many nights with tears in his eyes, and apparently she thought enough tears had been shed. Time to shape up or ship out. And as callous as that is, as cold as she was, she's the rule, not the exception. (You know I'm bitter over my ex when I'm bitter over how my ex treated *her* ex. Now *that's* bitter.)

If you cry about anything less than the death of a mother—a problem at work, a problem with the law, a problem with the crossword (or maybe your mother isn't dead but really, really sick)—you're doomed. Your relationship is over. Why? Because while it's true that the sympathetic-seeming woman sitting across the candlelit two-top from you thinks of herself as wanting to be with a guy who's in touch with his emotions and not afraid to cry, there's the rub: Women don't want to *be* that kind of woman; they want to *think* of themselves as being that kind of woman.

But, at heart, they're not.

You'll hear women say, "Honey, buy me a diamond." And mean it. You'll hear them say, "Honey, give me an orgasm." And mean it. You may even hear, "Honey, show me some emotion." And mean it. But you'll never hear, "Honey, cry me a river."

So this woman who seems to be dripping with empathy while you're dripping with saline—oh, she'll pretend to be there for you in your one and only time of blubbery need—she'll dry your eyes, hold you close, and tell you everything's gonna be all right. Then she'll break up with you two days later by calling you at work and muttering something about you not making her feel "safe."

And who you gonna cry to then?

She Said . . .

I was reading a magazine at the doctor's office recently when a survey caught my eye: The number one characteristic men say they're seeking in a potential mate is "attractive." Women, it reported, are overwhelmingly in search of "sensitive." For us, Mr. Right is Mr. Sensitive.

And we mean it.

Self-described sensitive men, though, will tell you that we're full of it. My guy friends come armed with tragic tales of being dumped after crying too many times in front of their girlfriends—although the girl-friends invariably say it's not because of the crying, it's just that "something's missing."

Usually my guy friend starts tearing up when he gets to this part of the story.

"I just [*whimper*] don't understand [*sniffle*] what's [*sob, sob*] missing," he'll say, his voice cracking, his face reddening, his nose beginning to run.

Hello? What's missing is your masculinity!

When I heard that my friend's new boyfriend said, "I think we should wait to have sex until we're more emotionally connected"; and then, when they did have sex, "I'm a bit self-conscious because I'm normally harder than this"; and then, a few months later, "I'm worried that you're not as committed as I am," my thought wasn't, "Wow, I wish I could find a sensitive guy like that!" No. It was, "Yikes! He's either gay or a total weenie!" In other words, *so* not sexy.

We want men to be sensitive enough to be empathic, but not so sensitive that they seem weak. Ultimately, the problem lies not in women misrepresenting what they want, but in the gender-specific definition of the word "sensitive." Sensitive *women* cry. Sensitive *women* are emotional. Sensitive *women* have lots (and lots) of feelings.

A sensitive man, on the other hand? He doesn't *have* feelings . . . he understands *our* feelings. He doesn't *act* emotional. He empathizes with *our* emotions. He doesn't crank up Norah Jones and spill tears onto his journal. He sucks it up and goes out to shoot hoops with the guys. He's stoic in the face of our meltdowns. He listens, he soothes, he assures us everything will be okay. Heck, he'll even give us an extra long backrub.

Women don't want to play this role for men. Seeing our boyfriend cry is creepy. It's like walking in on your parents during sex: We're aware they do these things, but please do them when we're at sleep-away camp.

Granted, we'll watch our man cry. We won't sprint out of the room. We may even feel flattered that, if push comes to shove, he feels close enough to be vulnerable with us. But we'll only do it once a year or so. Like a birthday. (Only our birthday wish is, "Please God, not for another 364 days.") Because vulnerable can turn into pathetic if he becomes a blubbering mass of tears as often as we do.

It's okay for me to cry if my boss yells at me. But it's just . . . awkward . . . for him to cry if he gets fired. He can yell, he can scream, he can curse the heavens, he can blow things up in his video games. But he shouldn't break down and cry. Double standard? You betcha. Men don't want dumpy women and women don't want wimpy men.

Remember Carrie Bradshaw's boyfriend Aidan on *Sex and the City*. Mr. Sensitive, right? Barely lasted a season. But the stoic Mr. Big—who caused Carrie to cry instead—made cameos for six seasons and then got her at the end.

Women, on the other hand, usually get the guy *because* they're crying. In *When Harry Met Sally,* Meg Ryan's a bawling mess—snot pouring out of her nose, mascara trickling down her face—when she calls Billy Crystal to come over to comfort her.

"It's not that Joe didn't want to get married," she whimpers through hiccups about her ex. "It's that Joe didn't want to marry *me!*"

They kiss, they make love, they ultimately live happily ever after. Had Billy Crystal's character been the gushing faucet, would Meg Ryan have slept with him that night? Not a chance.

There's only one time when a woman likes—in fact, desperately *wants*—to see a man cry: after they break up. She wants to know that he *cares,* that he *misses* her, that he has *feelings* for her. She wants to know that he *hurts* as much as she does.

So she'll call him late at night (sobbing, of course), and when he betrays no emotion about the breakup, she'll ask indignantly, "How come you're not crying? Didn't I mean *anything* to you?"

"Um, I gotta go," he'll say in a neutral tone, which only makes her cry harder. She may even call him "insensitive." Then she'll hang up and tell her friends what a heartless jerk he is. That he has no feelings. And when her tears finally dry up, she'll emphatically declare that next time, dammit, she'll make sure she finds a *sensitive* guy.

27

"If You Really Loved Me, You'd . . ."

WHEN DID YOU START DATING MACHIAVELLI?

He Said . . .

Since I prefer to date humans, and since all humans are flawed, there have always been small things that have annoyed me about my girlfriends. Nothing too serious. One, the way she demanded coffee like it was heroin. Another, the way she rolled her fingertips together when discussing even the most inane plan, as if she were a mustached silent movie villain hatching a dastardly scheme (first time cute, twelfth time annoying). Yet another, well, there's no good way to put this: her voice. (Sounds cruel, but just be glad this isn't an audiobook.)

But as the song says, I took all of them. I let the small stuff slide. Nobody's perfect.

When a woman has her sights set on us, however, we soon come to realize there is no small stuff. In her eyes, every hairline crevice between what we are and what she wants us to be is a Great Divide of Incompatibility that needs to be bridged before any forward progress can be made. Even if she was at first attracted to those qualities she found mysterious and intriguing ("How did God build such a wonder of the world?" we imagine her thinking), she'll soon go from asking, "What the heck is up with him?" to demanding "What the fuck is wrong with him?" It's not just that women want to figure us out; they want to fix us. Instead of marveling at the unique design of our canyons, they start digging here, plastering there, shoring up what they might have first seen as our charming little faults, but now see as our massive gaping deficiencies.

These things start small, and escalate. Not long after Katrina cajoled me into flossing every night (not the biggest sacrifice, I realize), she started making other slight alterations. No more licking my fingertips during meals. No more putting the wet towel on the bed. No more sleeping in past nine.

I don't make the same demands of my girlfriends. I cherish my girlfriends for who they are. Girlfriends, in return, seem to love me for who they think I can *become*. In their eyes, I've got serious potential. I've got a solid foundation, and I'm made of solid raw material. That's me: a very promising fixer-upper. Luckily, I have no allegiance to my bad habits, so if the woman I love is interested in helping me overcome them, who am I to leave my Christmas lights up until April? *Thanks for the heads-up.* Problem is, many women don't know when to stop ordering modifications.

The language may be different in different relationships, but the sentiment is universal: "If you loved me, you'd cancel that poker night." "If you loved me, you'd spend less time at work." All perhaps leading up to the granddaddy of them all: "If you loved me, you wouldn't ask for a prenup." (That last one is truly sneaky: Whoever made prenups

---

1. I recognize the temptation of a made-to-order relationship, because I too have succumbed to the satisfactions of our made-to-order culture. Hell, it's the history of my relationship with Starbucks. I started with "a cup of the house," then I graduated to a latte, then a nonfat latte, then a venti nonfat vanilla latte, and now I'm just making up words and expecting them to understand: "I'll have a venti vidi vici half-fat low-impact depresso. Extra foam." Problem is, once the baristas start giving us exactly what we want, we don't know when to stop asking. (My friend Danny is so addicted, he orders the crackaccino.)

the antiaphrodisiac did a great PR job.) Tweaking a lover in this way is clearly addictive.[1] Give her an inch and she'll start demanding a mile.

Trust me, ladies, it may be effective in the short term, but it's a recipe for disaster in the long run. Why? First of all, insisting that "if you really loved me, you'd [fill in the blank]"—that is, by using our love as leverage for behavior modification—does our love a great disservice. It implies that our love has street value, that it's simply currency to be spent. And all this time, we thought our love wasn't material. That it could not be bartered away. That it was priceless. Once you've put a price on it, no matter how high, you've cheapened it—in one fell irrational demand.

Worse, when a woman starts trying to change her man in profound ways, a man starts justifying his behavior. He feels threatened. Arguments ensue. But that push-pull soon becomes too tiresome, so he either acquiesces to her demands or he evacuates the building. Rarely does he simply stand up for himself, although—and this is the biggest irony of all—she'd probably respect him more for it. To this day I believe the truest thing I ever said to Katrina was this: "I don't think you want me to be the man you're asking me to become." *I wasn't subservient when you decided you wanted to be with me,* I was saying, *so why are you asking me to cower now?*

For these reasons, women, we beg of you, stop begging so much of us. We're not suggesting that you need to lower your standards, but we seemed to pass muster yesterday, so why is today so different? Think about that, and you'd stop trying to change us.

You know, if you really loved us.

She Said . . .

Many years ago, I was going through a career crisis. I was bored, and broke, and started doing some freelance television work. Then a producer suggested that I apply for an in-house job.

Meanwhile, my boyfriend had just gone from a temporary to full-time position at that network, and when I told him about the job, he tried to talk me out of it. He gave some valid reasons: Don't mix business and pleasure. If one person becomes more successful, you don't know whom you will hate more—yourself or the other person. I acknowledged these issues, but felt that since we'd be working on different shows at a large company, he shouldn't bar me from applying.

That's when he said it. "If you really loved me, you'd find another job."

Wow.

The thing is, I *did* love him. Also, I loved myself. And I didn't think that I should have to choose who I loved more. So what was my boyfriend really saying? *If you really loved me, you'd love me more than you?*

"And if *you* really loved *me,*" I replied, in counter-manipulation mode, "you'd want me to be happy in my career."

So there.

It seems shocking at first, but once you cross that linguistic threshold in a relationship, the phrase "If you really loved me, you'd . . ." slips smoothly off the tongue whenever you simply want to get your way. *If you really loved me, you'd spend your vacation with me instead of your brother. If you really loved me, you'd save me the last cookie in the box. If you really loved me, you'd close the bathroom door. If you really loved me, you'd stand up for me in front of my mother. If you really loved me, you'd do the dishes tonight. If you really loved me, you'd go to my colleague's wedding with me.*

"If you really loved me, you wouldn't apply for this job!" my boyfriend would yell.

"If you really loved me, you'd get help for your insecurity and competition issues!" I'd yell back.

My boyfriend became so resentful over this job impasse that I began to wonder if he was right. Maybe making myself happy and applying for that job meant that I didn't love him. Maybe I could show my love by picking a job I'd hate.

But I didn't think so.

It's hard not to get defensive when somebody tosses the "If you really loved me" grenade. The first time, your reaction might be shock and awe. *Did he really say that?* Later, it becomes swift retaliation—"If *you* really loved me, you'd . . ." But in the end, you realize it's just another futile attempt to change your lover. You either stop using the phrase or you withdraw the troops and get the hell out of a bad relationship.

When I broke up with this boyfriend, he took it in stride. I cried, he cried, we hugged, shared some tasty grilled salmon, and said a heartfelt good-bye. No "if you" this and "if you" that.

The next morning, though, he called sobbing, asking to get back together. I gently said no, I was ready to move on. He begged, he reasoned, and finally, when my answer was still no, he said, "If you really loved me, you'd give me another chance."

This continued all week. "I do love you," I'd say. "But I can't do this anymore."

"But if you really, *truly* loved me . . . ," he pleaded late Friday night, and this time, he didn't finish the sentence. Maybe he realized how ridiculous it sounded.

By Monday, we were back together (I know, I know—see chapter 33), and when he dumped me four months later (I know, I know, I know—see chapter 34), it was my turn: "If you really loved me," I said pathetically, "you'd wait until I'd find a job."

Desperate, I tried a bunch of combinations: "If you really loved me, you wouldn't spring this on me so suddenly." "If you really loved me, you'd give me a second chance the way I gave you one." And my most moronic: "If you really loved me, you'd . . . love me enough to want to stay."

Huh??? Even I couldn't follow that.

I knew right then that not only was our relationship over, but that we probably didn't love each other anyway. Because if we *really* loved each other, we never would have given each other these "If you really loved me" ultimatums in the first place.

28

Porn

IS OBJECTIFYING WOMEN ALWAYS
OBJECTIONABLE?

He Said . . .

Your girlfriend has found your porn.

Your tapes, your magazines, the whole stash. *Position: Impossible. Mutiny on the Booty. Casaboinka.* The whole shebang (not a porn title, but could be).

And now she's accusing you of being crude, insensitive, male. Keep in mind: There's no reason to panic. (When she throws it away, now *there's* reason to panic.)

You have the facts on your side. And the facts are these: You're a man. She's a woman. You're *supposed* to have different views on pornography—and by that I mean, you like to view it, she doesn't.

Men enjoy looking at naked women. Often. We're good at it, too. The only thing that can truly distract us from looking at a naked woman is another naked woman tapping us on the shoulder and screaming, "Hey, naked woman over here!" With a bullhorn. (I'm writing this at 7:30 on a Sunday morning. I should be at church. Instead, I'm *writing* about naked women, and wishing this was a pop-up book. That's it. After this chapter, I'm going to church.)

It's what men do. And not just oversexed college boys (or under-sexed television writers) with too much idle time on their hands. Truck drivers. College professors. Even Supreme Court justices. One porn-loving Supreme Court chief justice—to protect his identity, let's call him Feelgood Marshall—even admitted it in a landmark ruling on pornography. Asked to define when, exactly, naked pictures of women were no longer art and had crossed the line into "obscenity," he couldn't. His best guess? "I know it when I see it."

When I see it. Not *if*. So literally, it's the law of the land: We see pornography. And when we see it, we know it. Oh, how we know it.

However, because what constitutes obscenity is so darn subjective, judges in every local hamlet are assigned the task of determining whether pornography "violates the community standard." But here's the thing: Pornography doesn't violate the community standard. It *is* the community standard. A couple of years ago, the major hotel chains admitted that much of their profit is based on the pay-per-view adult movies they offer to lonely businessmen who would never admit they tuned in to *The Usual Suckfest* back in the usual board meeting. We're talking billions of dollars. Porn is common, porn is popular, porn is ubiquitous. And the best part is, it won't show up on your bill!

My point is, legally, you're in the clear.

Of course, by the time you explain all of this to your girlfriend, she'll be convinced that not only do you spend too much time look-ing at pornography, you spend too much time *thinking* about it, too much time building a defense (*I'll take it all the way to the Supreme Court!*). Defending your porn collection *legally* probably isn't the tack she's looking for. It's like defending murder as a population control measure.

So let's get personal.

The big criticism of pornography—aside from seriously crappy production values—is that it objectifies women. Objectively speaking, yes, that's pretty much the point. And objectifying women violates, well, let's call it "the femininity standard." Women insist—in op-eds, at rallies, over breakfasts—that they don't want to be treated as objects. Never. Ever. And yet . . .

I was at the library the other day—the library!—when a young woman walked past the card catalog wearing sweatpants with the word BOUNCY emblazoned in huge block letters on her butt. It used to be that women worried about panty lines; now women worry about what witty line to put on their pants. She had what can only be described as a vanity ass plate: BOUNCY. Mind you: not *near* her butt, not *framing* her butt. *On* her butt.

I'm not sure why: Was it *describing* her butt? Was it a warning in case small children drew too near and were suddenly bounced to the other side of the street? Who knows, but apparently her butt needed some sort of advertising to draw my attention. So it seems to me there's an obvious hypocrisy there: Women don't want to be treated as objects, yet they turn their ass into a billboard.

Women don't want to be treated as objects, except that they do.

And they start young. These days, twelve-year-olds wear "porn star" T-shirts. Sixteen-year-olds idolize porn stars. Eighteen-year-olds *are* porn stars. Young girls get sexy tattoos of birds and bees before they even learn *about* the birds and the bees. Even weirder, pick up any magazine. Flip through the pictures, and it won't be long before you say, "Wow, she's hot." Then you notice—it's an ad for Gap Kids. At this rate, it's only a matter of time before the Mickey Mouse Club starts charging a cover.

But back to the topic at hand: Your girlfriend has found your porn.

The best defense, as they say, is a good offense. And Lord knows she finds your porn offensive.

Keep this in mind: Women, as a rule, aren't against other women displaying, revealing, or piercing their sexuality however they may choose; rather, what upsets women most about pornography is that it creates an unrealistic ideal that most women—real women—can never attain.

Fair enough.

Porn *does* set a standard of womanhood and physical perfection to which women can never live up. Worse, it suggests to men that such women are out there—somewhere—and if they play their cards right, they might someday meet one (and, of course, have absolutely nothing to talk about).

But there's also a pornographer who sets a standard of *man*hood and emotional accessibility to which *men* can never live up. Worse, she tells women that such men are out there and that they might turn their husbands into one.

Her name is Oprah.

Oprah is pornography for women. Oprah objectifies men. Men have Hugh Hefner and Larry Flynt. Women have Oprah and Dr. Phil. (And, by the way, at least our purveyors of porn don't pretend to be doctors.) Every day in syndication, Oprah draws a portrait of the perfect man: He rips off your dress, and then mends it while you take a postcoital bath.

Oprah is selling women a bill of goods bound to disappoint. Like the many guarantees made to men in men's magazines—"How to Turn Your Girlfriend into a Stark Raving Nympho" comes to mind—it's a promise that's bound to fail. Venus can't turn Mars into Jupiter.

But it persists. It thrives. While *Penthouse* goes bankrupt thanks to decreased circulation (and if you've ever suffered from decreased circulation, you know how troubling it can be), Oprah is more popular than ever. She even has a glossy magazine—though its centerfold is more likely to be Alan Alda than Allan Quatermain.

Never mind that women don't actually *want* the sensitive man Oprah is pushing, any more than men want to bring Carmela Canyons to their kid's bar mitzvah. They think they do, but they don't. If women took Oprah's advice and changed their men into, well, Steadman, they'd merely be living Mia Farrow's nightmare: Go to bed with Frank Sinatra, wake up with Woody Allen.

So just look at your girlfriend—with her perfectly imperfect breasts and her "bouncy" vanity buttocks ("My other ass is a Porsche!")—and offer her a deal: "You stop expecting me to be in touch with my emotions, and I'll stop expecting Pamela Anderson to show up with a bullhorn."

Now let my *Playboy* go.

She Said . . .

Full disclosure about full disclosure: I write emotionally revealing memoirs, but won't wear see-through blouses. Which is to say, I'm not the type to post my naked picture on the Web. But when a women's magazine asked me to go to an "erotic amateur photo site and write about the experience," I was intrigued. Heck, I was flattered.

Okay, I know, I should have been offended. I completely understand why a friend threatened to break up with her boyfriend if he continued to keep *Playboy* on the coffee table. My friends and I spout the feminist rhetoric about how porn presents airbrushed, breast-enhanced, nipped-and-tucked objectifications of women, and how, as Naomi Wolf wrote in *New York* magazine, now that cyber porn has become such a natural part of even menschy guys' daily lives, "young women worry that as mere flesh and blood, they can scarcely get, let alone hold, male attention."

But this woman's magazine asked me—a petite Jewish woman who bears no resemblance to the cast of *The O.C.*—to play a porn star! Who wouldn't chuck political correctness for that?

And here was a perfect opportunity: an amateur porn site. Instead of competing with a gaggle of Heidi Klum clones, I figured these "real" women would have cellulite, lopsided breasts, and wrinkled skin. It seemed like going porno in the farm leagues might help me feel more comfortable with my body.

Or so I told myself.

So instead of going with a demure photo called "Left to the Imagination," I decided to take the plunge with "All Thongs Considered." The name was nerdy NPR, but the photo was pure porn star: I'm stretched across a sofa, face averted, hair wild, breasts bare, hips curved suggestively, thong covering my crotch. So what if I needed a bikini wax? I felt giddy!

The next morning, though, I woke up and thought: *Oh, shit.* What if I didn't—so to speak—measure up?

I raced to my computer to check my "feedback section." Bracing for a dis, I clicked to find fifty comments like "mouth-watering bite-sized titties," "legs to die for," and "awesome ass!" And who knew I had a "super sexy belly button"?

By week's end, instead of averting my eyes when men looked me over at Starbucks, I smiled back flirtatiously, bolstered by my thrilling secret: *"You, sir, can see me naked!"* Soon the cheesy feedback ("lovely Lolita!" "bodacious beauty!" "cum-hither!") went to my head. I posted two more photos, and even considered revealing my face. After all, if my body was getting rave reviews, shouldn't I get some credit?

Then it happened. One guy called me "scrawny" before adding that I had "the breasts of a twelve-year-old" and a cyber fight broke out. Other men came to my defense with comments like, "Hey, loser, she's a winner!" and "Go whack yourself" but suddenly I stopped caring. I realized I was as pathetic as guests on *Jerry Springer* baring themselves for public approval.

"You go, girl!" one guy wrote. So I did: I took my pictures off the site.

For the next week, I kept thinking about the men who had clicked on my photo. Instead of feeling uncomfortable, I wondered if they missed me. I *wanted* them to miss me.

And that's what most women won't admit: Naked women have tremendous power—and we enjoy that power. But we're also keenly aware (and afraid) of other women's power. *We* don't mind being gawked at or even objectified. It's the gawking at and objectification of *other* women that threatens us.

Which is exactly why men should keep their porn to themselves. Porn makes other women seem powerful, while we feel simply . . . bloated.

Recently my friend Aaron told me that his girlfriend was upset because while working on his computer, she noticed he'd been on a porn site. She said that if he was interested in women like that, he shouldn't be dating women like her. She said he had no respect for women in general.

"Isn't she being irrational?" Aaron asked.

I thought about my weeklong experience as a porn star, and how sexy it made me feel. I thought about how other guys' girlfriends might have thrown a hissy fit if they caught their boyfriends checking out my photos. I thought about the fact that back in the real world, I *am* that girlfriend throwing the hissy fit.

"Are you kidding?" I said, narrowing my eyes to imply that Aaron was a freaky pervert. "How can you even look at that stuff? It totally objectifies women."

29

Lie to Me, Please

SHOULD YOU ALWAYS TELL THE TRUTH ABOUT HOW YOU REALLY FEEL?

He Said . . .

Do these jeans make me look fat?"

I couldn't believe that Katrina was asking perhaps the single most clichéd question in the history of unanswerable questions. *Do these jeans make me look fat?*

It reminds me of the questions security screeners at the airport used to ask to determine whether or not you're a terrorist: "Did anyone unknown to you help you pack your bags?" "Have your bags been with you at all times?" How ludicrous: If you are, in fact, a terrorist, you're not going to spoil it right then and there. Even if the accurate answer is yes, the correct answer is no.

Same with relationships. Even if honesty is asked for, sometimes lies are expected.

Nonetheless, Katrina stood there expectantly, waiting for me to respond to her nonrhetorical, *Do these jeans make me look fat?* query, so I answered, "No sweetie, those jeans don't make you look fat. Your ass does." Luckily knowing she was quite skinny, she laughed at my joke, because I wanted to see her with the jeans off again someday.

Even if Katrina had gained a few pounds, my job at that moment, and the only reason she asked the question in the first place, was to bolster her ego before we hit the town for the night. It wasn't to tell *the truth, the whole truth, and nothing but the truth.* I was expected to be a boyfriend doting over his lovely girlfriend as she looked herself over in the mirror, not an eyewitness being deposed under oath in the case of *Katrina* vs. *her fat ass.*

The truth, the whole truth and nothing but the truth? No, sir.

The truth, after all, can hurt. Honesty is a trap. And asking for honesty is a form of entrapment. Too often I've forgotten that when a hot woman walks by and my girlfriend asks me, "Do you think she's pretty?" she doesn't want to know the answer, she just wants to see if I care enough to lie. The correct answer isn't an honest "yes" or "no." The correct answer is "Is *who* pretty?" The correct answer is to misunderstand the question.

The whole truth ain't so nice either. As a rule, honesty is generally appreciated, but brutal honesty is sometimes just that—brutal. Telling your girlfriend that yes, the jeans make her look fat . . . and a little trampy too, well, there's usually no need to be so rough with the one you love. The whole truth (that sometimes she looks butch when she puts her hair up, that her whiny voice kills nearby insects, that her parents smell funny) is what you tell your best friend, not your girlfriend. (And by the way, ladies, we men are under no illusions that you tell us nearly as much as you tell your girlfriends. I'm constantly harboring the suspicion that my girlfriends' girlfriends know infinitely more about my back hair than even I do.)

Nothing but the truth? Well, that's simple insanity. Sometimes telling the truth and a lie—"Yes, I'll spend the holidays with your parents, and you know what? I'm looking forward to it"—is exactly the kind of added detail that makes her realize what a sexy catch you are.

Having been brought up to think that honesty is the best policy, I used to be uncertain how to respond to questions to which the honest answer was the wrong one.

Do I tell the truth anyway? Do I pretend not to understand the question? Do I suddenly *no hablo inglés*? Once I thought that if I simply froze in my tracks, didn't move an inch, my girlfriend might become confused or get bored and move on. But girlfriends aren't like velociraptors. Their sight isn't based on movement. They can still see you even if you're evading the question by stiffening up. So you'll have to say something. A few choice lies keep a relationship humming.

Men, on the other hand, don't mind honesty, primarily because we rarely ask questions to which the correct answer is a lie. If we ask, "Does this tie make me look gay?" we actually want to know if the tie makes us look gay. We're not concerned that, oh my, we've been putting on a couple pounds of gay recently and we want our girlfriends to allay our fears by lying to us about how gay we don't look. We just want to know whether we should put on another fucking tie. Most of our questions aren't minefields. They're just questions. "Italian or Chinese?" is hardly an enigma. (Women, feel free to tell us you're in the mood for Chinese. We won't read anything into it.)

Women, however, will frequently, almost masochistically, ask questions where honesty can be painful. Not long into our relationship, Katrina, who had graduated first in her class from CalArts and was an accomplished sculptor and artist, brought me to her storage space and showed me her paintings. "So, what do you think?" she asked.

"They're great," I said.

"No, really. What do you really think?" she asked.

I hesitated for just a second too long before saying, "Amazing. Really amazing." She knew that I was lying.

Truthfully, I didn't spark to the paintings I saw—they seemed unfinished, for lack of a better word—but what did I know? I hadn't gone to art school like she had, and I was willing to admit my lack of qualifications. But it's not enough to say, "I'm unqualified to judge these things." It's like telling her she's bad in bed: "*But what do I know, I'm no sexologist.*"

Indeed, I thought her sculptures were stunning, and I praised them to high heaven, but I had already blown it. I knew better, too. When approaching a topic as sensitive as, you know, *a life's work,* I was perfectly aware I should tread lightly. Unfortunately, I tread too slowly.

For the slightest moment I forgot that even when honesty is asked for, sometimes lies are expected. What can I say: I'm not a very good liar.[1]

By asking me to judge her art honestly, Katrina did what many women do: expose themselves to pain. They do this not only to put themselves in danger (it's the female version of driving recklessly), but also as a test to determine if you're the kind of guy who will inflict pain. If you aren't to be trusted with their emotional security; if, frankly, you're an emotional terrorist.

You may not have learned about this little test in your last relationship, but ask yourself: How did that one work out? So take note this time around. No doubt your girlfriend is working on some new questions she's dying to ask you: "Has anyone unknown to me given you emotional baggage? Has your emotional baggage been with you at all times? Are you going to take your emotional baggage out on me? No? Okay then, prove it. . . . *Do these jeans make me look fat?*"

A relationship is one of the few places where honesty is not the

---

1. One special case of lying is worth noting. Even though lies and duplicity are the bread and butter of many healthy relationships, it's a sad truth that I—and many men— sometimes only become the best liar late in the relationship, and only when I want it to *end.* In those cases, we don't lie for the usual reasons: to save our hide or the relationship.

We lie to break up.

However, we lie to make ourselves look worse, not better. "I don't think I'll ever afford a house." "I'm not very good at my job." "I *like* how this tie makes me look gay." We want it to end, and at that point of no emotional return, instead of being honest with our feelings, and with her, and suggesting that we should move on like adults, we make up all sorts of self-deprecating excuses, reasons, and infirmities to paint a false portrait of ourselves as a really terrible guy, so that *she'll* want to end it all. Men aren't above making the women do the dirty work. A friend of mine once told a girl he was suicidal just to scare her away. Truth is, he was feeling rather peppy—he just didn't want to waste it on her. Sad, but true.

same thing as sincerity. Even if we don't tell the truth, we sincerely want to make you happy. Ask me a question, and I'll tell you a few lies, but you'll never doubt my good intentions. And if you only knew my good intentions, you'd let me get you out of those jeans.

She Said . . .

The truth is, I lie in relationships. Not malicious lies, just lies to grease the well-oiled machinery of mutual admiration and support. In fact, every woman I know tells these lies to her significant other. And every man I know is shocked—shocked!—to learn that we're such liars.

I don't know what these guys are so upset about. Do they really want, as they say self-righteously, "honesty at all times"? Women certainly don't.

Obviously, certain lies are disturbing. Like the guy who assured my friend that he was leaving his girlfriend, but who (of course) didn't and thereafter became known as Asshole Liar. (A typical exchange: "How's Asshole Liar?" "Still with his girlfriend.") Or like the guy who told me when I was out of town that although his cell phone was off and he didn't call me until the next day, he'd gone to dinner alone—when, in fact, he'd been out with his ex-girlfriend. (Typical exchange: "You're still dating Pinocchio?" "Maybe he'll change.") (Yes, women also lie to themselves.)

Generally speaking, though, women don't want the truth. Maybe it's because we're not used to it since our girlfriends have always lied to us—in a good way. Women are raised to distinguish between lies that are soothing and those that are hurtful. It's a simple calculus: We gloss over anything that might damage a person's self-esteem. We do our best to tell the truth about everything else.

And we want the same from our lovers.

But men have a less empathetic system of honesty. Either they lie to deceive (like Asshole Liar and Pinocchio) or they go the brutally honest route. My last boyfriend even wrote on his online dating profile under "Traits I seek in a mate": "I want brutal honesty." I don't get that. Who wants brutality in their relationship? Wouldn't gentle honesty be a lot nicer? Brutal honesty may sound evolved—you're mature enough to "handle the truth"—but it has its drawbacks. This isn't "Truth or Consequences"; it's "Truth *with* Consequences."

"Yes, I'm attracted to Daphne," Brutally Honest Boyfriend replied when confronted about a coworker he clearly had a crush on. "But it's not like I'd act on it."

"Would you go out with her if we broke up?" I asked (masochistically).

"I don't know. Probably," he shrugged.

"Probably?"

"What?" Brutally Honest Boyfriend asked. "I work with a lot of very attractive women. If I said I didn't think about them that way, I'd be lying."

"Then lie!" I said.

How does this level of honesty, as Brutally Honest Boyfriend claimed, make us "feel closer as a couple" (especially when he's sent to sleep alone)? This may sound counterintuitive, but if my boyfriend had simply lied to me, I would have trusted him more. Because a lie like "I'm not attracted to Daphne" would show that he cared about my feelings. Telling the cold, hard truth meant he didn't give a shit.

Women can understand men who lie to, say, avoid arguments. *Yes, I'd still love you if you were a paraplegic. Of course you're my best friend* (after Sam, Paul, Henry . . . and a few others). *They were out of your tampons* (instead of *I forgot to buy your tampons again*). But men also lie about innocuous things, just because they can. "I went to the gym with Mark," a boyfriend said, when actually they'd gone to a movie. Why would I care? When I asked why he lied, my boyfriend replied, "Because I wanted some privacy."

Most frustrating for women are men who want praise for simply telling the truth. "I didn't have to tell you the truth," another boyfriend said, "so shouldn't I get some credit?" To him, the truth was optional. Which might explain why he told only part of the truth ("I'm missing your cousin's wedding because I have to go to New York for business") and later, after I become angry at him for leaving out the rest of the story ("I stopped in Vegas for a bachelor party on the way back") he complained that he was being "punished" for telling the truth.

"No," I replied. "You're being punished for telling a *half*-truth."

While men tell half-truths to save their asses, women tell half-truths to save their dignity. (Things women lie about: orgasms, food consumption, how long ago they graduated from college. Things men lie about: orgasms with others, alcohol consumption, how long the baseball game really lasted.) For women, though, lying is primarily a form of reassurance. So whenever my boyfriend would express insecurity about being the only one in his family not to have gotten into medical school, I assured him that his current job was much more fulfilling and equally prestigious—whether I believed it or not. Whenever he asked "Did you come?" I said, "Of course! Couldn't you tell?" When he noticed that his coworker gave me the once-over during a visit to his office, I told him I had no idea what he was talking about.

In this way, intimacy should never be confused with honesty. Guys who say, "I'm telling you this hurtful-painful-negative thing because I love you" are clueless. Love is soft-pedaling the truth to spare each other's feelings. My boyfriend saying, "You shouldn't wear crop tops because you have a Buddha belly" or pointing out, "You're really insecure about the way you dance" (people love it when you call attention to their insecurities) doesn't necessarily speak to the depth of our connection. Quite the opposite: Unconditional love means *conditional* honesty.

But even well-intentioned white lies have their limitations. Women are so hard-wired to be sensitive to people's feelings that often under the guise of "protection" we err on the side of omission, or worse.

Take my friend Dana, who went on vacation with her long-term boyfriend. Their first night in Spain, he leaned over and whispered in her ear, "I love you. I think I may want to spend my life with you." In fact, Dana was considering breaking up with this boyfriend, but she hoped some time away together might help her decide how she felt.

"I love you, too," Dana said. "I want that, too."

She dumped him a week after they got back. When I asked her why she'd said those things in Spain, she replied, "I didn't want to hurt his feelings."

"But don't you think your lie was confusing?" I asked. "Don't you think it made it harder for him to get dumped when you got home?"

"Maybe," Dana said. "But it was our first night on this romantic trip, and we had two weeks ahead of us. He saved up an entire year for this and I didn't want to ruin it for him. I mean, what would you have said?"

I thought about it for less than second. "The same thing," I replied. "I would have said exactly the same thing."

30

Fighting Etiquette

IS ALL FAIR WHEN LOVE IS WAR?

He Said . . .

Even though women are said to be better communicators, men are supposed to be better fighters. Men are from Mars, after all. We are the gods of war.

Well, it's all a myth. Men are no better at fighting than women are. If we were, don't you think we would have won by now? On the contrary, fighting has become yet another front on which men and women have reached common ground. On this we can agree: We are both quite skilled at disagreeing.

What's more, since we're both "in it to win it," both men and women will do whatever it takes to be victorious. We'll win at all costs. We'll be remarkably cruel, nasty, malicious, heartless, and harsh to the one we love, because we're convinced that in the heat of the moment, the ends justify the mean. Worse, there are no rules of engagement, no Marquis of Queensbury regulations that dictate how a war of words is supposed to be waged. It's simply "may the best man win," even if he's a woman.

And so the battle between the genders rages on, with both men and women sticking to their unique bag of tricks.

PICKING A FIGHT

Katrina had actually made up a word to describe me when she thought I was in the mood for a fight. "You're just being *awchity*" she'd say. (It rhymed with "crotchety." Don't know if that was a coincidence.) About half the time she was right—I was rarin' for a fight—and the other half of the time *she* was the one in the mood for a fight, and she knew that by accusing *me* of being in the mood for a fight, I'd accuse *her* of trying to start a fight and—whaddaya know—soon we'd be fighting.

No one can deny that we're occasionally just "in the mood" for a fight. It's why so many people pony up to view a pay-per-view on HBO, and why Don King is a multimillionaire. We're all just a little *awchity* on occasion. And when that's the case, there's usually no way—no way—to avoid the fight, so there's no use trying. Whoever wants a fight will find a way to get it started.

It's simply a matter of picking your first move, so that you can be the one to pick the fight. Take, for example, the way women will make accusations they don't actually believe, just to get their man talking: "You'd rather watch *Celebrity Poker* than make love to me." Or the way men will be nonresponsive, not because they have nothing to say, but merely because they secretly want women to start asking provocative questions.

FIGHTING A FIGHT

Katrina actually gave me a book about fighting etiquette once (apparently she thought she had given me so many lectures on fighting, it was about time I also read the syllabus). It was called *Don't Be So Defensive,* which of course immediately put me on the defensive.

But because I loved her, I read it from cover to cover, twice. I even put notes in the margins in case she thought I was lying. I underlined. I highlighted. I dog-eared. I learned a lot. She soon regretted giving me the book, because not only did it make *me,* out of the two of us, the fighting etiquette expert, it gave me a whole new menu of fighting tricks to add to my repertoire. It wasn't a self-improvement book; it was a handy cheat sheet. (Funny how we usually give our loved ones their most effective artillery against us. I remember when we were kids my older brother used to kneel on my stomach, grab my arms, and make me pummel myself. "Stop hitting yourself! Stop hitting yourself!" he'd say. We do the same in adult relationships: Share with our significant others our deepest darkest secrets and our most painful vulnerabilities, so that they can, of course, pummel us with them. Remember that next time you think you're confiding in your significant other: You're only hitting yourself.)

Anyway, the book confirmed what I have always believed. In the war between men and women, men are seriously outgunned, in large part because women don't fight fair.

Consider: Women can *put us on the defensive* simply with their tone. When a woman has something important to say to us, for example, she'll often talk slowly, as if talking to a child. It's effective, but condescending. Hard not to be defensive when our own girlfriend is implying we're either a baby or retarded.

Some women will *raise the stakes irrationally,* as when she threatens to break up with us over the most trifling complaint, just to get us to comply. "If you can't take it upon yourself to do something as simple as the dishes once in a while," she'll say, "I don't know . . . I just wonder if we're right for each other."

"Don't be so dramatic," we'll say . . . right before we offer to both wash *and* dry.

Then there's passive-aggression, which some women have made into an art form. "No, that's fine," she'll say, when things aren't fine. "I don't need you to [fill in the blank], I'm sure we'll both be perfectly happy when we sit on our asses not [fill in the blank]."

Perhaps most infuriating, women are the queens of *misdirection.* As soon as we've made a good point that deflates her argument, she'll bring up some other complaint that is entirely irrelevant to the topic at hand. Suddenly we're playing argument whack-a-mole, desperately trying to bat down the latest topic she brings up.

"Why didn't you call me today? I told you I want you to call me every day, and you didn't call me!" Katrina once accused.

"Actually I did," I assured her.

"You did not," she insisted.

"Have you picked up your cell phone messages?" I asked. I had left two messages on her cell phone telling her I had brought my friend Ryan to the hospital.

"Oh," she demurred. "That still doesn't explain why you never hung up your wet towel in the bathroom."

Whack-a-mole!

"That was your towel," I pointed out.

"I know that. I'm the one who bought it. Because you never do any of the shopping!"

Whack-a-mole!

This can go on for quite a time. Instead of admitting defeat, she'll choose a different battleground, she'll pop up someplace else. Once Katrina and I went so far afield from what we were originally arguing about that we joked we needed to take a break to consult MapQuest. (Another time our argument got so heated about something so irrelevant, we both just starting giggling. Apparently the *I hate you* part of the brain is located right next to the part of the brain that appreciates ridiculousness.)

EXTENDING A FIGHT

Perhaps no argument is more frustrating than an argument that devolves into an argument *about* the argument. Instead of arguing about wet towels on the floor, you start arguing about who's not listening to whom. Who's focusing on the wrong part of the accusation. Who's presuming things that haven't been said.

In my case, Katrina actually accused me of developing an argument fetish—specifically, of not being willing to let the argument end. (Actually, she accused me of having unresolved issues with my mother. *Whack-a-mole!*) She insisted that I seemed to want to prolong arguments rather than let them peter out, unresolved. Though I took issue with the suggestion that I had a fetish, I allowed that she might be on to something. I explained to her what I knew: That growing up, my parents fought often (likely no more often than other parents, but I didn't share a house with other parents). That as an eight-year-old, I couldn't bear to hear them yell at each other. That while my older brother would respond by riding his bike around the block, I responded by shuttling back and forth between my parents *begging* them to stay together. That I was sure if my parents didn't fix their problems right then and there, they would leave each other. That by leaving each other, they'd abandon me and not love me anymore. That it was my responsibility to keep that from happening. "And so," I told Katrina, "if I can't seem to let an argument die, it's because I was once an eight-year-old who was desperate to keep his parents talking."

Katrina seemed satisfied with that answer, until the next time *she* wanted to continue arguing and *I* was nonresponsive. Armed with the new knowledge that arguing, for me, meant commitment, she immediately got worried: "What, don't you love me anymore?"

REVISITING A PREVIOUS FIGHT

A girlfriend once told me, "I forgive, but I don't forget." That seems unfair. If you've done your penance, shouldn't your record be cleared? Sadly, the opposite is often true for me. *I forget, but I don't forgive.* I'll sulk around the apartment for days not remembering what the hell got me sulking in the first place.

"What's wrong with you?" she'll ask. "What did I do?"

"I don't know," I'll say, "but I'm sure it was something."

And then, just to confuse matters more, I'll make her apologize and swear that she'll never do it again.

But because neither side can completely remove ourselves from earlier arguments—by both forgiving *and* forgetting—we'll often have the exact same one over again, simply because it feels familiar. It's remarkable how exactly this new argument will mirror the one we had a week ago, or a year ago. Frankly, I've never understood why we go through the trouble of replaying the tape, just as I've never understood why people watch ESPN Classic—you know how it ends, so what's the point?

Winning a Fight

Oh, there's no winning. If we convince her she's wrong, she'll resent us for being right. If we apologize when we sincerely don't think we're guilty, she'll accuse us of simply appeasing her. If we throw in the towel, she'll yell at us for not hanging it up in the bathroom where it belongs. Sometimes the best we can hope for is to go to bed angry.

Ending a Fight

Since there's never a winner, one of the toughest parts of an argument is discerning when it's over. I sometimes wonder if we'd all be happier couples if the moment an argument ended, a bell rang, or the credits would roll.

Even when the argument seems to have an organic, obvious ending, how many times have you just stood there, feeling foolish, wondering what you're supposed to do now? You're still pumped with fighting endorphins, still eager to go for the jugular, so often you'll just continue the argument without anything really being said:

"All right then."

"All right."

"Good."

"Good."

"Because I—"

"Yeah, I know. Me too."

"Good."

"All right then."

"Good."

And on and on. I don't think it's a matter of "getting the last word." It's just not knowing what the *first* word of the next conversation is supposed to be. Come to think of it, it might not be such a terrible idea to agree on a prearranged word or topic before the argument starts—what's sometimes called a "safety word," I'm told—that would indicate when to stop.

"All right then."

"All right."

"Good."

"Good."

"Because I—"

"Yeah, I know. Me too."

"Good."

"All right then."

"Good."

"Would you like some pie?"

THE AFTERMATH

Women are supposedly so fragile, and yet in most of my arguments with them, I tend to be the one who stays wounded. There is, I think, a reason for that. Men can fight with other men and the moment it's over, it's over. When women fight with other women, usually grudges arise that are never forgotten. When the sexes confront each other, the roles reverse: After an argument with a man, a woman will feel better, exorcised and exercised. After an argument with a woman, a man will feel worse—even if he "won" the argument, he likely lost the war, because what kind of a boyfriend would make his girlfriend feel so defeated?

Arguments, much like the discussions that prompted them, are inherently feminist. It's no big secret that men would rather avoid having a discussion (which is why women are often the ones to deem them necessary). By nature, arguments are designed to get something off *her* chest, not his, and usually something having to do with his bad behavior. So by the end of the conservation, men have inevitably gotten the short end of the argument stick.

She's been heard; he's been hurt. Even if he won, he lost.

GETTING BACK IN FIGHTING SHAPE

It's important not too let the last fight take all of the wind out of you, or to dread your next one. Don't be afraid of a good fight. Fighting, after all, is a form of intimacy. Sometimes if you can't have sex, you can at least have at it. So get right back on that horsey.

But try to fight *fair,* especially if the fight's about nothing, and you're standing there at the end, compelled to wonder aloud, "Why'd we even have this argument in the first place?"

"I don't know. You started it."

"I did not."

"You did *so.*"

And you're off and rolling again, when you'd much rather be enjoying some pie.

She Said . . .

When women fight with women, it's like fighting bulimia—we emotionally binge and purge. But when women fight with men, men label our bursts of emotion "illogical," even though there's nothing logical about love.

If love were logical, would anyone ever say, in the heat of an argument, "Stop being so controlling . . . why can't you just do what I said?" or "I hate you . . . don't leave me!"

"I can't believe you won't kill a spider for me!" I once said to my boyfriend after we'd had this same fight for months. "What, are you gay?"

"It's cruel to kill a living thing," my boyfriend said. "That makes me gay?" (Secretly, I thought he was gay—during fights, our true feelings pop out.)

We can't help it. The more in love we are, the more we treat our loved ones like adversaries during disagreements. And as generals fighting our own private battles, we employ a variety of strategies from our arsenal of psychological warfare:

◆ *There's eye-to-eye combat, the silent but nuclear stare across the dinner table after a particularly nasty comment (and the contest to see who blinks first).*

◆ *There's commenting on your lover's inadequacies in front of other couples ("Don't ask Rob, he can't fix anything") or while on the phone in front of him ("We can't meet you for dinner tonight— Rob's in one of his moods").*

◆ *There's pointedly addressing your lover by his given name ("Nick") instead of his pet name ("Foonie").*

◆ *There's taking the moral high ground ("I may not clean up as much, but at least when I do, I recycle").*

◆ *There's sulking (code for: "I'm going to make you guess what's wrong!").*

◆ *There's accusing your lover of being defensive after saying something that would make anyone defensive ("I am NOT selfish!" "Jeez, don't be so defensive." "I am NOT defensive!").*

◆ *There's saying something provocative and anxiety-provoking to your lover first thing in the morning that causes him to ask,*

"What's that supposed to mean?" then leaving him in the lurch by adding, *"Oops, I'm late for work, we'll talk about this later tonight."*

◆ There's invoking the authority of friends (*"My friends think you're overreacting"*).

◆ There's comparing your lover unfavorably to his friends (*"John gives Susan massages even when he's tired"*).

◆ There's deflecting the current argument by bringing up an old wound (otherwise known as *"The Lifetime Vendetta Bait and Switch"*).

◆ There's the classic picking a fight for no reason. (Maybe you're bored and want a little excitement. Maybe he hasn't shown passion in months and you want to know that he's still alive. Or maybe you want to break up and hope he'll dump you if nag him enough about shaving his goatee. This works best if you not only pick the fight, but cut him off when he tries to respond by insisting on having the first, last, and in-between words to yourself.)

A particularly powerful strategy for women is Trojan horse fighting: presenting a conversational topic that appears perfectly harmless, but that is, in fact, lethal.

WOMAN:	Julia broke up with Matt.
BOYFRIEND:	Really?
WOMAN:	Yeah, Matt cheated on her and she left him.
BOYFRIEND:	Wow. How'd she find out?
WOMAN:	Why? You want to learn how not to get caught cheating? Should I be worried?
BOYFRIEND:	Of course not.

WOMAN:	Would you tell me if you were cheating?
BOYFRIEND:	Probably not. I mean, what kind of cheater admits that they're cheating?
WOMAN:	Oh, great. So basically you're saying that you're cheating.
BOYFRIEND:	But I didn't say *anything.*
WOMAN:	Exactly.

Ideally, bickering couples should fight in front of a judge who could enforce basic procedural rules like no fighting below the belt: "I never really liked the way you kiss anyway. You want me to be honest, I'm being honest!" (This is the male variant of the girlfriend who says any cruel thing about her boyfriend's inadequacies before adding, "What? Can't I even express my *feelings*?")

Another rule: No bringing your lover's family into the fight. Unless, of course, the fight is about your lover's family—in particular, his unresolved feelings of anger toward his mother.

"You're yelling at me when you should be yelling at your mother," you'll tell him.

"Thanks for the tip, Dr. Freud," he'll spit back.

"I just think, sweetie, that you should *maybe possibly consider* looking at your issues with your mother," you'll say as gently as possible, which will never be gently enough.

Most men, especially the ones who hate their mothers, will end up hating you instead for merely broaching the subject. In fact, your lover will probably accuse *you* of hating his mother, and say that he can't love anyone who hates his mother, even though in truth he loves *you* and hates *his mother*. Or else he loves his mother so much that he hates you for demanding a portion of that love. Either way, you lose.

Whoever said that the definition of a genius is someone who can simultaneously hold two conflicting thoughts in their head must have been talking about couples who love the person they want to choke to death. In a weird way, it's reassuring that you can go from adoring to despising to adoring each other again and again.

In fact, the whole point of fighting is to restore the bond that breaks as you vacillate between craving for and irritation of each other. Soon it's hard to tell which came first, the chicken or the egg: You feel unloved, so you criticize your boyfriend for being distant. He stonewalls. You blame. He withdraws. You act like a bitch. He criticizes. You get defensive. He blames. You withdraw. He feels unloved. You get in a big fight and soon you're back at equilibrium.

As loud as the screaming gets and as hard as the doors slam, it doesn't take long before you realize that you *do* love the person you said you hated (if not directly to him, then to your friends, your mother, your siblings, and yourself). Often you'll feel guilty for your bad behavior and want to apologize. You'll want to make amends.

Don't be an idiot.

Apologizing will only lead to another fight. Oh, it may start off all touchy-feely. But nobody stops with a simple, "I'm sorry." There's always a "but," as in "I'm sorry, but you really should get over this." Even if you take responsibility for your nutty behavior, part of you also feels the need to explain—and justify—what provoked it. And before you know it, one of you is trying to be heard, the other is acting defensive, you're talking around each other—and you're in the same exact fight you thought you'd resolved an hour before. You're recycling insults and metaphors that failed a mere ninety minutes earlier, clinging to the notion that this time, the conversation will go differently.

It won't.

So forget the apology. Instead, to keep the peace, give your lover a massage and call it a night. And when he says "Ouch" after you "accidentally" press too hard on his spine, then—and only then—can you safely say, "Oh, sweetie—*I'm so sorry.*"

31

Cheating Without Actually Cheating

CAN YOU DEFINE THAT PLEASE?

He Said . . .

I was sure Katrina was having an affair with her chiropractor. It had started years ago, long before I had met her, after Katrina had fallen off a ladder while on a job assignment and was prescribed physical therapy, which developed into a six-year, once-a-week, fifty minutes at a time, unbridled romantic relationship with Dr. Halsted. As I recall, she had originally paid for the whole thing through worker's comp, so not only was she having an affair, but as a taxpayer *I* helped foot the bill.

I had met the guy—a man's man, burly, chiseled, perfect posture and, needless to say, good hands. His office was near my apartment, so Katrina would often schedule an appointment for either on the way over to my place, or upon leaving the next morning. I started noticing a peculiar pattern emerging. If she scheduled the session before her arrival, she'd show up at my door feeling very . . . frisky. At first, I didn't mind. Sex is sex. If she was going to show up hot for me, I wasn't going to worry when or how her coals were stoked.

But one morning, after a night that included—well, there's no other way to put it—great sex, I awoke to hear her on the phone . . . canceling her appointment.

"Why?" I asked, as soon as she hung up.

"I don't know," she said. "I guess I'm no longer in the mood."

In the mood? Since when do you have to be "in the mood" to go to your chiropractor, to endure an ostensibly *medical procedure*? Does anyone cancel an appointment with her dentist or proctologist because they just don't feel inspired? My mind went all sorts of places, most of them bad. It didn't help that one of my college friends who occasionally went to a massage parlor (where massage wasn't the only thing on the menu) would refer to the whole trip as going to get his "back fixed." And here was Katrina, *getting her back fixed.* Or in this case, not getting it fixed, because apparently I had done just the trick the night before.

By the way, say what you will about the spotless integrity of even the most professional massages, but make no mistake: They are sexual. Once, thinking I was being romantic, I brought Katrina to Ojai for a spa getaway and signed us up for a "duet massage," having only a vague understanding of what that would entail. Turns out we were in the same treatment room at the same time, she enjoying the hands of some male stranger and I enjoying the touch of some female stranger. Uh . . . that's not a massage. That's an orgy. When Katrina reached over and took my hand mid-massage, I realized I hadn't touched this many people at once since I played Red Rover, Red Rover in elementary school.

Perhaps because Katrina never showed the slightest hint of guilt (sometimes I wondered if she was even capable), I never confronted her about her chiropractor. I suppose it's poetic that I was spineless about the whole thing.

For the record, I never suspected Katrina had actually consummated her affair with Dr. Halsted in any definitive sexual way. They just had that "same time, next week" thing going on. And yet I contend that Katrina was cheating on me. Simple math: The physical pleasure she derived from the experience with her chiropractor overlapped with the physical pleasure she derived when we had sex. That's why she canceled the appointment—she didn't want too much of a good thing.

Years later, when I told my friend Bonnie about Katrina's chiropractor, Bonnie confided in me that she, too, was having a "same time, next week" thing going on with her acupuncturist. I was curious to know what exactly she meant by "thing." I wondered if he was sticking more than just needles in her.

"Have you ever—?" I asked.

"Oh, no. God no. Nothing like that," she said. "We're just flirting."

I then asked what exactly she meant by "flirting," and she explained: They had discussed their mutual attraction to each other, and lamented that both of them were in exclusive relationships.

"That's not flirting," I told her. "Flirting is when you stare at each other a little too long. Flirting is when you try to sound sexier when you talk. And as far as *what* you talk about, at most it's an occasional use of innuendo. What you're doing is not flirting."

"Then what are we doing?" she asked.

"You're having an affair," I confirmed.

"Yeah, that's what I thought," she said, guiltily.

Flirting with each other is one thing; explicitly addressing the fact that you're flirting with the object of your flirtation is quite another, and it's the latter that rises to the level of cheating.

Keep in mind, at some point everyone *wants* to cheat. Everyone feels the pull. On that, both genders can agree. The problem, from a male point of view at least, is when women make their indiscretions no longer discreet, but explicit. Women usually think they can get away with this kind of emotional infidelity as long as it doesn't get physical. They rationalize their behavior by insisting that a few surreptitious stolen words are acceptable as long as they stay PG-13. *Men don't care what I say to someone,* they'll say to themselves, *as long as I keep my pants on.*

Wrong. While it's true that we're astonishingly visual beings, and that the *image* of our girlfriends in flagrante delicto with some strapping guy is sheer torture (in our minds, as he smothers her with his manli-ness, she makes faces she never made when we were with her, faces we didn't know she could even conjure), we're equally tortured by the *thought* of it as well. We are just as susceptible to heartbreak when we think of our girlfriends having *emotional* affairs in which they merely spin mutual flirtations and fantasies about what might have been, with the actual people she might have been *with*.

Because that's not flirting. That's an affair.

She Said . . .

As someone who's slipped and said "monotony" when I meant to say "monogamy," I understand the temptation to cheat. There's a differ-ence between being committed and comatose (no, I've never made *that* slip), and we all have thoughts about getting naked with anyone from our coworker to our lover's best friend. Temptation is like standing on the edge of a cliff and wondering what would happen if you jumped off. Would you get a few scrapes, be paralyzed, or die?

If a boyfriend ever cheated on me, he'd probably get a few scrapes (depending on the length of my fingernails), then die (or rather, our re-lationship would). No explanations, no second chances, no three shtups and you're out.

"Wait," my friend Linda might remind me. "Alec cheated on you, and you stayed with him for another two years."

Oh, right. I forgot about Alec.

Maybe Linda's right. Maybe Alec did cheat on me. I don't know. How could I, when cheating can mean so much more (or, actually, less) than shtupping? In fact, there's a whole group of people who believe that only very specific combinations of body parts constitute cheating. ("If body part A touches, but is not inserted into, body part B, that's okay. But if body part C is involved, that's cheating.") Still, aside from the occasional wacko who insists that kissing someone who's not you is "contextual," most of us pretty much agree on what's kosher.

Then there was Alec.

Alec and I had been dating exclusively for three months when he told me after a Saturday of "doing his own thing" that he'd gone to the outdoor market with his friend Chloe. I'd never heard of Chloe, but since I didn't yet know his entire friend roster, I thought nothing of it. Sunday morning, he said he'd be spending the day working and getting to sleep early, since he had to be up at 5:00 A.M. on Monday.

So when I called Alec later to say good night and he wasn't home, I tried not to jump to any conclusions. Maybe he's still at work, I thought. Heck, maybe he got hit by a bus. Maybe I should be worried about his well-being.

But when he wasn't home two hours later, I actually preferred the possibility that he'd been hit by a bus than that he was out with Chloe. I vacillated between praying he wasn't dying on a gurney and hoping he was. I Googled Chloe (somehow, reading about your boyfriend's mistress makes you feel more in control of the situation—like, *Hey, lady, I've got your number*—when really, it just makes you seem more pathetic). I hung up on Alec's machine every half hour. Eventually, I took two tablespoons of NyQuil and still couldn't sleep.

When Alec called me back Monday morning, he explained that the day before he'd dropped something off at a colleague's house and—lo and behold!— he was in his friend Chloe's neighborhood, so he stopped by before going home to bed. Then he turned off his phone because of the early morning ahead.

This might sound innocent enough, except that upon further inquiry, I learned that Chloe had gone on a blind date with Alec just before Alec and I had met. She was interested, he wasn't and, as Alec put it, "end of story." My gut told me something wasn't right, but I reasoned that if Alec had cheated, he would have lied about where he'd been. And since he didn't seem the least bit guilty, whatever felt wrong to me must be, as Alec said when I shared my suspicions, "just you" (and, it turned out, my mother, my therapist, and twelve of my friends).

Weeks later, when I asked if I might meet Chloe, Alec copped to the fact that it would be awkward because his "friend" Chloe (nervous laughter) . . . had a crush on him. And—oh yeah—he hadn't exactly told her right away that he had a girlfriend. ("It didn't come up," he explained. "Am I supposed to announce to every person I talk to, 'Hey, I've got a girlfriend'?")[1]

"You cheated, didn't you?" I asked. No, Alec insisted, because when he and Chloe were *in her hot tub* ("to relax from all his work stress," Alec added quickly) he realized he "needed to tell her" about me. In other words, it was potential cheating, until Alec decided at the eleventh hour not to cheat, at which point Chloe learned that the guy who got together with her twice in one weekend and who was half-naked in her Jacuzzi sipping margaritas did, in fact, have a girlfriend.

Throughout our relationship, Alec insisted that the Chloe Incident wasn't cheating.

"I wanted to have sex with her, and I could have, but I didn't," he'd say whenever the topic came up—implying that not only had he not cheated, but that he should get bonus points for *almost cheating* but not going through with it.

He even held my hand, looked me in the eye and said, "I will never cheat on you. I promise. You can trust me." (Note: It's always the sanctimonious ones who cheat. Be especially wary of "ethics professors" who sleep with their students.)

Another time, I was sitting at Alec's computer about to type in "www.nytimes.com." As soon as I typed "www.n" his computer automatically filled in the rest: "www.nerve.com." I knew that he'd been on the Nerve dating site before we met, but that was more than a year earlier. This had to have been a recent search.

---

1. Yes.

"Have you been on Nerve?" I asked, cautiously.

"No," he said, without blinking. "Why?"

I showed him the screen, and he mumbled something about "cache" and "memory." It sounded dicey to me.

So Alec hugged me, then pressed his nose to mine. "No," he repeated with conviction. "I haven't been on Nerve since before we met." I asked him twice more, and twice more I got the same seemingly sincere response. But like a police interrogator wearing down the witness, I asked him repeatedly during the week, and finally he admitted that yes, he'd been trolling women on Nerve—"but only because you were out with your agent and some attractive producer, and I was jealous."

The reason he hadn't come clean the first time? *If I'd told you, you would have broken up with me.*

Is this in the *Guys' Guide to Cheating* handbook? Most women have heard this line at one time or another. And what happens is, because you didn't tell us, we *do* break up with you. We're not cool with the "If a tree falls in the forest and nobody hears it . . ." philosophy of cheating. It's like saying, *I wanted to come clean, but if I came clean, I knew you'd overreact. What I did was 10 percent wrong, but you'd think it was 90 percent wrong, then overreact by 180 percent. So I'll just keep quiet instead.*

(*The Girls' Guide to Cheating* also needs some revising, especially the line, "It's not the sex that bothers me as much as the lying!" Actually, the sex does bother us, probably *more* than the lying. The lying we can get over. For a while, we'll replay all the "working late" excuses and try to figure out which were lies. But eventually, we'll let it go. The sex, on the other hand, leaves us in a state of perpetual masochistic fantasy. The images of our boyfriend having sex with another woman are indelible.)

Lately, the term "emotional affair" has become trendy, probably because everyone with a computer is having one. Some people see this as the safe sex version of an actual affair. Like my friend Eric who was dating Natalie, but suggestively IM'd my other friend Jane every day.

"I'm not cheating," he told Jane. "You're my *virtual* girlfriend." (She promptly blocked him from her IM list.)

Near the end of my relationship with Alec, I too had an emotional affair. My love interest and I would e-mail flirtatiously all day, and talk on the phone hours past midnight. Although we never had sex, I knew I was cheating. And I felt justified. Most people think the worst that can happen if you cheat is that the person you really love leaves you. Not true. The worst that can happen is that the person you really love cheats on you back—then leaves you.

Sorry, Alec. But think of it this way: I wanted to have sex with this guy, and I could have, but I didn't. Like you with Chloe, I placed my-self in the throes of temptation, then resisted it. Doesn't that make me a fabulous girlfriend? Don't I deserve some bonus points?

32

Couples Therapy: Your Place or Mine

He Said . . .

Right off the bat, I'd like to point out that the term "therapist" is a conjunction of the article "the" and the noun "rapist." The . . . rapist. *Therapist.* It's what entomologists call an "elided cotransformative derivative."

Of course that's not true. There's no such thing as an "elided cotransformative derivative." And not all therapists are rapists. For that matter, an entomologist is someone who studies bugs, not words. But I wanted to joke around here at the top of this essay to get it out of my system, because if I had actually joked around in *therapy* my girlfriend wouldn't think it was funny, mainly because we went to *her* therapist and I'm now embarrassing her and *see, doctor? This is just the kind of thing he does: tell stupid jokes that aren't really jokes and embarrass me in front of other people and it's like he doesn't even care and shouldn't we break up?*

Ah, couples therapy. Probably a good idea. In fact, you probably should have started going to couples therapy before your first date. (Nice to meet you. Same time next week?)

I can't know for certain, since both times my most recent ex-girlfriend broke up with me (a twofer!), she did it exactly one day after we agreed to go to couples counseling. So thanks to my lack of any real-world experience, and not having any clue as to what I'm talking about, I can no doubt assume that couples counseling is the . . . let's see . . . *third* stage in Kubler-Ross's five stages of grieving. (Or was it Maslov's hierarchy of needs? I can't remember. And now I'm wasting time. And the clock is ticking! *See doctor, this is just the kind of thing he does. Doesn't he know that the clock is ticking? And shouldn't we break up?*)

Again, that's exactly how it works. I'm assuming.

Now, this third stage—going to couples counseling—is preceded only by the second stage: agreeing to go. Which is preceded only by agreeing to talk about whether *to* go. The fourth stage, after going to counseling, then, is agreeing to go back. And finally, of course: acceptance. Of the fact that the relationship is doomed.

To review:

Talking About Going

Agreeing to Go

Going

Going Again

Acceptance (of the fact that the relationship is doomed)

So let's say you've already agreed to go. Congratulations: You're only about three weeks away from reentering the exciting dating world. And so what the heck? Why not spend a couple hundred bucks and kill a few hours sniping at each other for all the pain you've caused over the many, many days you've known each other.

But even more important: If you've already lost the war, how do you at least win the last battle?

Maybe you're already in therapy—individual therapy, that is. Odds are if one of you is, you both are. (Or, in my case, she was, so it was only a matter of time before she insisted that I be. Apparently I'm very fucked up.) So supposedly paying to talk to a stranger for one hour a week has made you happier and healthier. Not just older and poorer.

Say you both are. So then: Whose therapist do you go to? Likely, she'll want to go to hers, because she's comfortable there and she and her therapist have a shorthand. And here's where you make your first move. Call it "the Bleyer opening." It's simple: *let her.* Let her have her way.

Why, you ask?

With therapy, there's no such thing as home-couch advantage. In fact, if you're a man (and we'll assume you are, never mind that you agreed to go to couples counseling), you're already at a significant *dis*-advantage. Each and every therapist's office is inherently a feminine world (this explains the throw pillows) in which your manhood, so po-tent outside these diplomaed walls, has exactly zero currency. Inside counseling, the role-playing field is not level.

Counseling was *designed* to give women the edge. It's talk, talk, talk, not fix, fix, fix. Feelings, not reason. It's about addressing problems, not solving them. If counseling were really about *solving* problems, there'd be a buzzer and cash prizes.

But like in any good head-to-head matchup, the underdog can still come out on top. He need only follow a couple simple rules:

First thing—toss the throw pillows to the floor. It will prove that you're willing to throw things (a little testosterone can't hurt), and yet you *choose* to throw things that are harmless (a little throw pillow can't hurt). But . . .

Don't get emotional. As soon as you get emotional, you're toast. It's too easy for a therapist to paint you as irrational, or unstable, or (heaven forbid) capable of anger. As men, we're innocent until proven moody. Remember that.

After all, one reason you agreed to go to her therapist—not a terri-ble one, in fact—is not to solve your problems, but rather to prove to her therapist that you're not nearly the monster she's been describing all these years. Your simple challenge is to overcome expectations—if she's been doing her job, she's been spending every minute telling her therapist you're a bad, bad man. Bless her. She's lowered the bar for you. All you have to do is step over it.

At least, just knowing that you've made a good impression on her therapist will be that perfect ego boost you'll need when she breaks up with you and you're back out in the dating world. Because until a girlfriend actually makes good on her promise to take me to couples counseling (odd event to look forward to, yet I do), I can only assume the truly relevant message you and your significant other should take away from your therapy session is the last four words: *Our time is up.*

Our time is up.

She Said . . .

I knew my relationship had turned into *Groundhog Day* when my boyfriend and I kept having the same arguments each night. We'd be sitting at dinner and a thorny topic would come up (our future, our finances, our bathroom habits). I'd get angry, he'd get mean, I'd cry, he'd get defensive. Then, after threatening to break up, we'd make up. By that I mean, we'd "agree to disagree." And by that I mean, he thought he was right and eventually I'd come to my senses, while I thought I was right and eventually he'd come to his senses.

In other words, we resented the hell out of each other.

Soon we went from "agreeing to disagree" to insisting that the other person was a nutcase—and that any rational person could see this. One night, my boyfriend said he had evidence:

"My therapist says I'm right," he gloated over fettucine alfredo.

"Of course he says you're right," I shot back. "He gets paid $150 an hour to say that."

But over enchiladas the next evening, I quoted my own therapeutic authority. "Dr. K says *I'm* right."

"Of course he says you're right," Alec laughed. "He's only heard your side of the story."

My boyfriend had a point. So for once we agreed to agree: We decided to go to couples therapy to present our respective cases.

The question remained: My therapist or his? My boyfriend suggested we go to mine, which instantly made me suspicious.

"Are you worried your shrink will reveal something about you that you don't want me to know?" I asked.

"Are *you* worried *your* shrink will reveal something about *you* that you don't want *me* to know?" he replied.

We didn't need a shrink to tell us we had "trust issues."

Still, I figured bringing Alec to my therapist would be like bringing an accused man before a judge. In Cuba. After all, my shrink had already declared I was right. This would be a fixed trial, a kangaroo court. The verdict was already in.

But after we sat on the soft leather couch in Dr. K's office and explained the various problems, Dr. K nodded, exhaled slowly, then pronounced: "You're both right."

"What?!" I said.

I looked over at Alec, expecting him to be equally outraged, but he sat calmly with his hands folded delicately in his lap. I'd never seen his hands folded in his lap before. Normally he'd be making little stabbing gestures in my direction to punctuate each of the following words: "You. Have. No. Idea. What. You're. Talking. About."

"Dr. K has a point," Alec whispered soothingly. "I understand where you're coming from, and I think we both have some . . . processing . . . to do."

Processing?! When had he become Mr. Therapy? I looked from Alec to Dr. K and back to Alec again. "What do you mean you understand where I'm coming from? Last night you said I was completely irrational!"

That's when it hit me: By acting like the sane one, Alec could peg *me* as the basket case.

In the sessions that followed (his idea, of course), Alec began using bogus touchy-feely phrases like "I'm sorry you feel that way," "I validate your experience," and "I respect your boundaries." He called me "Sweetie" and looked at me with doe eyes while I called him "Fuckface" and glared back at the alien beside me.

Instead of blaming me or acting defensive like he did at home, in therapy he'd only use "I feel" statements. "Elly," he'd say, buttering me up with my pet name. "When you get angry at me for expressing my true feelings, I feel shut down."

"Well, how in the hell do you expect me not to get angry when you tell me you're more attracted to the girl you met Rollerblading at the beach than to me?" I'd scream. "How is a normal person supposed to put up with this crap!"

Then Alec would look at Dr. K, and Dr. K would look at Alec, and they'd both shake their heads, as if to say, "Well, we're trying."

Occasionally I'd shout, "WHO ARE YOU?!" and try to tell Dr. K that Therapy Alec was a completely different person from Boyfriend Alec who calls my feelings "stupid." Secretly, though, I was falling in love with Therapy Alec. I wanted to date the sensitive guy that Alec had become in the shrink's office. (Only I didn't—see chapter 26.)

Outside of therapy, meanwhile, Alec would do things like show up two hours late for dinner without calling ("I couldn't call because I was already on the cell phone with my brother") and when I said I'd be bringing that up in therapy, he'd reply sarcastically, "You're telling on me to our therapist?"

Instead, he beat me to the punch by admitting his wrongdoings before I could. He seemed to revel in misbehaving in ways that gave him plenty of Sensitive Guy material for our sessions.

"Sweetie," he said at an early session. "I know we talked about forgiveness, and I have something to tell you." Then he took a deep cleansing breath and smiled sheepishly. "I went through your computer files."

"You what?" I yelled, but Dr. K gave me an admonishing look.

"Remember the four 'F's of forgiveness," Alec whispered in his Dalai Lama tone.

"You mean fuck, fuck, fuck, and YOU?" I asked. I was too angry to count.

"Relationships are work," the therapist would say when I looked despondent enough to quit.

"If relationships are work," I replied, "when do the benefits kick in?"

Alec, on the other hand, couldn't wait for each session. He'd treat me badly during the rest of the week, but because he *felt bad* about treating me badly, it meant he was a caring person. It meant he had a conscience. And so for him, couples therapy became his version of confession: admit your sins, and save your soul (and ass). If I got angry at him for, say, "forgetting" that something I told him in confidence wasn't to be shared with his entire family, he'd hold my hand and reply serenely, "But I regret doing it, and at least I'm admitting it. Isn't honesty the most important thing?"

No. It wasn't. Because couples therapy, I learned, isn't about honesty. It's about currying favor with the therapist, manipulating your misdeeds so they seem like confessions, and, above all, never having to deal with the issues that brought you to the therapist's soft leather "love seat" in the first place.

In the end, it's probably best to agree to disagree, and skip the therapy entirely. Your therapist? His therapist? Doesn't matter—he'll fool them all, and leave you with the bill. (Remember, you'll need the money for all the online dating services you're about to sign up for anyway.)

PART

FOUR

IT'S ALL OVER BUT THE POUTING

33

Knowing When It's Over

ARE WE DONE, OR IS THIS FINAL BREAKUP
JUST TEMPORARY?

He Said . . .

My friend Sean has survived life-threatening cancer three times. Each time his doctor had assured him it was gone, and each time it came back. He'd lose his hair, vomit a bunch, and lose twenty pounds, before beginning the Sisyphean task of rebuilding his health.

"When do you know it's all over?" I asked him.

"You never know," he said.

Hmmm. *You never know.*

One thing I *do* know is that the first time Katrina broke up with me—which is one of the saddest phrases I have ever written—it was over dinner at the Café Delfini[1] in Santa Monica.

"This just isn't working out for me," she said, soon after we had ordered a very expensive meal and wine to go with. Though her timing

---

1. I just now realize that "Delfini" may in fact mean "of the end"—*del fini*—not, as I had originally thought, simply "dolphin." Hmm. *The End Café.* Let me just chew on that sour morsel for a moment, won't you?

was crap, I took her words to heart. She was breaking up with me. Over the first and second course, she proceeded to explain why we were incompatible. By the third, I was in tears.

By dessert (yes, we ordered dessert) I wasn't quite as distraught. Even as the breakup was happening, there was something about her decision that made me think it wouldn't last. Not the relationship, mind you. The breakup. Even as I sat there crying (men, forgive me), even as my entire world seemed to be crumbling around me (along with my manhood), I oddly felt what I can only describe as . . . hope. There was something in those moments—perhaps the way Katrina looked at me, perhaps the slightest bittersweet tone in her voice, perhaps the sheer force of my good intentions—that made me think things would get better. Or perhaps it was the fact that, yes, we ordered dessert.

It so happens I wasn't delusional. We did get back together. Much later (but before the second and final breakup), Katrina confided in me that she actually hadn't planned on breaking up with me that first night. That when she said, "This just isn't working out for me," it wasn't meant as a prelude to a kiss-off, but rather the prompt for a discussion about what we should work on as a couple, and how we could turn something that just "isn't working out" for her into something that is. And yet, when I incorrectly interpreted her statement as a breakup, she just "kind of . . . let it happen." (To this day, I don't believe I overreacted. "This just isn't working out for me" is a classic breakup icebreaker. What else was I supposed to think? She was unhappy with the restaurant?)

What's more, she was using the "we need to have a talk" tone of voice. In my experience, when a woman brings up a subject in the "we need to have a talk" tone, she already knows how the talk will end. It's a foregone conclusion.

When these big decisions are made, why aren't we consulted? Why doesn't a woman need to discuss it with us? Simple: Because she's already discussed it with her friends. This is what women do. They discuss life-and-death matters with their girlfriends, leaving us out of it, and then when they mention it to us and we're shocked at the news (which is, after all, *news* to us), *they're* shocked we didn't see this coming. *C'mon*, she'll say, *hasn't it been the elephant in the room for a while now?*

No, we'll say, *I didn't even know you had an elephant! You've been keeping the elephant at your friend Julie's place, remember?*

But this time, something about *how* Katrina was breaking up with me—how we walked back to her house hand in hand, how she let me pet her dog Ralph without interrupting—led me to think that there was still hope for us.

And there was.

Exactly three weeks later, there was a knock on my door around midnight, and I opened it to find Katrina standing there, her eyes welling with tears. Before I said a single word, Katrina admitted she had made a terrible mistake and begged for my forgiveness. In an instant, I gave it to her. She fell into my arms as if she had never left. As if we were back in the hammock, on the sailboat, heading out from the San Diego harbor to fall in love all over again.

Which we did, until six months later, when she broke up with me all over again.

This time, I waited three weeks, hoping to hear a knock on my door and a plea to take her back. But three weeks turned into two months, which turned into news that she had met someone else.

"Is it serious?" I asked our mutual friend Ryan.

"They're engaged," he said. Never before have I wanted to shoot the messenger quite so badly.

"But they just—"

"Yeah, I know," he said. "They met and got engaged within four days! That's insane! I tell you, you really dodged a bullet with her."

Maybe so, but at that moment I wanted nothing more than to lean into the bullet's path. The wedding, Ryan told me, was set for less than three months later. The faster she ran to him, the farther she ran from me. Worse, the news reports of their romantic developments kept coming in. Ultimately, within a year of meeting someone new, Katrina had gotten engaged, had gotten married, had moved out of the country, had gotten pregnant, and had twin daughters named Angela and Jasmine.

I hadn't even gone on a date.

Seriously? *Jasmine?*

When a woman tells us she doesn't love us anymore, the temptation for a man is to reinterpret the entire relationship as a sham. Men refuse to believe that a woman's feelings for us may have *changed*. We simply decide (although we're inclined to say that we simply *recognize*) that she was lying when she told us she loved us in the first place. When I think back on so many of the things Katrina said to me during our relationship—"I can't wait to grow old with you," "I'm yours," "I'd love you even if you were a farmer" (long story)—I can't comprehend they came from the same mouth as "This just isn't working out for me." They don't jibe. How can the person who said, "I'll never leave you" be the same person who left us?

Katrina and I are *del fini*. I'm sure of it.

And yet, I remember thinking, 50 percent of marriages end in divorce. Things fall apart. People reunite. Continents shift. You never know. For years, I wondered if it was really over.

I mean, *really*.

Because with love, just like with vomit-inducing, body-ravaging, life-threatening cancer . . . you never know.

She Said . . .

It happens with nearly every breakup. Within a week of losing love, you begin to worry about never finding love again. But just as the panic sets in, suddenly you *do* find love. It's right where you last left it—in your ex's apartment.

That's the thing about the end: Even when the end is clear-cut to everyone else, it may not be clear-cut to you. Your boyfriend might say,

"I'm not in love with you anymore, I don't want to have sex with you anymore, and I'm attracted to Nina at work, but I hope we can still be friends," and you'll think, "He's just afraid of commitment. He doesn't *mean* that."

Yes, he does—except that in his own cocoon of denial, he's not sure he means it either. So the next day, he'll tell you that he's afraid of commitment and Nina's slightly cross-eyed, so will you please take him back? When you know it's over but haven't accepted it's over, your lover will talk about ending the relationship—or just disappear and mail the key back—and you'll think, "He needs some space, he'll come back." And he does, because *he* doesn't know it's really over either.

So you go through a series of breakup dress rehearsals.

Once I was at my friend's party when she told us she couldn't find her boyfriend. He'd been there a few hours ago—they'd gotten into a fight and he'd yelled, "I'm out of here!" Everyone (except for the couple in question) knew their relationship had been over for months. So we told our friend, "It seems like he's finally left." And she said, "No, no, we're fine, we're working things out. He just went to cool down and get some fresh air. But now I'm worried he's been mugged."

We, her friends, knew he hadn't been mugged. Her boyfriend wasn't stupid. He must have figured out that the only way his girlfriend would truly understand their relationship was over would be for him to leave in front of witnesses, so that her friends could confirm that he did, indeed, break up with her. He was leaving no room for interpretation on the phone the next morning. ("Yeah, he said he was leaving, but I thought he meant, 'to get more drinks.'")

Is it any wonder that most states make you wait twenty-four hours before filing a missing persons report? The police probably got sick of hearing from women who didn't accept that their relationships were over. The cops knew that within twenty-four hours of a boyfriend's disappearance, the dumpee's friends would be notified and give the spurned woman a reality check.

"No need to call the police," these friends would tell their dumped soul sister. "Your relationship is truly over this time. In the interest of saving our tax dollars, please do not report John missing."

Unfortunately, our friend's boyfriend returned the next day—having "made a mistake." So when he left for good eight weeks later (and after two more false alarms), it took our friend months before she finally accepted that he wouldn't show up on her doorstep, sobbing and declaring his love all over again. After all, he had disappeared, reappeared, disappeared, reappeared, disappeared, reappeared, and finally disappeared—all in the span of a year. Each time he claimed he wanted his ex back, but really he wanted her to make the breakup less lonely for him.

It's not uncommon. The longer you stay together, the harder you'll need to slam on the breaks before you two grind to a complete stop. And even then, you might get whiplash. You'll tell him that you need to break up because you never really communicated, then realize that you're really communicating for the very first time—and wonder whether you should stay together. You'll be confident you're making the right decision to move out, until he carries your stuff out of his apartment, then sweetly offers to help you home.

But just as you're imagining what it might be like if it were *really* over, he'll do something to confirm it. He may, for instance, offer you alimony. He won't call it that, of course. Instead he'll say magnanimously, "You keep all the stuff" and although you'd like to interpret that as a sign he'll be back (for his stuff *and* you), on some level, you know better. You know he's really saying, "Now that I've wasted your five most fertile years . . . that Nelson lamp and those antique bookshelves—my treat!" It's like war reparations to clear his conscience. He gets rid of you and his guilt in one fell swoop, while you're just left with the delusion that he'll come back. (Sadly, he will.)

Maybe it's the hesitant wording we use. Your boyfriend doesn't break up by saying, "When I see you sitting across the dinner table, I'm overcome with revulsion." Instead he holds your hand and says, "I'm just not sure about us, but maybe if we take time off, we can work it out." You don't break up with your boyfriend by saying, "I stopped loving you a long time ago. I was just acting out my abandonment complex and since I've figured that out, you can go now." Instead you say, "I'm feeling disconnected, but maybe it's temporary." Even our body language is ambivalent. If he really wants you gone, how come he's convulsing with tears and won't let go when you're hugging good-bye?

It's hard to let go of somebody who loved you, and now says he doesn't. "Why do you love me?" you may have asked, playfully, when you were sure of his love. "Because you're *you*," he'd say, tickling you, until the pattern became a game. Now, in moments of desperation, you ask, "Why *don't* you love me?" And although he looks away and doesn't answer, you know the answer is the same: "Because you're *you*."

Even when you do break up for good ("It's over-*over* this time," you'll say as your friends roll their eyes), you won't think of yourself as single right away. True, you're no longer in contact and you're dating other people, but in your mind, you and your "ex" (whom you still re-flexively call your "boyfriend"—even on dates) are simply "on hiatus."

Besides, in some ways you *are* still a couple: the broken-up couple. You're connected not just by your history, but by your current mutual heartbreak. You're pining away for him in your apartment while he's pining away for you in his apartment. You're psychically communing (even if he's physically communing with a different woman each night).

Meanwhile, you'll try to convince your friends that you've accepted the breakup.

"We're on an indefinite hiatus that will probably last forever," I told a friend, showing her that I could joke about my breakup *and* knew the score.

But secretly I wondered, "How long, exactly, is forever?"

34

It's Not Me, It's You

IS IT BETTER TO DUMP, OR BE DUMPED?

He Said . . .

Throughout the ages, man has had two options to end a relationship. He can either break up with his girlfriend, or treat his girlfriend so poorly that she finally gets sick of his shit and breaks up with him.[1] It's always a dilemma, because while the former can be uncomfortable and always feels cruel—no man who's truly a man wants to inflict pain on a woman—the latter is manipulative and frankly does his ego no service, even though, the deed done, he achieved the goal he wanted in the first place: to end the relationship. Ultimately, he got dumped.

No one wants to get dumped. Better by far to be the one who does the dumping. So most men choose the first option.

A woman, on the other hand, has three options: a) break up with her boyfriend; b) treat her boyfriend so poorly that he finally gets sick

---

1. A third option—beheading à la Anne Boleyn—thankfully seems to have receded with the times.

of her shit and cheats on her, thereby giving her *no choice* but to break up with him; or—and this I've only come to realize lately is an option many women select—c) break up with her boyfriend *without telling him,* and continue to date him until she has mourned the relationship, accepted the loss, and can truly move on.

Then, and only then, will she break up with him. Or, more accurately, *tell* him that she's breaking up with him. Even though she has long ago, in fact, broken up with him.

Brilliant! This last option is a work of pure feminine evil genius (feminevil genius?), and while I have suffered its slings and arrows, I am in awe of its methodology. Don't you see? If, as the poet says, breaking up is hard to do, why would any woman want to do it alone? Why not keep her boyfriend around while—unbeknownst to him—she mourns the end of their relationship? That way, as things fall apart, she won't be sad and lonely. She'll just be sad. And when it's all over, she'll just be lonely. But not both at the same time.

We men should be disabused of the notion that her decision to break up with us was even a remotely recent one—that, say, the night before she cut us loose she had a long conversation with her sister or her best friend or her therapist and they came to the conclusion that the relationship was going nowhere and that the next time she saw us she'd let us know. If our girlfriend is telling us the relationship is over under the Christmas tree, it's likely something she decided over corn dogs at our cousin's Fourth of July barbecue.

That's the dazzling sleight of hand we men rarely see coming: When a woman breaks up with us, she's not actually breaking up with us. The transaction happened long ago: We're simply being debriefed. She's just getting us up to speed. When a woman musters the courage to broach a subject as serious as a breakup, although we're hearing the thunder for the first time, the lightning struck long ago.

Even if she does accidentally drop a few clues about her impending vanishing act, most men don't notice; the fact that she evacuated her panties and T-shirts from the drawer we lent her doesn't mean she's leaving. It simply means that our socks finally have some breathing room. It's cause for celebration, not alarm.

Oh, if pressed, she'll tell us—and herself—that she stayed in the relationship in case things got better. But that's not what happened. She stayed in the relationship because she wanted to wait until *she* got better—so that when she finally *did* break up with us she wouldn't have to waste months being miserable. It's not that women don't grieve the end of a relationship. It's that women grieve the end of the relationship while the relationship is—or so we think—still chugging along nicely.

The genius of it still astounds me.

Now, how can this possibly be? How can a woman whisper sweet nothings into our ear while she's planning her escape route? Consider: Katrina dumped me approximately forty-eight hours after she had told me—in what I took to be a charming conversation about our future together—"I would love you even if you were a farmer." (I wasn't contemplating becoming a farmer, she was merely confirming her love for me—although with my dumping right around the corner, the thought of fleeing to Iowa would soon have a certain appeal.) To be honest, how exactly one develops that particular talent, I'm not sure. Nonetheless, women have an astounding—I'd even say sociopathic—ability to appear to be present in a relationship, including all the trappings, affections, and terms of endearment, while in truth they're psychologically cutting us out of their photographs.

Thus, with a kiss, I lie . . .

We men aren't so devious. When we've begun to check out of a relationship, we can't put on an act. We're unable to anaesthetize ourselves with chocolate or anything chocolate-covered. We can't distract ourselves with pedicures, or facials, or yoga. Worse, when we're with our girlfriend, we can't hide our detachment, or mask it with smiles, or pretend to still be interested in having an in-depth conversation about our feelings. Heck, the only thing we can do with any semblance of our previous interest is have sex. Sex is the exception. (Because for us, sex is always exceptional.)

A woman, of course, can fake it . . . right up until she doesn't need to fake it any longer, and she leaves us, shell-shocked, jaws on the floor, alone.

Sad *and* lonely. If only we had seen your going coming . . .

She Said . . .

Women may be guided by emotion, but when it comes to ending a relationship, we're as cold-blooded as Saddam Hussein. Our motto: Dump first, and never let him see it coming.

I'm not sure why women do this more than men. Maybe dignity is more important to us. And by taking the reins and doing the dumping, at least we can engineer a respectable breakup. If we leave it up to men, we risk being given the axe immediately after having sex, at a family holiday dinner, on vacation, in a speeding car (a state not safe for operating a motor vehicle), during the first week of moving in together, or in bed at 3:00 A.M. the night before an important meeting at work. Women are more considerate: We even know that if we don't dump the guy by mid-November, we're morally obligated to stay with him through Christmas and New Year's—and buy him gifts.

With proper planning, we can also make sure to have the appropriate medications around. While we sleep soundly with our surrogate lover, Ambien, let our ex-boyfriend be the one who suffers the side effects of that bitter pill called "I'm Breaking Up With You": nausea, vomiting, insomnia, depression, weight loss, minor aches or pains, hives, bloating, shock, and heart palpitations.

Isn't that better than having your boyfriend hold your hand, his eyes shifty, telling you in his gentle but condescending tone, "I don't think I can give you what you're looking for"?

"What am I looking for?" you'll ask, taking perverse pleasure in watching him squirm as he draws a complete blank.

"Um, not me?" he'll say lamely.

By dumping him first, we avoid hearing his soul-crushing, valedictory speeches: "You know how amazing I think you are, right?" (Well, no, because he's about to dump you.) "I'm not attracted to you. I thought I could get over it, but I just . . . can't." (Yet somehow he managed to have sex with you four times in the past week.) "I don't think this can work. I think we should nip this in the bud." (The "bud" being "two years.") "You deserve better." (Nobody's that selfless. He thinks *he* deserves better.) "You're too good for me." (In other words, "I'm cheating on you.") "I care about you so much, I don't want to hurt you." (The fact that he cares hurts even more.) And the topper: "It's not about you—it's about me." (This only reminds you how irrelevant you are in his life. If it's all about him, you could have been anyone—that's supposed to make you feel *better*?)

Even more important, we spare ourselves the disgrace of the exit interview when a guy blindsides us with a breakup. Instead of walking away, most women want to know *why* we're being let go. We want a performance review—is there anything we could have done differently? (Sadly, we're such team players that we'd be willing to become an entirely different person to keep our girlfriend gig.) We'll even try to talk the guy out of firing us by reciting why we're so qualified for the job. So rather than enduring the double indignity of both the rejection and our pathetic reply ("But I can change!"), we empower ourselves by preemptively delivering the pink slip.

Remember: We've learned the hard way that when we think our boyfriend is about to break up with us, nine times out of ten we're right. And no amount of good behavior (breakfast in bed, back rubs) or bad behavior (crying jags so he'll feel sorry for us) will change his mind. Therefore, as soon as we suspect he wants out, it's time to get out ourselves.

That said, achieving one-dumpsmanship can be tricky business. Because even if you "win"—let's face it, being the one to pull the plug has its glory—it might be a Pyrrhic victory. When my friend Sara broke up with her boyfriend, he kept calling her anyway. Finally, she wrote him a nice but firm e-mail explaining that they couldn't have contact for the rest of the summer, that they needed space in order to move on.

So what did her ex-boyfriend do? He *listened* to her! It's a catch-22. Had he continued to contact her, she'd say he had no boundaries. But when he stopped contacting her, she felt rejected. So who broke up with whom? She had the paper trail proving she'd done the dumping, but she still felt like the dumpee.

(If a man crawls back and fights for you, he's romantic. If a woman crawls back and fights for a man, she's pathetic. But if a man doesn't crawl back and fight for you, *you're* pathetic. Even those guys who say they "won't accept" the breakup are considered cute, not crazy.)

A married friend says that even if you're dumped, you can still feel like you have the power. If you really hope to get rid of the guy, she reasons, it doesn't matter who ends it. You got what you wanted: out of the relationship.

That's all very enlightened, but my friend is forgetting about the Relationship Report Card. Every time you meet a new guy and share your relationship history, the story of your breakups will be broached. Which of the following would you rather have on your permanent record:

1. "We weren't right for each other, so I broke up with him. It was very sad—I didn't want to hurt him."

2. "I thought things were great, but suddenly he dumped me."

An ideal breakup history consists of a ratio of 70 percent dumping to 30 percent dumped (nobody wants someone who bails every time). If you reverse that ratio, it affects not just your fragile ego, but what future boyfriends may think of you. Instead of "Hmm, that guy clearly had major psychological problems to reject this fantastic woman," he'll more likely think, "Hmm, something must be wrong with her if she keeps getting the boot."

Plus, if you actually hope to become "friends" with your ex, protocol dictates that only the dumper can call the dumpee months later to "check in." The dumpee calling is always interpreted as a "pining away" for the dumper (even if the dumpee is simply calling to say, "Hey, I'm engaged, I thought you should know").

So plan early. With my last boyfriend, I began about six months prior to the actual breakup. We were fighting because I was depressed and moody (unbeknownst to him, I was depressed and moody because I was in the middle of a breakup—with him). We argued because he thought I was cheating. (I wasn't cheating, I was platonically lining up a possible future boyfriend. Besides, the argument can be made that being left for somebody else is better than just being left. If someone leaves you for *nothing,* that means they really can't stand you. So actually, it's a compliment.) We bickered about money (why should I spend money on my soon-to-be-ex-boyfriend?). And when, the week after Valentine's Day (so I could say I was considerate enough to wait until after the holiday to dump him), I uttered those fateful words—"I think we need to end this"—he kept saying, over and over, "I can't believe it. I can't believe this is over."

No wonder: He was where I'd been six months earlier. He wanted to know why. He wanted to get back together. He promised to change. He called in the wee hours, unable to sleep.

Me? I had my bottle of Ambien. I slept like a baby.

35

Ex-Sightings

CAN YOU RUN INTO YOUR EX
WITHOUT TRIPPING ON YOUR SANITY?

He Said . . .

My ex-girlfriend Katrina came in to work today. Which is odd, because my ex-girlfriend Katrina lives in Dublin with her new husband, Simon. So imagine my surprise when my ex-girlfriend Katrina came in to work today—in Los Angeles. Hell, you don't have to imagine it. I'm telling you—I was surprised.

Except, in truth, her name's not Katrina, and she's not my ex-girlfriend. She's not even my friend. She's a woman who works in the audience department on the TV show I produce, and when I say my ex-girlfriend Katrina came into work today, what I really mean is that a woman who *looks* like my ex-girlfriend Katrina (who now lives in Dublin with her new husband, Simon) in fact looks *so much* like my ex-girlfriend Katrina (light brown hair, green eyes, skinny, five-feet-one-inch, long legs) that the first time I saw her walk into the office I was so sure that she *was* my ex-girlfriend Katrina that I muttered something like, "Oh my god, my ex-girlfriend Katrina!" and dove under my assistant's desk. This, I realize, doesn't entirely prove that she looks like my ex-girlfriend Katrina, because I can't recall ever diving under my assistant's desk when my actual ex-girlfriend Katrina entered a room I was in (I mean, how healthy of a relationship would that have been?), but you'll have to trust me that if my actual ex-girlfriend Katrina entered the room I actually *was* in, today, having not seen my actual ex-girlfriend since the night before she broke up with me by calling me at work three years ago (different office, different job, different assistant, different desk), I would, most likely, at that point, in that situation, confronted with my actual ex-girlfriend Katrina, dive under my assistant's desk.

Which is actually, exactly, precisely what I did the first time this woman, who looks like my ex-girlfriend Katrina, showed up at my work. Don't believe me? Ask my assistant.

So, that's what I mean when I say my ex-girlfriend Katrina came in to work today. As she does every day. Hell, she works there. If she *didn't* come in to work every day, I'd have her fired. (Come to think of it, maybe I *should* fire her just to get back at my ex-girlfriend for firing *me*.) And although I've overcome the compulsion to dive under my assistant's desk, I still suffer the other physical responses I originally suffered each time I laid eyes on my ex-girlfriend Katrina (the actual one) when I began wooing *her* four years ago. The breathing halts. The sweat beads. The saliva collects. The tongue paralyzes. The feet shuffle. (Or what I call my "charm offensive.") In sum, I crumble in her presence, despite never even having been introduced to or holding an actual conversation with my ex-girlfriend Katrina (the fake one).

What am I supposed to say? "You broke my fucking heart. So nice to finally meet you."

For that very reason, ours is the oddest of relationships. When I see her, I remember my ex-girlfriend, and my heart hurts a little. Call it "déjà voodoo." (One has to be impressed by the evil genius my ex-girlfriend has displayed by her ability to keep reminding me of *her* without her having to remember *me*. It's as if she sent her doppelgänger into my life to stand sentry.) Running into your ex, even if she's a fake, can make the most secure man weep.

And I have to do it *every day*. Kind of.

When I, told my coworkers the uncanny resemblance this woman bears to my ex, it quickly became something of a hot topic around the watercooler. Actually, I was surprised by their first response: Why not ask her out?

It's a fair question: Why shouldn't you date your ex's doppelgänger? I mean, you were naturally attracted to your ex (the actual one), so isn't it natural that you'd be attracted to your ex (the fake one)? And your ex (the fake one) isn't actually your ex (the actual one), so why hold her accountable for anything untoward or heartbreaking your ex (the actual one) actually did to you? Doesn't your ex (the fake one) deserve a shot at the happiness you generously offered your ex (the actual one)? After all, why punish your ex (the fake one) for the heartless way your ex (the actual one) punished you? And even then, on second thought, don't first impressions deserve a second chance in the first place? What a shame, really: Katrina has clearly ruined it for both of us.

It's too bad, when you think about it, that exes can spoil so much in their absence. Thanks to the memories that haunt me from my exes, there are restaurants I can't frequent (Vincenzo's on Montana, Café Delfini, Xiomara), singers I have trouble listening to (Rufus Wainwright, Sting, Israel Kamakawiwo'ole), and vacations I am reluctant to take (Maui, Big Bear, sailing off the coast of San Diego). Farther down the road (and by the way, every time I see a green Jeep Cherokee, I want to drive off a cliff), thanks to my exes I can never name any of my children Cheryl, Elyse, Stephanie, Kate, Kristen, Dawn, Gloria, or Katrina.

Exes have the reverse Midas touch: Everything they touched turns our stomach.

More roiling than those exes who haunt us with bad (or worse, good) memories are those who drop back into our lives, live and in person. Even on the rare occasions the breakup was mutual, there are times when you absolutely don't want to run into your ex—except with your car. Sadly, most men run into their actual exes at some point, either because of the serendipitous ways of the world or because our exes engineered the happenstance meeting and pawned it off as an accident. I've dated two actresses who were never more convincing in their professional lives than when in their personal lives they mustered an "Oh, *hi!*" upon "bumping into" me at a crowded Starbucks. Where she "just happened" to be shopping for a "buzz grinder."

These moments are the definition of *fraught*. The most inane small talk takes on all sorts of deep meaning. The encounter is always fleeting and superficial, and since we can't say what we really want to say without sounding like a petty Annie Oakley—"Anything you have done, I have done better!"—even we men hope that at least we have a good hair day goin'. At these moments, we consider it might be that looking good, not living well, is truly the best revenge. It's impossible, in the slight six minutes allotted to this exchange, to say anything truly impressive or explain with any eloquence how easily we've gotten over her. I suppose that's why so many men trot out new trophy girlfriends after a breakup—when words fail, men need a physical prop to imply the many competitions they must have won to deserve such a beautiful accessory.

Fortunately, my Katrina doppelgänger aside, most of the exes who have reappeared in my life lost their powers-of-devastation over me long before the "Oh, *hi.*" Seeing them postbreakup usually has been relatively pleasant, if uncomfortable. The shorthand is still there, but we derive very little intimacy from it.

"How are—"

"Good."

"And how 'bout—"

"Still plugging away."

"Are you still—"

"As much as I can."

"Give my best to—"

"I will."

"Gosh. It's so good to—"

"I know. Me too."

I'll take awkward over painful any day. If seeing my ex for the first time since she fled my life doesn't make me want to double over in agony, chew off my tongue, or dive under my assistant's desk, I'm grateful. It's great news: She may have moved out, but I'm ready to move on.

She Said . . .

I have a massive fear of running into my ex. Not just the last ex, but *all* of them. I can be completely over someone I dated years before, but if that person were to walk into a restaurant—even if he's alone, even if I'm with a new boyfriend—my pulse would start pounding. I'd laugh too hard, talk too loudly, and generally make a fool of myself.

So after a breakup, weekends can be particularly dangerous. Not just because they lack the structure and distraction of the workweek, but because they increase the likelihood of running into an ex.

At a certain point, though, you have to get out because nothing's worse than running into your ex at home. Admit it, he's right there in your apartment. Everything you look at reminds you of him. The desk you made love on. The rug by the fireplace where you'd read to each other. The doorknob where he used to drape his jacket. He's hanging out in each room, telling you that he's gone forever.

So you resolve to get out, but deciding where to go is tough. There's no post-breakup demilitarized zone. If you didn't get sole custody of the deli, coffeehouse, market, movie theater, pharmacy, post office, dry cleaner, Blockbuster, or bookstore that you went to together, either you'll spend forty-five minutes getting dressed to leave the house, or you'll never leave it all. (And thanks to online shopping, you don't have to. You can order your flannel pj's, floppy socks, and Chinese takeout with the click of a mouse.)

This is when long-distance dating comes in handy. "Geographically undesirable" becomes "geographically preferable" as soon as one of you pulls the plug. I don't mean opposite sides of town (because the new *She*—and eventually, there will be a new *She*—may live near you and frequent your deli, coffeehouse, market, movie theater, pharmacy, post office, dry cleaner, Blockbuster, bookstore, and, God forbid, even your manicurist). I'm talking about different cities. In fact, if you can swing it, try different states. After a breakup with a serious boyfriend who lived in Minnesota, I experienced a true luxury: I could look blemished and pale and wear three-day-old clothes without ever worrying about running into him. (Of course, at the time, I was devastated precisely because I never ran into him.)

If you live in the same town, though, you don't even have to run into your ex to feel that machete slicing through your heart. A ninety-second encounter with your ex by proxy can have the same traumatic effect. Imagine running into an acquaintance you haven't seen in a while. She asks how you're doing, then tosses out this zinger: "And how's your guy? You know, that adorable, funny writer? He seemed so great! Any news?" (Unfortunately, by "news" she means "wedding announcements," not "obituaries.")

Or how about running into his friend when you look your worst, only to get a call from the ex himself who asks, gloating with phony concern, "Jeremy said you looked exhausted and stressed out. I'm worried. Are you okay?"

Paradoxically, you both do and do not want to run into our ex. If dating well is the best revenge, you might resort to taking your hot rebound boyfriend to your old haunts in hopes of an ex-boyfriend sighting. But in not seeing your ex, you wonder, "Where is he? How come he's never at Starbucks on Saturdays at ten anymore? Is he luxuriating in bed with some other woman?" In seeing him, on the other hand, you're disappointed when there's no passionate reunion, or at least a sign that he's as miserable as you are (signifying a tinge of regret on his part that you got away, even though he was the one who asked you to go away).

It's not that you wish him ill—it's that you wish you better. You want him to be happy—as long as you're happier. (On the happiness meter, he should be you minus two points.) And it makes sense to feel competitive. When you were together, you were on the same team. Now that you're broken up, you've been traded to a different ball club—one that, quite distinctly, isn't his. No wonder we keep detailed stats on our exes' progress. They've become the rival team.

If you don't run into your ex right away, you can always settle for the next best thing: Date someone who reminds you of your ex. Maybe the new guy has the same face, or voice, or résumé. Maybe he's an insufferable mama's boy. Whatever. Take him to all of your ex-boyfriend's places and create new dysfunctional memories. Eventually, the unpleasant associations should help you to find a brand-new deli, coffeehouse, market, movie theater, pharmacy, post office, dry cleaner, Blockbuster, and bookstore. Then you can make a clean start.

When you do, eventually, run into your ex (and you will, when you least expect it, two neighborhoods away in the middle of a workday), remember that the guy giving you the finger as you make an illegal left turn into the crosswalk is not a very pleasant person. He's your ex, and even when you realize it's your ex and your ex realizes it's you, and he raises his remaining four fingers into a wave, do not for a second think, "Hey, maybe we can be friends."

You can't.

Look in your rearview mirror, check out the woman crossing the street beside him, and see how friendly you feel. Notice that she's basically a better version of you (also short and skinny but with bigger breasts; also has curly hair but hers is wavy to your frizz). She's you, version 2.0. Which is even worse than had she been a 5'10" Swedish bimbo. At least you'd know you're not his type. But if you are his type and he traded you in for someone else, how crummy does that feel?

No matter how the encounter happens (maybe you simply see him from a distance, walking into the bank) you'll likely have to write off the rest of your day for emergency phone calls with your girlfriends. You'll spend the next twenty-four hours wondering whether the fact that he was wearing the blue-striped sweater you gave him for his birthday means that he's still thinking about you, or that he's moved on to such a degree that he's forgotten the gift was from you in the first place. If he's wearing a T-shirt you've never seen before, you'll talk about how he's changed completely, that you don't even know *who he is* anymore. You won't only bemoan the loss of intimacy of knowing his entire wardrobe—you'll feel stabbed when he calls you by your given name, instead of that awful pet name you hated when you were dating (see chapter 24). You'll try to hurt him in exactly the way he hurt you by calling him by his actual name, too.

In a way, running into your ex is like hammering the last nail into the coffin. You know you broke up, but it isn't until you see him on the street, without you, that the finality truly hits you. You're seeing his life from the outside now, like everyone else walking by. It's strange to think that the person to whom you would have donated a kidney a mere month ago is the same person you're now trying to avoid by going to a different supermarket. And when you see him, it feels like you're dying, not just because the relationship did, but because that part of your life died right along with it.

So forget all those scenarios you've rehearsed in your head about what might happen if you run into your ex. Forget that you "want to get it over with" or "are ready to see him" or "miss hanging out with him." It'll feel like a funeral, not a reunion. So dress appropriately for the occasion. Besides, you'll look thinner in black anyway.

36

Moving On

He Said . . .

A few years ago, a woman named Terry Lynn Barton was depressed that her man had left her. Presumably, friends advised her how best to get over the loss: Try a new hairstyle, pick up a hobby, start drinking. All these nuggets of wisdom fell on deaf ears. Instead, she went into the forest, started a bonfire, tossed in all of his old love letters, and accidentally burned down Colorado. Unfortunately, her man wasn't the only one that got away. So did the fire. By the end of the summer, her *Ya-Ya Sisterhood* cleansing ceremony had devastated well over a hundred thousand acres in *the worst wildfire in Colorado history*. Her healing effigy demolished homes, destroyed fragile ecosystems, and widened the hole in the ozone. What makes the episode especially absurd is that Terry Lynn Barton wasn't just your average heartbroken woman, she was a veteran *forest ranger*. She was the walking definition of "should have known better."

And yet, we all know the feeling, don't we? Poor thing—Terry simply wanted to move on, to put her heartbreak behind her. And maybe, while she was at it, eat a S'more.

We've all been burned, so to speak. We'll do almost anything to get that pain behind us so that we can be emotionally available to yet another person, project unreasonable hopes and dreams onto this poor sap, and with unbridled optimism, look forward to all sorts of new pain.

We'll do anything to move on.

At some point in a breakup, each of us wants nothing more than to ex-out our exes, and everybody's got a theory about how best to do so. Some, the Ms. Bartons of the world, take it to the extreme. In the wake of a broken heart, they burn down forests, wage wars, and conquer kingdoms. I heard that Hitler invaded Poland because Eva stopped returning his calls. That's not really moving on at all.

Some say recovery can't be engineered, and is just a "matter of time." They say things like, "It takes half the length of a relationship to get over the relationship." Which is a little like saying it takes half your life to get over your death. For those of us who have experienced it, it feels like there's no possible recovery. In fact, we'd prefer you take your nifty equations and stuff them up your ass.

I haven't exactly broken the speed record in getting over my relationships. For a full two years after Katrina and I broke up, her phone number was still programmed into my cell phone. In fact, it had its own unique ring tone, and the one time she called me after the dumping—once again, *at work*—my face went white upon hearing the chime. My coworkers said I looked like I was going to faint.

I was one of Pavlov's dogs, but instead of salivating for food, I had an instinctual urge to beg for a second chance.

Despite the stereotype that men are callous, thoughtless, insensitive egotists, men take breakups especially hard, particularly when we're the ones being dumped. This is because we're callous, thoughtless, insensitive egotists. Brace yourselves, ladies: If you took a poll, you'd find that the average man would rather have a girlfriend die in a fiery plane crash than break up with him. It sounds cruel and selfish—and it is—but it's also oddly rational: one is a loss, the other is a loss *and* a rejection. The plane crash is a singular horrific tragedy; the dumping is a twofer. (It's much easier to move on, frankly, when staying together is not an option. And if you haven't noticed by now, we men like it easy.)

Frankly, being dumped leaves us asking too many questions.

Even though I've reached that glorious day when I can honestly say I'm better off without her, for years one particular question regarding my relationship with Katrina haunted me, as I expect it haunts many men who have loved and lost: Did she *learn* on me?

If it's true that people enter your life when you need them, was I just a lesson in her romantic higher education? The thought needles me; like the beneficiary of a breakthrough scientific advance resulting from experiments done on a dying patient, her new husband is benefiting from our DOA relationship. *He* is reaping the rewards of *Katrina's* revelation that *she* might have actually been complicit in *our* demise (and therefore might have been too hasty in breaking it off).

What do *I* get? Merely to say, "I told you so."

Thanks to her mistakes with me, she will have lived and learned. Maybe she won't be quite as demanding of him, for example, because she recognizes what she put *me* through. Maybe she won't be quite so selfish when it comes to him, because she realizes she was no altruist when it came to me. Maybe she'll realize that he's arguing with her not because he's pathologically confrontational (as she thought I was), but merely because he disagrees with her (as I sometimes did). I dread that my loss, and her growth, is his gain.

For better or for worse.

It's thoughts like these that make moving on so hard for so many. Paradoxically, the more we think about whether *she's* moved on, the less *we've* moved on; and the more *we've* moved on, the less we wonder if *she's* moved on. It's a zero-sum catch-22. To this day, I wonder how long after Katrina broke up with me did she experience a full day—sun up to sun down—in which she didn't even *think* of me. I don't mean didn't pine for me, or didn't long for me, or even didn't remember me fondly. I mean didn't *think* of me. I mean didn't allow me to enter her consciousness. When did I first disappear from her daily thought routine? When didn't my name come to mind when she was idly scanning her mental Rolodex? Sadly, I suspect it was long before I experienced a non-Katrina day.

Truthfully, when I set out to write this book, I'm not even sure I *had* experienced a pure non-Katrina day. I *think* I had, but I'm not sure. (If a tree doesn't fall in the forest . . .) All I can say with any certainty is that I had strung together a few non-Katrina hours. Like when I had ankle surgery under general anesthesia and dreamt of Julianne Moore eating a pizza.

When a relationship ends, it's understandable to want to forget it cold turkey, but there are no shortcuts to take, no maps to follow, no drugs to swallow, and no sacrificial forests to burn to the ground to help us get over it. The best you can do is practice a little tough love with yourself: *Get over it, and move on.* Remember, you're a callous, thoughtless, insensitive egotist. Surely you can do this.

She Said . . .

If only we could fall out of love as quickly as we fell into it. What if, like the millisecond in which you see a guy across the room and decide you're smitten—poof!—you could forget him just as fast? What if you never had to wonder if you made a mistake, or whether he's changed, or whether the timing was wrong and if you met now things might be different?

I went through all those feelings with Alec. Partly, it was my digital camera's fault. How was I supposed to get over Alec when I had hundreds of photos of us on my hard drive? Sure, I could delete them, but I was haunted by these images, each giving rise to another painful memory: Alec tenderly pressing his cheek to mine on the beach; Alec grinning lovingly at me on vacation; Alec and I in goofy costumes. Was he lying then about his love? Was I? When we caressed each other, whispered soothingly to each other, laughed together, showered together, talked about spending our lives together—did we mean it?

Probably. But it's easier to pretend that we were both lying than to accept that love is so fragile and transient. It's easier to believe that all the passion and acts of selflessness were deceitful, than to accept that love alone isn't enough. Because if love isn't enough, why should we go looking for it again?

For a while, I reveled in my sadness. I held on to Alec's stuff for an extra few months, not so I could hang on to him, but so I could hang on to the sadness of losing him a little longer. But eventually I came to realize that I was sadder about the loss of what might have been, than the loss of the actual person.

It wasn't that I missed Alec anymore. It was that I didn't miss him at all—and that's why I was crying. I was crying because when I walked by his apartment, I completely forgot it was his street. I didn't feel even a twinge of nostalgia when I saw his show on TV. Worst of all, I'd wasted two and a half years on a doomed relationship because I didn't have the guts to find something better. I didn't have the guts to move on.

Perhaps falling in love again is the socially acceptable version of mental illness—more crazy than just plain courageous. Because even once you stop falling, once you're just *there,* love is confusing while it lasts, and it may not last forever.

In the movies, most love stories end at the wedding, when the couple finally gets together. But in real life, love stories end when the couple finally breaks up. I have no idea how my next love story will begin or end.

And for now, I like it that way.

EPILOGUE

We Said . . .

Love is never a sure thing. Love is twenty-three hours of unsure things topped off by an hour of nakedness. And that's on a good day.

So we wonder, is there such a thing as a happy ending? If something ends—especially if it's something *good*—is that ever happy? Is that ever an occasion for celebration? How many times have you told yourself, *Wow, that was the best sex I've ever had. Thank God it's over!*

Not many, we hope.

That's the thing about love. It's a gamble. It's a one-in-a-million chance. So why do we do it? This time, it might work out. This time, it might not end. This time, we might find the happiest of all happy endings: one that doesn't.

In the meantime, we've got our anecdates.